TIME-DRIVEN
ACTIVITY-BASED
COSTING

TIME-DRIVEN
ACTIVITY-BASED
COSTING

A SIMPLER AND MORE POWERFUL PATH TO HIGHER PROFITS

Robert S. Kaplan
Steven R. Anderson

HARVARD BUSINESS SCHOOL PRESS

BOSTON, MASSACHUSETTS

Library of Congress Cataloging-in-Publication Data
Kaplan, Robert S.
    Time-Driven Activity-Based Costing: a simpler and more powerful path to higher
profits / Robert S. Kaplan and Steven R. Anderson
        p.   cm.
        Includes index.
    ISBN-13: 978-1-4221-0171-1 (hardcover: alk. paper)
    1. Activity-based costing. 2. Time management I. Anderson, Steven R. II. Title.
    HF5686.C8K267   2007
    658.15'52—dc22

                                                                              2006035423

*To Robin Cooper, for his creativity and friendship,
and to Ellen, for everything*

—Robert Kaplan

To my wife, Chelsea, and sons, Wyly, Blake, and Teddy

—Steven Anderson

CONTENTS

PREFACE

THE ORIGINS FOR THIS BOOK go back to 1995, when Steve Anderson, then a second-year MBA student at Harvard Business School (HBS), took a course, Cost Measurement and Management, taught by Bob Kaplan. The course featured how companies design, implement, and act on activity-based costing (ABC) systems. It concluded with a summary lecture in which Kaplan described new material from his forthcoming book with Robin Cooper, *Cost & Effect*, on "Stage IV" cost systems. These systems could access enterprise resource planning (ERP) systems, making possible a new ABC approach that would feature time consumption and capacity utilization as central components.

Anderson, while at HBS, had already been working with a classmate to apply ABC techniques to several medium-sized private companies. They had built a homegrown software model to analyze cost and profit information across an enterprise. Their early clients used the output from the new software system to negotiate with key customers and were pleasantly surprised by the size of the profit opportunities they could identify and capture.

After graduation, Anderson worked as a consultant at McKinsey & Co. to do similar work for *Fortune* 1000 companies. Despite these companies' excellent senior management, sophisticated use of information technology, and advanced applications of business process improvement techniques, their ABC systems were labor-intensive and limited in scope. Anderson saw an opportunity for a consulting/software company that could help companies better automate their ABC systems and extend ABC concepts across the enterprise.

In 1996, he founded Acorn Systems, Inc., to focus on medium-sized enterprises. Acorn initially partnered with a leading ABC software vendor, but the software and methodology from this firm could not even replicate the analysis that Anderson and his classmate had done while at business school. At Acorn's first client, Wilson-Mohr ($15 million in revenue at the time), the commercial ABC software took weeks to drive the company's general ledger to the hundreds of activities in the model, took even longer to download the customer and product files, and then spent several more days running the enterprise model. As Anderson thought more about the problems at his short list of clients, he realized how a new approach could improve enterprisewide ABC implementations.[1]

The new system would start by driving general-ledger costs directly to departments, a simple task. For each department, he defined the principal process performed. Then, he selected time, a common measure across all the activities and subactivities done within the process, as the unit of work performed by the department. Anderson rejected the approach of existing ABC software, which focused on either a product or a customer as the unit of analysis. He saw how ERP systems enabled him to work directly and naturally at the transaction level to measure the drivers of process time consumption. He developed time equations to describe how different types of orders or transactions consumed process time in departments.

In the spring of 1997, Acorn built its first time-driven activity-based costing (TDABC) solution.[2] The company applied it successfully to Wilson-Mohr and another client, Hendee Enterprises, in the summer of 1997, and then to a broader set of medium-sized companies, especially those with high transaction volumes. Several years later, Anderson expanded Acorn's management team by hiring experienced software executives, including Leland Putterman as president, Alex Fernandez as vice president of sales, Torsten Weirich as vice president of development, and Chris Fraga as vice president of alliances. Acorn soon learned that TDABC had much wider applications than it originally thought. By 2006, the model has been successfully implemented in more than two hundred companies, including many enterprisewide applications in midsize and *Fortune* 1000 companies.

Meanwhile, Kaplan, after coauthoring and publishing *Cost & Effect*, had focused on his Balanced Scorecard work with Dave Norton. The work led to several *Harvard Business Review* articles, three more books, and numerous HBS case studies and *Balanced Scorecard Report* articles.

But Kaplan retained his interest in sustaining and extending activity-based costing.

Kaplan joined Acorn's board of directors in 2001 and began to collaborate with Anderson and the Acorn team on how to make their approach even more powerful. These discussions led to an integration of the capacity-costing approach that Kaplan and Cooper had advocated in *Cost & Effect* with Anderson's time algorithms for modeling transaction complexity. Kaplan and Anderson described the integrated TDABC approach in a November 2004 *Harvard Business Review* article and agreed to collaborate on the current book. This book explicates the theory of TDABC, provides examples of its successful implementation with several case studies of Acorn clients, and introduces extensions of TDABC to new, innovative applications.

With all these new applications and extensions, many have asked Kaplan how his dual interests of ABC and Balanced Scorecard intersect. The short answer is that ABC and the Balanced Scorecard are distinct but complementary. They are distinct since TDABC provides complex enterprises with an accurate model of the *cost* and *profitability* of producing and delivering their products and services, and managing their customer relationships. Activity-based costing generalizes the economists' classic single-product supply curve to capture the economics of multiproduct, multicustomer businesses. It provides companies with vital cost-curve information but says little about what their customers value.

The Balanced Scorecard fills this void by describing how companies create *value* for customers and shareholders. The Balanced Scorecard measures the customer value proposition and links critical processes and intangible assets to customer and shareholder value creation. The Balanced Scorecard generalizes the economists' demand curve by representing how price and all the other critical attributes of the product or service create customer value.

Thus, ABC provides a model of cost while the Balanced Scorecard describes a model of value creation. They provide different levers for measuring and implementing a company's strategy. Companies whose Balanced Scorecard describes a low-total-cost strategy need ABC for accurately measuring the costs of critical processes. Otherwise, they run the considerable risk of implementing a low-cost strategy with faulty information about their fundamental cost drivers. Companies that use a Balanced Scorecard to describe and execute a differentiation strategy need ABC to measure whether the value they create from their differentiation for customers exceeds the cost of achieving this differentiation.

The complementary nature of the two approaches becomes even more tangible when companies contemplate adding customer profitability information to their Balanced Scorecard customer perspective. The ability of TDABC to measure, simply and accurately, profitability at the individual customer level allows companies to consider new customer metrics such as percentage of unprofitable customers and dollars lost in unprofitable customer relationships. Such customer profitability metrics complement conventional customer success metrics, such as satisfaction, retention, and growth, to signal that customer relationships are desirable only if these relationships generate increased profits. The profitability measurements provide the link between customer satisfaction and loyalty and improved financial performance. Scorecard measures of the incidence of unprofitable customers and the magnitude of losses from unprofitable relationships focus the organization on managing customers for profits, not just for sales.[3]

Perhaps the most powerful linkage between the Balanced Scorecard and ABC is articulated in chapter 5. We illustrate there how a TDABC model bridges the gap between the Balanced Scorecard's strategy focus and the budget, which authorizes spending for the resources required to create, produce, and deliver on the company's strategic plan. Time-driven ABC's focus on measuring and managing the costs of a company's capacity resources can now be tightly linked to the fulfillment of the company's strategy, as articulated in its strategy map and Balanced Scorecard.

ACKNOWLEDGMENTS

This book is the synthesis of ten years of work to develop Time-Driven Activity-Based Costing. It started in 1997 as just an idea and evolved into a more formal framework through the contributions of countless people. Employees at Acorn, outside consultants, members of academia, and, of course, numerous clients at Acorn were critical to this process. We will always be indebted to them.

We would like to first thank the folks at Acorn throughout these formative years. Robert Mills; Anderson's HBS classmate James Brigman; Manisha Fernando; and Acorn's first employee, Steve Schulist, all helped set the wheels in motion by applying this approach to real clients and by creating a software application focused on TDABC. Years later, many Acorn consultants, including Scott Skorupsky, Pete Henderson,

Bernard Chaval, Mike Roeltgen, Ian Robertson, Snehal Talati, Richard Drobner, Deniz Batuman, and David Michie, tested TDABC at larger customers and new applications. And with the expansion of the team with individuals like Boyd Meiers, Emma Browning, Ken Williams, and Vice President of Technology, Torsten Weirich, the marriage of TDABC to software became even more scalable.

We are indebted to members of the Acorn management team. Chris Fraga carried the banner of TDABC worldwide through consulting partnerships and alliances. Leland Putterman leveraged his twenty years of experience in software to recruit a highly seasoned team, which included Alex Fernandez, Lien Kingston, Kim Box, Jeff Duncan, Rich Lasalle, and Ken Knickerbocker, to make the TDABC solution mainstream. The experiences of many of the companies referenced in this book are the result of this go-to-market team. In addition, Leland provided numerous helpful suggestions that improved our exposition of TDABC and its contrast to conventional ABC.

Many representatives from industry and consulting also contributed. Anderson's HBS classmate (and Kaplan's student) Vince Keller helped develop complex equations to more accurately drive costs at IJ Foods, which eventually led to the more general time equation concept described in this book. Ron Nixon at Catalyst Hall in Houston embraced the technique and helped identify several of Acorn's first clients to test the approach. Paul Woods of IBM promoted the role for TDABC in high transaction-volume environments. Mitch Max and Larry Maisel from DecisionVu taught us how to apply TDABC effectively to the financial services industry and contributed significantly to the Compton Financial, Global Insurance, ATB, and Citigroup Technology Infrastructure experiences described in the book. Jack Haedicke of Arena Consulting played a similar role in introducing and implementing TDABC for Acorn's retail clients, such as Harris Teeter, Spartan, Supervalu, Target, and Petco. Werner Bruggeman, Kris Moreels, Thierry Bruynee, and Thierry Vandekerkhove of B&M Consulting provided the Sanac case, as well as additional material on building complex time equations. Dick Barry was instrumental for his input on the role TDABC can play with lean management.

Of course, none of this would have been possible without the indispensable role played by Robin Cooper in codeveloping ABC in the 1980s, describing it in numerous articles and books, capturing the pathbreaking innovations in best-selling cases, many still being taught widely today, and demonstrating the viability and effectiveness of ABC through proof-of-concept consulting assignments in the 1980s and 1990s. When we contrast what we call conventional ABC with the time-driven variation advocated in the book, we are not critiquing Robin's contributions, which are enormous. His creativity and grounded theory development gave us a platform on which to improve and make the vision he had in 1985 even simpler and more practical.

We also thank the companies that supported the effort by implementing TDABC and allowing us to share their experiences with the readers. Listed below alphabetically are the companies referenced in the book, along with the individuals who played a central role in the TDABC implementations. These individuals not only served as great champions for their respective TDABC initiatives, but also helped customize the approach to their industries.

American Beverage	Tony Battaglia, Dave Anderson
ATB	Jim McKillop, Amolak Grewal, Lenka Stuchlik
Citigroup	Jeff Nachowitz, Tom Veljacic, Bob Michta
Coca-Cola, Belgium	Pascal Platteau
Conco	Pete Algero, Jerry Kurzweg
Denman & Davis	Dave Deinzer
Hendee	Chuck Hendee
HSBC	Daniel Stusnick
Jackson State University	Troy Stovall, Edmond Donald, Rod Deane
Kemps	Christopher Thorpe, James Green, Paul Kunkel, Joe Schmitz
Lewis-Goetz	Jim Thieman, Paul Franz, David Goetz
PNC	Mike Vallo, Dan Hodge
Questor	Kevin Prokop, Dennis Kirby
Sanac	Gert-Jan Decreus
TW Metals	Aldo Miceli, Ed Waas
Wilson-Mohr	Dennis Floro, John Wilson

We thank those who were involved in publishing this book, particularly our editors, Astrid Sandoval and Hollis Heimbouch, who guided us throughout the process and solicited valuable reviews to an early manuscript that led to substantial improvements. We appreciate Jen Waring's excellent and timely leadership of the production process. We thank four anonymous reviewers for their encouragement and valuable suggestions. Cynthia Joba of Acorn and David Porter at Harvard Business School provided valuable assistance to produce a well-crafted manuscript copy.

Finally, we thank our respective families, who showered us with support all along the way. For Steve Anderson, his wife, Chelsea; children, Wyly, Blake, and Teddy; parents, Robert and Judith; and brothers, David and Brian, were a continual source of ideas on how to make this a better book. Bob Kaplan acknowledges the support and constructive, insightful criticism of his wife, Ellen, and the enthusiasm of his daughters, Jennifer and Dina, for their dad's work.

Robert S. Kaplan, Boston

Steven R. Anderson, Wayne, Pennsylvania

NOTES

1. The clients were Wilson-Mohr, a process control distributor and systems fabricator; Hendee Enterprises, a custom awnings manufacturer; Denman & Davis, a steel service center; and Lewis-Goetz, a hose and belt distributor and fabricator.
2. The name *Time-Driven ABC* did not come into use until 2001. At the time, Anderson and Acorn called it Transaction-Based ABC.
3. B. P. Shapiro, et al., "Manage Customers for Profits (Not Just for Sales)," *Harvard Business Review*, September–October 1987, 101–108.

The Fundamentals of Time–Driven Activity–Based Costing

## CHAPTER ONE

THE EVOLUTION OF TIME-DRIVEN ACTIVITY-BASED COSTING

Introduction

CONSIDER THE CONVENTIONAL activity-based cost (ABC) system used at a large financial services firm several years ago. The system attempted to measure product cost and customer profitability each month, certainly desirable goals for stimulating process improvement, product pricing, and customer relationship actions. But the process required seven hundred employees at more than 100 facilities to submit monthly surveys of their time. The company employed 14 full-time people just to collect and process the data and prepare management reports, which took more than thirty days to prepare.

Hendee Enterprises, a far smaller Houston-based manufacturer of awnings, encountered similar implementation problems with its ABC model. The software took three days to calculate costs for its 150 activities, 10,000 orders, and 45,000 line items.

These two experiences, unfortunately, were not atypical. Many companies, because of the time-consuming surveying and data-processing costs of ABC systems, either abandoned ABC entirely or ceased updating their system, which left them with out-of-date and highly inaccurate estimates of process, product, and customer costs.

Contrast these experiences, however, with the current situation at the financial services firm, described in detail in chapter 10. It has implemented a new ABC approach that uses automatic data feeds from its enterprise resource planning (ERP) system to provide managers throughout the system with monthly reports on capacity utilization and customer profitability. The system summarizes, within a few days after each monthly close, the profit impact of over 50 million transactions conducted by its more than 3 million clients in the previous month. Managers have already used this information to lower process costs by several hundred million dollars annually and to align better their product pricing and account management to the company's diverse client segments. Two employees maintain the system's accuracy and capabilities.

The new approach, which we call Time-Driven Activity-Based Costing (TDABC), gives companies an elegant and practical option for determining the cost and capacity utilization of their processes and the profitability of orders, products, and customers. TDABC enables companies to improve their cost management systems, not abandon them. Managers obtain accurate cost and profitability information to set priorities for process improvements, rationalize their product variety and mix, price customer orders, and manage customer relationships in ways that benefit both parties.

ACTIVITY-BASED COSTING: A BRIEF HISTORY

As originally introduced in the 1980s, ABC corrected serious deficiencies in traditional standard-cost systems.[1] The traditional systems typically used only three cost categories: labor, materials, and overhead. While manufacturing companies could generally trace the labor and materials used by their individual products, their cost systems allocated the indirect and support costs—the "overhead"—with measures already being recorded, such as direct labor hours and direct labor dollars.

As the direct labor content of products decreased, through automation and industrial engineering–driven efficiencies, the percentage of total costs represented by the somewhat arbitrary allocations of overhead had continually increased during the twentieth century. In addition, many companies had shifted from mass-production strategies to those that offered customers more variety, features, and options. The customer-focused strategy attempted to attract, retain, and grow business by offering services such as the following:

- Producing and stocking a greater variety of products
- Supporting more order-entry and order-tracking channels
- Producing and delivering in smaller order sizes
- Delivering directly to customers' end-use locations, often in expedited and narrow time windows
- Providing specialized technical applications support

All these new services created value and loyalty among customers, but none came for free. To offer the expanded variety and the new options, features, and services, companies had to add (overhead) resources for engineering, scheduling, receiving, storage, inspection, setup, materials handling, packaging, distributing, order handling, marketing, and selling. Overhead costs increased both relatively and absolutely as companies diversified into more product lines, customers, channels, and regions, and offered specialized features and services.

By the 1980s, the standard cost systems designed during the scientific management movement seventy-five years earlier no longer reflected the current economic reality. Companies were now operating with distorted information about the profitability of their orders, products, and customers. For example, while traditional cost systems might show that all customers were profitable, the economic reality was that a minority of customers earned between 150 and 300 percent of profits, and unprofitable customer relationships lost 50 to 200 percent of profits.

Activity-based costing seemingly solved the inaccurate allocation of overhead from standard cost systems by tracing these indirect and support costs first to the activities performed by the organization's shared resources, and then assigning the activity costs down to orders, products, and customers on the basis of the quantity of each organizational activity consumed. Managers used the more accurate ABC and profitability information to make better decisions about process improvements, order acceptance and rejection, pricing, and customer relationships. The decisions led to near-term and sustainable improvements in product and customer profitability.

ABC PITFALLS

Despite its attractive value proposition, however, ABC was not universally accepted. In an annual survey of the adoption of management tools, ABC ranked below the median, with only a 50 percent adoption rate.[2] For a system that gives companies insights into the cost and profitability of products, processes, services, and customers—insights not otherwise available—the low adoption rate seemed surprising.

Some companies failed to adopt ABC, or abandoned the tool, because of behavioral and organizational resistance that accompanies any new idea, particularly one as seemingly radical as to treat most organizational costs as variable and to acknowledge the possibility of unprofitable customers.[3] But much of the resistance to adopting and sustaining ABC was rational and justified. As our opening example documents, ABC systems were expensive to build, complex to sustain, and difficult to modify. People also questioned the accuracy of cost assignments based on individuals' subjective estimates of the percentages of their time spent on various activities. Apart from the measurement error introduced by employees' best attempts to recall their time allocations, the employees—anticipating how the data would be used—might bias or distort their responses. As a consequence, operations, sales, and marketing managers argued about the accuracy of the model's estimated costs and profitability rather than addressing how to improve the inefficient processes, transform unprofitable products and customers, and cope with the considerable excess capacity that the model had revealed.

Many managers raised an additional concern. Despite the large number of activities in the ABC model, they knew that the model was not accurate or granular enough to capture the complexity of actual operations. For example, consider an activity *ship order to customer*. Rather than assume a constant cost per order shipped, a company may wish to recognize the cost differences when an order is shipped in a full truck, in a less-than-truckload (LTL) shipment, by overnight express, or by a commercial carrier. In addition, the shipping order may be entered either manually or electronically, and it may require either a standard or an expedited transaction. To allow for the significant variation in resources required by the different shipping arrangements, new activities would have to be added to the model, further expanding its complexity. When employees must be reinterviewed and asked to estimate their time across a broader and more complex set of activities, cost assignments generally become even more subjective and inaccurate.

Further, as ABC system designers expand the activity dictionary to reflect more granularity and detail about activities performed, the demands on the computer model used to store and process the data escalate nonlinearly. For example, a company using 150 activities in its enterprisewide ABC model, applying the costs to 600,000 cost objects (products, SKUs, and customers), and running the model monthly for two years requires data estimates, calculations, and storage for more than 2 billion items. Such expansion causes many ABC systems to exceed the capacity of generic spreadsheet tools, such as Microsoft Excel, and even many commercial ABC software packages. The systems take days to process one month of data, assuming the solution converges at all.

Because of the difficulties that conventional ABC software solutions had in scaling to enterprisewide models, companies (and their consultants) frequently built isolated ABC models for individual facilities, departments, and businesses that could not link with each other, or the companies built separate models for product and customer analysis that did not link. Because of the proliferation of models across units, the companies could not take a holistic view of cost and profitability. Improvements were incremental and local. The benefits from the siloed ABC models could not justify the models' high cost to maintain and run.

These estimating and data-processing difficulties became obvious to most ABC implementers. But a subtle and more serious problem arises from the interview and survey process itself. When people estimate how much time they spent on a list of activities handed to them, invariably they report percentages that add up to 100 percent. Few individuals record a significant percentage of their time as idle or unused. Therefore, almost all ABC systems calculate cost driver rates assuming that resources work at full capacity. But operations at practical capacity are more the exception than the rule. ABC cost driver rates should be calculated at practical capacity, not at actual utilization.[4]

In summary, implementing conventional ABC encountered the following problems:

- The interviewing and surveying process was time-consuming and costly.
- The data for the ABC model were subjective and difficult to validate.
- The data were expensive to store, process, and report.
- Most ABC models were local and did not provide an integrated view of enterprisewide profitability opportunities.
- The ABC model could not be easily updated to accommodate changing circumstances.
- The model was theoretically incorrect when it ignored the potential for unused capacity

TIME-DRIVEN ABC: AN ELEGANT, MORE ACCURATE APPROACH

Fortunately, a solution to all these problems with conventional ABC now exists. We have recently devised, tested, and implemented a new approach, which we call Time-Driven Activity-Based Costing. As we will demonstrate, TDABC is a rare example of a free lunch; it is simpler, cheaper, and far more powerful than the conventional ABC approach.

TDABC simplifies the costing process by eliminating the need to interview and survey employees for allocating resource costs to activities before driving them down to cost objects (orders, products, and customers). The new model assigns resource costs directly to the cost objects using an elegant framework requiring only two sets of estimates, neither of which is difficult to obtain. First, it calculates the cost of supplying resource capacity. For example, consider a department or process for handling customer orders. In this first step, the TDABC model calculates the cost of all the resources—personnel, supervision, occupancy, equipment and technology—supplied to this department or process. It divides this total cost by the capacity—the time available from the employees actually performing the work—of the department to obtain the capacity cost rate.

Second, TDABC uses the capacity cost rate to drive departmental resource costs to cost objects by estimating the demand for resource capacity (typically time, from which the name of the new approach was chosen) that each cost object requires. Staying with our example of the customer order department, the model requires only an estimate of the time required to process a particular customer order. But TDABC does not require that all customer orders be the same. It allows the time estimate to vary on the basis of the specific demands by particular orders, such as manual or automated orders, expedited orders, international orders, orders for fragile or hazardous goods, or orders from a new customer without an existing credit record. The TDABC model simulates the actual processes used to perform work throughout an enterprise. It can therefore capture far more variation and complexity than a conventional ABC model, without creating an exploding demand for data estimates, storage, or processing capabilities. Using TDABC, a company can embrace complexity rather than being forced to use simplified, inaccurate ABC models of its complex businesses.

We illustrate the fundamental differences between the conventional and TDABC approach with a simple numerical example. Let's consider the analysis of a customer service department whose total operating expenses are $567,000 per quarter. This amount includes the customer service personnel, their supervisors, and the cost of the department's information technology, telecommunications, and occupancy. Let's also assume that the $567,000 is committed for the quarter and won't vary with the quantity of work performed by the customer service department.

Conventional ABC

Conventional ABC starts with a project team interviewing supervisors and departmental personnel to learn about the various activities they perform. To keep the example simple, let's assume that the ABC team determines that the department performs the following three activities:

- Process customer orders
- Handle customer inquiries and complaints
- Perform customer credit checks

In the next step, the team interviews and surveys the employees, asking them to estimate the percentage of their time spent (or that they expect to spend) on these three activities. This part of the analysis is generally time-consuming and difficult for people to respond to. A typical employee question is, "Do you mean what I did yesterday?" The reply is, "No, I would rather that you think about an average three- or six-month period and estimate the proportion of time you are processing customer orders, dealing directly with customer questions or complaints, and checking and maintaining customer credit reports during this extended period." The ABC team cannot really validate employees' subjective time distributions unless it is prepared to spend weeks observing the actual mix of time spent among the three activities.

Let's assume that interviews and surveys reveal that the time mix among the three activities is 70 percent, 10 percent, and 20 percent, respectively. The ABC team assigns the total cost of the department ($567,000) to the three activities using these time percentages. The team also collects data about the actual (or estimated) quantities of work for the quarter in these three activities, as shown below:

- 49,000 customer orders
- 1,400 customer inquiries
- 2,500 credit checks

The project team makes an additional assumption to keep the analysis simple: all orders take about the same quantity of resources (time) to process, all customer inquiries take about the same amount of time, and each customer credit check also takes about the same level of effort. The ABC system now calculates the following average cost driver rates:

Activity	Time Spent (%)	Assigned Cost	Cost Driver Quantity	Cost Driver Rate
Process customer orders	70	$396,900	49,000	$8.10 per order
Handle customer inquiries	10	$56,700	1,400	$40.50 per inquiry
Perform credit check	20	$113,400	2,500	$45.36 per credit check
Total	100	$567,000		

The ABC project team uses these cost driver rates to assign the customer service departmental expenses to individual customers on the basis of the number of orders handled, complaints processed, and credit checks performed for each customer.

Time-Driven ABC

TDABC skips the activity-definition stage and therefore the need to allocate the department's costs to the multiple activities the department performs. The time-driven approach avoids the costly, time-consuming, and subjective activity-surveying task of conventional ABC. It uses time equations that directly and automatically assign resource costs to the activities performed and transactions processed. Only two parameters need to be estimated: the capacity cost rate for the department and the capacity usage by each transaction processed in the department. Both parameters can be estimated easily and objectively.

The capacity cost rate is defined below:

$$\text{Capacity cost rate} = \frac{\text{Cost of capacity supplied}}{\text{Practical capacity of resources supplied}}$$

The cost of capacity supplied is, of course, the $567,000 per month. To estimate the practical capacity, the TDABC team identifies the quantity of resources (typically, personnel or equipment) that actually perform work. Assume that the department employs 28 frontline people (this doesn't count supervisors or support staff). Each frontline employee works an average of 20 days per month (60 days per quarter) and is paid for 7.5 hours of work each day. Each employee shows up at work, therefore, for about 450 hours, or 27,000 minutes per quarter.

Not all the time paid for is available for productive work. Employees in the customer service department spend about 75 minutes per day in breaks, training, and education. Thus, the practical capacity for each employee is about 22,500 minutes per quarter (375 minutes per day multiplied by 60 days per quarter). With 28 frontline employees, the department has a practical capacity of 630,000 minutes. The cost rate (per minute) of supplying capacity, the first estimate for a TDABC model, can now be calculated:

$$\text{Capacity cost rate} = \frac{\$567,000}{630,000 \text{ minutes}} = \$0.90 \text{ per minute}$$

Estimating the practical capacity for an employee or a piece of equipment should be straightforward. Calculate how many days per month, on average, employees and machines work, and how many hours or minutes per day employees or equipment are available to do actual work, after subtracting time for scheduled breaks, training, meetings, maintenance, and other sources of downtime. This amount need not be calculated precisely; an error of a few percentage points will rarely be fatal, and major errors will be detected through unexpected shortages or excesses of capacity.

The second estimate required for the TDABC model is the capacity required—in this and most cases, time—to perform each transaction. Conventional ABC uses a transaction driver whenever an activity—such as *set up machine*, *issue purchase order*, or *process customer request*—takes about the same amount of time. TDABC, instead of using such transaction drivers, simply has the project team estimate the time required to perform each of these transactional activities. The time estimates can be obtained either by direct observation or by interviews. As with the estimate of practical capacity, precision is not critical; rough accuracy is sufficient. And unlike the percentages that employees subjectively estimate for a conventional ABC model, the capacity-consumption estimates in a time-driven model can be readily observed and validated.

Returning to the numerical example, suppose that the TDABC team obtains estimates of the following average unit times for the three customer-related activities:

Process customer orders: 8 minutes

Handle customer inquiries : 44 minutes

Perform credit check: 50 minutes

The team now simply calculates the cost driver rate for the three types of activities performed in the customer service department by cross-multiplying the capacity cost rate with each activity's estimated unit time:

	TDABC COST DRIVER	
Activity	Unit Time (minutes)	Rate (at $0.90/minute)
Process customer order	8	$ 7.20
Handle customer inquiry	44	$39.60
Perform credit check	50	$45.00

Alternatively, we can replace the three customer service activities in the conventional ABC model with a single time equation for the department:

Customer service time (minutes) = 8 × number of orders processed +
44 × number of customer inquiries +
50 × number of customer credit checks

The TDABC cost driver rates are somewhat lower than those estimated by the conventional ABC model. The reason for this discrepancy becomes obvious when we recalculate the cost of performing the three activities during the recent quarter.

Activity	Unit Time	Quantity	Total Minutes	Total Cost
Process customer order	8	49,000	392,000	$352,800
Handle customer inquiry	44	1,400	61,600	55,440
Perform credit check	50	2,500	125,000	112,500
Used capacity			578,600	$520,740
Unused capacity (8.2%)			51,400	46,260
Total			630,000	$567,000

The analysis reveals that only about 92 percent of the practical capacity (578,600 divided by 630,000) of the resources supplied during the period was used for productive work; hence only 92 percent of the total expenses of $567,000 is assigned to customers during this period. The conventional ABC system overestimates the costs of performing activities because its distribution-of-effort survey, while quite accurate (the estimated percentage mix of 70, 10, and 20 is quite close to the actual mix of 67.7, 10.6, and 21.6 percent of the productive work across the three activities), incorporates both the costs of resource capacity used and the costs of unused resources. By specifying the unit times to perform each instance of the activity, the organization gets a more valid signal about the cost and underlying efficiency of each activity as well as the quantity (51,400 hours) and cost ($46,260) of the unused capacity in the resources supplied to perform the activity.

While the TDABC model is initially estimated on historical data, its main power is to help predict the future. Suppose, in the next period, the quantity of activities is expected to be 51,000 customer orders, 1,150 customer inquiries, and 2,700 credit checks. During the period, the company can operate the TDABC model as a standard cost model—though, of course, with many more cost drivers than a traditional standard cost model—and assign costs to orders and customers on the basis of the standard rates, calculated at practical capacity: $7.20 per order, $39.60 per customer inquiry, and $45.00 per credit check. This calculation can be performed in real time to assign customer administration costs to individual customers, as their transactions occur. The standard cost rates can also be used in discussions with customers about acceptance and pricing of new business.

Assuming that the actual quantities at the end of the period correspond to those expected, as specified above, the company obtains a simple and informative report shortly after the end of the period:

Activity	Quantity	Unit Time	Total Time	Unit Cost	Total Cost Assigned
Process customer order	51,000	8	408,000	$7.20	$367,200
Handle customer inquiry	1,150	44	50,600	39.60	45,540
Perform credit check	2,700	50	135,000	45.00	121,500
Used capacity			593,600		$534,240
Unused capacity (5.8%)			36,400		32,760
Total			630,000		$567,000

The report reveals the time required to perform the three activities, as well as their resource costs. It also highlights the difference between capacity supplied (both quantity and cost) and capacity used. Managers can review the $32,760 cost of the unused capacity and contemplate actions to determine whether and how to reduce the costs of supplying unused resources in subsequent periods.

Rather than reduce currently unused capacity, managers may choose to reserve that capacity for future growth. As managers consider new product introductions, expansion into new markets, or just increases in product and customer demand, they can forecast how much of the increased business can be handled by existing capacity. For example, the vice president of operations at Lewis-Goetz, a hose and belt fabricator based in Pittsburgh, saw that one of his plants was operating at only 27 percent of capacity. Rather than attempt to downsize the plant, he decided to maintain the capacity for a large contract he expected to win later that year. Managers can also forecast where capacity shortages are likely to arise if forecasted increases in demand will exceed currently available capacity.

TIME EQUATIONS

Time-Driven ABC easily incorporates variation in the time demands made by different types of transactions. It does not require the simplifying assumption, made so far, that all orders or transactions are the same and require the same amount of time to be processed. We can allow the unit time estimates in a TDABC model to vary on the basis of order and activity characteristics.

Companies can usually predict the drivers that cause individual transactions to be simpler or more complex to process. For example, consider the department of a chemicals distribution company that packages customer orders for shipment. A standard item in a compliant package may require only 0.5 minutes. If the item requires a special package, then an additional 6.5 minutes is required. And if the item is to be shipped by air, an additional 0.2 minutes is required to place it in a plastic bag. Rather than define a separate activity for every possible combination of shipping characteristics, or estimate transaction times for every possible shipping combination, the time-driven approach estimates the department's resource demand by a simple equation:

$$\text{Packaging time} = 0.5 + 6.5 \; \{\text{if special handling required}\} + 0.2 \; \{\text{if shipping by air}\}$$

While seemingly complicated and demanding of data, in fact time equations are generally quite simple to implement since many companies' ERP systems already store data on order, packaging, distribution, and other characteristics. These order- and transaction-specific data enable the particular time demands for any given order to be quickly calculated with a simple algorithm that tests for the existence of each characteristic affecting resource consumption. TDABC models expand linearly with variation by adding terms in a time equation.

The accuracy of a TDABC model arises from its ability to capture the resource demands from diverse operations by simply adding more terms to the departmental time equation. Returning to the packaging department, let's say that the chemicals company wants to offer a new differentiating feature by giving its customers access to hazardous materials. To capture the cost of this feature, packaging personnel do not need to be reinterviewed to learn what percentage of their time will be required for packaging orders for hazardous chemicals. The TDABC model manager simply adds one more term for this possible variation in the packaging activity. The new equation becomes

$$\text{Packaging time} = 0.5 + 6.5 \; \{\text{if special handling required}\} + 0.2 \; \{\text{if shipping by air}\} + 30 \; \text{minutes} \; \{\text{if hazardous material}\}$$

In contrast, conventional ABC requires a geometric expansion to capture the increase in complexity. The packaging department's work would be decomposed into four distinct activities:

- Packaging standard product
- Packaging product with special handling requirements
- Packaging product for air shipment
- Packaging hazardous material

Each period (e.g., month), personnel in the packaging department would be surveyed for estimates of what percentage of their time is spent with each activity. This survey is time-consuming and subjective. The TDABC model allows all these activities to be combined into one process, with one equation. A typical TDABC model requires fewer equations than the number of activities used in a conventional ABC system, while permitting much more variety and complexity in orders, products, and customers. Complexity in the process, caused by a particular product or order, may add terms, but the department is still modeled as one process with one time equation. This feature adds accuracy to the model at little additional cost and effort. And once a time equation is built for each process, through interviews and time studies, as will be described in chapter 2, the model dynamically reflects the actual activity in each period.

The time equations in a TDABC model also provide managers with a capability for simulating the future. The equations capture the principal factors that create demands for process capacity, including changes in process efficiencies, product volume and mix, customer order patterns, and channel mix. Managers can use their TDABC model to perform dynamic what-if analysis of various scenarios. The model can easily be incorporated into a new budgeting process that analytically calculates the required supply and spending on resource capacity that is needed to deliver on future periods' sales and production plans. For example, at Citigroup, managers use the TDABC model for business planning, determining the level of staffing necessary to deliver anticipated customer service demands.[5]

MODEL UPDATING

Managers can easily update a TDABC model to reflect changes in their operating conditions. As already noted, they don't have to reinterview personnel when more activities are added to a department. They simply estimate the unit times required for each new activity identified. Managers can incorporate the effect of complex versus simple orders by estimating the incremental unit time required when a complex transaction must be handled. For example, one food service company modified the algorithm for customer service time to reflect the additional time required to process special orders and those that required credit memos. The algorithm subtracted time if the order came via an electronic data interchange (EDI) connection. In this way, TDABC models evolve seamlessly as managers learn more about additional variety and complexity in their processes, orders, suppliers, and customers.

Managers can also easily update cost driver rates. Two factors cause a cost driver rate to change. First, changes in the prices of resources supplied affect the capacity cost rate. For example, if employees receive an 8 percent compensation increase, the cost rate increases from $0.90 per supplied minute to $0.97 per minute. If new machines are substituted or added to a process, the analyst modifies the capacity cost rate to reflect the change in operating expense associated with introducing the new equipment.

The second factor affecting the cost driver rate is a shift in the efficiency of the activity. Quality (six sigma) programs, other continuous improvement efforts, reengineering, or the introduction of new technology can reduce the time or resources needed for the same activity. When permanent, sustainable improvements in a process have been made, the TDABC analyst modifies the unit time estimates (and therefore the demands on resources) to reflect the process improvement. For example, if a computerized database is made available to the customer administration department, the people may be able to perform a standard credit check in 12 minutes rather than 50 minutes. The improvement is simple to accommodate; just change the unit time estimate to 12 minutes, and the new activity cost driver rate automatically becomes $10.80 per credit check (down from $45.00). The new rate may be somewhat higher than $10.80 after the unit cost rate has been increased (above $0.90 per minute) to reflect the department's cost for the newly acquired database and computer system.

In summary, TDABC models are updated on the basis of events rather than by the calendar (once a quarter, or annually). Any time that analysts learn about a significant shift in the costs of resources supplied, or changes in the resources required for the activity, they update the capacity cost rate. When they learn of a significant and permanent shift in the efficiency with which an activity is performed, they reduce the unit time estimate to reflect the lower time required. Best-practice TDABC companies assign an operational owner to each process time equation, thereby ensuring that each equation remains accurate as business processes evolve and become more efficient.

— Duration
Drivers

TIME-DRIVEN ABC:
"OLD WINE (DURATION DRIVERS) IN NEW BOTTLES?"

Some have attempted to minimize the TDABC innovation by claiming that conventional ABC always had the capability to use time as a cost driver. They cite the role of duration drivers in conventional ABC—an idea introduced by Robin Cooper in a seminal article.[6] Cooper observed that early ABC systems used a large number of transactional cost drivers to count the number of times an activity was performed. Examples of transaction drivers include number of production runs, number of setups, number of shipments, number of purchase orders, and number of customer orders. When the resources required to perform each activity vary, such as when some setups are more difficult or complex than others, or when some customer orders require more time and effort to process than others do, Cooper observed that ABC systems introduce *duration drivers* to estimate the time required to perform an activity. Examples of duration drivers are setup hours, materials handling time, and, of course, direct labor hours and machine hours. Duration drivers are generally more accurate than transaction drivers, but they are also more expensive to measure. Therefore, most ABC designers strive to use transaction drivers whenever these drivers reasonably approximate resource demands by each occurrence of an activity.[7]

Conventional ABC systems, however, use duration drivers in a fundamentally different way than the role of "time" in TDABC. Conventional systems apply duration drivers in the second stage of a cost assignment process, after resource costs have already been mapped to different activities using the expensive and time-consuming interview or survey approach. For example, in our numerical example of the customer service department, instead of assuming that all customer inquiries take the same amount of time, an analyst building a conventional ABC model could estimate the *duration* of each inquiry. But the analyst still has to first interview and survey all customer service personnel to get their subjective estimates about the percentage of time they spend to handle customer orders, process customer inquiries, and perform credit checks. The duration driver adds accuracy to the conventional ABC model at some additional measurement cost. The important distinction is that the higher cost for using duration drivers in conventional ABC is over and beyond the high cost still required to map resource costs to activities before using the duration driver. Duration drivers add more accuracy, but in a conventional ABC model, they do not eliminate the high cost of first driving costs to activities. The TDABC innovation, in contrast, uses time to drive costs directly from resources to cost objects, skipping entirely the tedious and error-prone stage of first assigning resource costs to activities.

SUMMARY

Since the mid-1980s, Activity-Based Costing has enabled managers to see that not all revenue is good revenue, and not all customers are profitable customers. Unfortunately, the difficulties of implementing and maintaining a conventional ABC system have prevented this innovation from being an effective, timely, and up-to-date management tool. The Time-Driven ABC approach overcomes these difficulties and has the following advantages:

1. Easier and faster to build an accurate model
2. Integrates well with data now available from ERP and customer relationship management systems (this makes the system more dynamic and less people-intensive)
3. Drives costs to transactions and orders using specific characteristics of particular orders, processes, suppliers, and customers
4. Can be run monthly to capture the economics of the most recent operations
5. Provides visibility to process efficiencies and capacity utilization
6. Forecasts resource demands, allowing companies to budget for resource capacity on the basis of predicted order quantities and complexity
7. Is easily scalable to enterprisewide models via enterprise-scalable applications software and database technologies
8. Enables fast and inexpensive model maintenance
9. Supplies granular information to assist users with identifying the root cause of problems
10. Can be used in any industry or company with complexity in customers, products, channels, segments, and processes and large amounts of people and capital expenditures

These characteristics allow ABC to move from a complex, expensive financial system to a tool that provides accurate and actionable data to managers, quickly, frequently, and inexpensively.

Part I of this book provides an in-depth explanation of how to build a TDABC model as well as extensions of the approach to new applications. This chapter introduced and defined TDABC, giving a brief tour of the history of ABC and how it has evolved.

Chapter 2 explores the principal innovation in TDABC, showing how the model estimates demands for resource capacity, principally time, by transactions and other cost objects. The chapter provides more in-depth treatment of the important innovation of time equations.

Chapter 3 describes how to calculate capacity cost rates, the second component in a TDABC model. It discusses when to capture cost at a department or a process level, how to incorporate all relevant costs in the numerator of the capacity cost rate, and how to measure practical capacity. Also addressed are the impact of seasonal and peak-load capacity and options for using actual or budgeted costs.

Chapter 4 discusses the project and implementation steps typically used to build a TDABC model in practice.

Chapter 5 introduces the powerful new extension to perform what-if analysis and, especially, activity-based budgeting with a TDABC model. Activity-based budgeting has been discussed for some time, but now becomes far more practical with a TDABC model. The budgeting process culminates with authorizations for resource spending. This decision is all about how much capacity the company needs to supply in future periods. By using the TDABC model as the core of its budgeting process, a company can now easily link its strategic plan and sales and production forecast to the specific demands for capacity required to implement the plan and realize the forecast. Budgeting is often a painful, tedious negotiating process. Time-driven activity-based budgeting for resource capacity substitutes analytic rigor for endless and frustrating negotiations.

Chapter 6 presents a fascinating application to the merger and acquisition due-diligence process. Several firms have constructed quick and approximate TDABC models of potential acquisition candidates to estimate the magnitude of potential near-term profit turnarounds from rationalizing product mix, renegotiating terms with customers, and implementing process improvements.

Chapter 7 extends TDABC to integrate with several contemporary improvement initiatives: lean management, supply chain management, and benchmarking. These applications are still in the embryonic stage, but we do have early evidence that they offer significant benefits to companies.

Part II of this book contains short case studies that illustrate various aspects of TDABC and its application to different industry settings.

Appendix A at the end of the book summarizes the actions that companies take with the information from an ABC model. The material is not unique to TDABC; it would be equally applicable for a conventional ABC model, but we include the action options for readers relatively new to ABC. Appendix B presents answers to frequently asked questions (FAQs) about TDABC.

NOTES

1. R. S. Kaplan and R. Cooper, "Measure Costs Right; Make the Right Decisions," *Harvard Business Review* (September–October 1988): 96–103; and R. S. Kaplan and R. Cooper, "Profit Priorities from Activity-Based Costing," *Harvard Business Review* (May–June 1991): 130–135.
2. Darrell Rigby, *Management Tools 2003* (Boston: Bain & Company, 2003).
3. Sources of organizational resistance to ABC and some suggested solutions to this problem are described in C. Argyris and R. S. Kaplan, "Implementing New Knowledge: The Case of Activity-Based Costing," *Accounting Horizons* (September 1994): 83–105.
4. Cooper and Kaplan, "Profit Priorities from Activity-Based Costing," and "Measuring the Cost of Resource Capacity," in R. S. Kaplan and R. Cooper, *Cost &*

Effect: Using Integrated Cost Systems to Drive Profitability and Performance (Boston: Harvard Business School Press, 1998), 111–136.

5. S. Anderson and L. Maisel, "Putting It All Together at Citigroup: How IT Value Management Is Leading CTI into the Next Millennium," Acorn Systems white paper (Houston: Acorn Systems, April 2006).

6. R. Cooper, "The Two-Stage Procedure in Cost Accounting: Part Two," *Journal of Cost Management* (fall 1997): 39–45.

7. If different amounts of resources are used each time an activity is performed, then even time estimates (duration drivers) may not be adequate. In this case, an intensity driver that directly charges resource cost for each incident of the activity may be required. See Kaplan and Cooper, *Cost & Effect*, 95–99, for a discussion on the nature of, and trade-offs between, transaction, duration, and intensity cost drivers.

## CHAPTER TWO

ESTIMATING PROCESS TIMES

The Role of Time Equations

TIME-DRIVEN ACTIVITY-BASED COSTING, as the name implies, uses time to drive resource costs directly to objects such as transactions, orders, products, services, and customers. The use of a resource capacity metric, time, as the primary cost driver enables TDABC to skip the complex stage, in conventional ABC, of allocating resource costs to activities before driving them to cost objects. TDABC uses time as its primary cost driver since most resources, such as personnel and equipment, have capacities that can be readily measured by the amount of time they are available to perform work. Some resources, however, as shown below, measure capacity with other units:

Resource	Capacity Measure
Vehicle capacity (volume), warehouse space	Cubic meters
Vehicle capacity (weight)	Kilograms
Data storage capacity	Gigabytes
Data bandwidth	Bauds

In this chapter, we focus on developing equations that estimate the demands for time on capacity resources. But the approach generalizes readily to other resources, such as those above, whose capacity is measured in units other than time.

Conventional ABC drives activity costs to products with transaction quantities, such as numbers of setups, customer orders, customer requests, production runs, material receipts, material movements, and vendor payments. It uses transaction drivers for two reasons. First, candidly, the full theory of ABC as a mechanism for driving the *costs of using capacity* down to the triggering demands for capacity had not been articulated or fully understood at the birth of ABC in the mid-1980s. The early ABC articles, cases, and adopters, therefore, used simple mechanisms for allocating indirect and support costs down to cost objects rather than using capacity-based drivers. This practice still persists in most conventional ABC applications.

Transaction drivers were also convenient since the operating processes and information systems of the 1980s were not up to the task of estimating the demands for capacity from individual transactions and orders. Companies operated with informal, ad hoc processes and had dispersed, legacy computer systems. They did not have systematic, machine-readable data on the incidence and intensity of transactions. To run early ABC models, project teams often had to perform quite heroic data collection efforts to bring together even surrogate measures for transaction counts from multiple databases and information systems.

Today, fortunately, the situation is dramatically different. The central role for measuring the cost of capacity utilization in ABC models has now been developed.[1] And most enterprises today have enterprise resource planning (ERP) systems that collect and store transaction data such as order header, customer identity, order detail, bill of materials, and other order features.[2] Further, since the mid-1980s, companies across the globe have invested hundreds of billions of dollars in applications, databases, data warehouses, and the like to capture key data elements across the enterprise in ERP, CRM (customer relationship management), call center, supply chain, logistics, transportation, and warehouse systems.

Beyond their data collection and reporting capabilities, ERP systems impose a process management discipline on companies. This discipline is reinforced by the widespread adoption of improvement methodologies such as total quality management, six sigma, lean manufacturing, and process reengineering. These methodologies transform ad hoc and non-repeatable activities into consistent, efficient, and well-documented processes that require systematic data collection.

Once the processes have been stabilized, standardized, and documented, major process changes are infrequent. Continuous process improvements do occur, and sustainable changes can and should trigger an update of the TDABC time standards, as described in chapter 1. But considering the extensive effort needed to standardize critical processes within an organization, management does not uproot their structure very often.

Even previously nonstandardized and unmonitored activities in research, marketing, and sales departments have become more systematic and documented. For example, Conco Food Service incorporates several definable drivers—last year's sales, forecast volume, and the number of product categories purchased—in the sales plans of each sales representative. It then tracks the actual quantities for these drivers in the company's information system. The company also tracks, in machine-readable form, sales call information (e.g., number of calls and call times), travel distance, number of rush deliveries, how items are shipped, and travel and entertainment expenditures. It feeds these data into a sales process time equation so that management can accurately estimate how much time the salespersons are spending with each customer. Companies like Conco also record data on their distribution system by employing global positioning system (GPS) and radiofrequency identification (RFID) technologies to track the movement of trucks and inventory.

With TDABC, a company can easily tap into these databases to estimate the resource demands on processes triggered by a production, sales, distribution, delivery, or payment event. TDABC exploits these rich data sets online and inexpensively. In summary, the synergistic combination of new theory, streamlined and standardized processes, and new systems has provided the platform on which accurate and inexpensive time-driven cost and profitability models can be built.

ESTIMATING TIME CONSUMPTION

The key input into a TDABC model is the time (capacity) required to perform an activity, such as processing an order, performing a production run, or servicing a customer. For more than a century, industrial engineers have estimated standard times for the work performed by direct labor or machines. These engineers have typically focused on repetitive frontline work by production workers or service deliverers, such as bank tellers and call center operators. This experience has both good and bad implications for TDABC. The good news is that standard procedures exist for measuring the time required to perform all kinds of different activities. While industrial engineers have historically focused on employees thought to be "variable costs," that is, direct production workers who touch and build the product, or customer service workers who deliver services and respond to customer transactions, it is simple to extend the industrial engineering approach to the work performed by almost all indirect and support employees. Thus, the time estimates for TDABC system require a measurement capability that many organizations already have or can easily acquire.

The bad news is that industrial engineers have historically focused on making incremental improvements in the use of labor and machine resources. They attempt to reduce, by a few percentage points, the standard times required to produce a product, deliver a service, or meet a standard customer need. Because many short-run improvement opportunities are small, the engineers perform costly measurements to calculate standard times out to three or four decimal digits per transaction. In many people's minds, the idea of letting their industrial engineering staff loose to measure process times throughout the enterprise at this level of precision is too horrible to contemplate.

But for the strategic costing purposes of a TDABC model, companies need accuracy, not precision. Knowing the first digit accurately, being close on the second digit, and then placing the number of zeros and decimal point correctly are more than adequate for TDABC. This level of accuracy and precision can be obtained easily and inexpensively by "industrial engineering lite."

These so-called lite measurements are obtained by multiple methods: direct observation (the venerable stopwatch and clipboard approach), accumulating the time required to process fifty to one hundred similar transactions and calculating the average time per transaction processed, interviewing or surveying employees, utilizing existing process maps, or leveraging time estimates from elsewhere in the company or industry. In conventional ABC, the project leader asks employees to fill in surveys of how they spread their time across multiple types of activities. The TDABC surveys are quite different; the project leader solicits direct estimates of the time required to perform the specific steps of a process, such as performing a credit check or entering a line item or placing a rush order. In our experience, employees find it far easier to estimate the time required to perform a standard activity than to estimate the percentage of their total time that an activity, in aggregate, consumes over a three- to six-month period. And, should the employee be unsure about the estimate, the project leader can always directly observe the time someone takes to perform the transaction, a measurement that can be accomplished in minutes or hours, rather than weeks or months. As in much management accounting, TDABC strives to be approximately right rather than precisely wrong.

Regardless of the method of gathering the process times, it is even more important to ensure that the estimates correspond to actual events.

We recommend discussing time estimates during interviews with department personnel and supervisors. The discussion engages department personnel and encourages them to take a proactive role in, and ownership of, their departmental time estimates.

TIME EQUATIONS

Typically, transaction characteristics cause processing times to vary. In these cases, simple time estimates are inadequate. For example, a production order can be routine or expedited, a customer order can be standard or complex, and shipping can be local or international. Each variation leads to different demands for resource capacity.[3]

Conventional ABC handles variation by expanding the dictionary of activities so that all the major known variations are treated as separate activities. *Cost & Effect*, a book coauthored by one of us, illustrates a standard high-level activity dictionary commonly used.[4] The dictionary consists of seven high-level operating processes and six management and support processes. Each of these thirteen processes has between three and eleven subprocesses. For example, *process customer order* is a subprocess within the *market and sell* operating process. Even this two-digit-level subprocess, however, has variations within it. The ABC activity dictionary, as shown below, shows further detail down to a five-digit sub-sub-sub-subprocess level.

4. Market and sell
     . . .
     . . .
   4.2 Process customer order
       4.2.1 Create customer file
       4.2.2 Obtain rate quote from sales
       4.2.3 Verify special charges and credits
       4.2.4 Create transportation document
             4.2.4.1 Domestic
             4.2.4.2 International
                     4.2.4.2.1 Prepare customs forms
                     4.2.4.2.2 Prepare shipper's declaration
                     4.2.4.2.3 Arrange for consular clearance
       4.2.5 Create document to describe special services or handling
       4.2.6 Prepare document for dangerous-goods handling

Each subactivity within subprocess 4.2 represents an important varia-tion in a customer order; each requires a quantity of resources to handle its features. And subprocess 4.2 is just one of 72 two-digit subprocesses in a standard ABC activity dictionary. One can readily see the complexity of attempting to drive costs down to each three-, four-, and five-digit sub-activity level by asking employees what percentage of their time is spent performing each subactivity. Yet such granularity in the model may be critically important since, otherwise, the model fails to capture the differ-ential cost between very different orders. Consider, for example, the cost of an order for a standard product in standard packaging delivered in bulk using standard delivery vehicles versus an order for a customized product produced in small batches, shipped in special packaging, and em-ploying a customized distribution and delivery option. Such activity de-tail in a conventional ABC model causes the quantity of data estimates, storage, and processing to increase exponentially with the number of ac-tivity variations.

In contrast, TDABC does not need an activity dictionary. The analyst simply estimates the demands for resource capacity for each activity vari-ation. Consider process 4.2, above, *process customer order.* For this activity, the TDABC analyst develops an additive, linear equation to represent the basic time required to process a standard customer order, plus the incre-mental time associated with each variation that can occur. Consider the following time equation for subprocess 4.2:

$$
\begin{aligned}
\text{Order processing time (minutes)} = {} & 10 + 5 \ \{\text{if new customer}\} \\
& + 2 \times \text{number of line items} \\
& + 4 \times \text{number of rate quotes} \\
& + \{\text{if international order}\} \\
& \quad (2 \ \{\text{if customs form}\} \\
& \quad + 5 \ \{\text{if shipping declaration}\} \\
& \quad + 10 \ \{\text{if consular clearance}\}) \\
& + \{\text{if special services}\} \\
& \quad (5 \ \{\text{if rush order}\} \\
& \quad + 10 \ \{\text{if credit hold}\} \\
& \quad + 2 \ \{\text{if hazardous material}\})
\end{aligned}
$$

This equation states that the processing time for a standard domestic order from an existing customer with 5 line items and no special handling or services takes 20 minutes to set up [10 + (2 × 5)]. If the order requires that a new customer file be set up, this takes an additional 5 minutes. It takes about 4 minutes to obtain each special rate quote from the marketing department, 2 minutes to prepare a customs report for an international shipping document (but no shipping declaration or consular clearance required), plus the additional time for special services—a rush order, credit hold, or hazardous-material document. For this time equation, the analyst requires ten parameter estimates, none of which would be difficult to obtain from actual observations of the incremental work required to handle each special feature.

This example reveals that model size increases only linearly with real-world complexity, not exponentially, as in a conventional ABC model. This is a huge benefit from using time equations rather than transaction quantities. One medium-sized food distributor replaced its conventional ABC model of more than 900 activities with a TDABC model that captured more detail about activity variation with a far smaller model that consisted of about 100 time equations.[5] One national retailer built a time-driven model that captured all processes and transactions across more than a thousand stores. The model required 25 terabytes of data, but this was economically feasible, given the benefits from capturing profitability at the SKU-store level. The same level of accuracy in a conventional ABC model would have required a 250-terabyte model, even assuming the relevant parameters could be sensibly estimated.

Also, if the initial model happens to omit some important variation in a process or subprocess, the analyst simply adds one additional term to the time equation to reflect the incremental resource capacity (typically, time) required for this previously omitted variation. In conventional ABC, in contrast, a new subactivity requires reestimating all the percentage allocations before the new subactivity can be incorporated into the model. One can readily understand how conventional ABC models inhibit reevaluating the model and adapting it to the changing reality of an enterprise's operations.

Typically, activity times are stable for several periods. Many companies review the average or standard times annually to assess the cumulative impact of process changes made during the year. Or if a reengineering or major process improvement has occurred, they reestimate and enter the new activity time at project completion. As stated previously, best-practice TDABC customers assign process equation accuracy to the process owner, thereby ensuring a continually accurate model.

Some companies' information systems already capture actual time consumption for every transaction. Managers may certainly use actual rather than estimated or standard times when such times are readily available.

But this is not always a good idea. Actual times are not more accurate than standard times if actual times reflect random variation, individual employee variation, and nonrecurring factors that should not be incorporated into product and customer costs. The goal is to estimate expected (or standard) times for an activity, not to report on actual times, transaction by transaction. For example, a customer service employee who starts an order late in the day and finishes it the next morning would reflect a 17-hour time consumption in the company's information system, whereas in reality the order took 10 minutes on the afternoon of day one and 10 minutes on the morning of day two.

CASE STUDY: WILSON-MOHR

We illustrate the derivation of a departmental process time equation with an example of the inside sales department at Wilson-Mohr, an industrial controls distributor in Houston.[6] This department has seven employees located at four offices: Houston, Dallas, Corpus Christi, and Denver. The inside sales process across each of these locations is virtually identical (figure 2-1). The department receives customer orders, sets up new ac-

FIGURE 2-1

Inside Sales Process at Wilson-Mohr

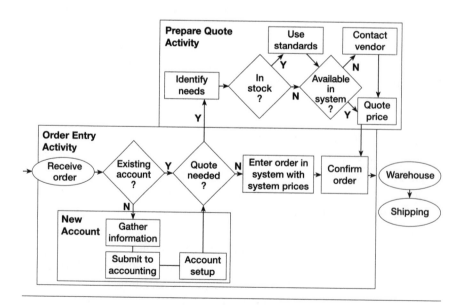

counts, prepares quotes, confirms availability for custom items, and transmits accepted and completed orders to the warehouse for shipping. The two core activity steps of order entry and quoting are the same in all four sites.

Wilson-Mohr estimates the *average time required to perform* each of the activities shown in figure 2-1. It uses a standard software package for order entry. All the company's inside sales representatives go through the same training, so activity times are standard, stable, and easily estimated. The computerized order entry system reinforces this consistency. Variation in order entry time is caused by order characteristics, such as whether the customer is an existing or a new one, whether the order uses a list or a quoted price. Figure 2-2 shows the incremental times associated with particular order characteristics.

The time equation for inside sales can now be easily determined:

> Inside sales time = order entry time + new-account setup time
>   + quoting time + order confirmation time
>   = receive order + enter order
>   + account setup {if new account}
>   + (identify need + contact vendor + quote price)
>   {if quote needed}
>   + confirm order
>   = 2 minutes + 2 minutes × (number of line items)
>   + 5 minutes {if new account}
>   + 1 minute {if quote needed} + 5 minutes
>   {if contact vendor}
>   + 6 minutes × (number of line items in quote)
>   + 1 minute

For the mathematically inclined, we can represent a time equation as a simple algebraic expression:

> Process time = sum of individual activity times
> $$= (\beta_0 + \beta_1 X_1 + \beta_2 X_2 + \beta_3 X_3 + \beta_4 X_4 + \beta_5 X_5 \ldots + \beta_i X_i)$$

where β_0 is the standard time for performing the basic activity (e.g., 10 minutes)

          β_i is the estimated time for the incremental activity i (e.g., 2 minutes)
          X_i is the quantity of incremental activity i (e.g., number of line items)

FIGURE 2-2

Times Applied to Process Steps

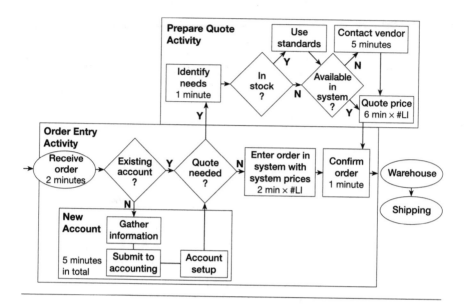

Estimating a time equation requires describing the basic activity and all major variations around it, identifying the drivers of the variations, and estimating the standard time for the basic activity and each variation. Figure 2-3 contains the information for estimating the time for Wilson-Mohr's inside sales process. The data from Figure 2-3 can be represented by the following time equation:

$$
\begin{aligned}
\text{Inside sales process time (in minutes)} = {} & 2 + (2 \times \text{LI}) + 5 \ \{\text{if NEW}\} \\
& + 1 \ \{\text{if CONF}\} + 1 \ \{\text{if QUOTE}\} \\
& + 5 \ \{\text{if NS}\} + 6 \times \text{LI} \\
& \{\text{if QCONF}\}^{[7]}
\end{aligned}
$$

If the company determines other factors that help explain variations of inside sales process time, it easily incorporates them into the time equation by adding new terms. For example, if rush orders take an additional 10 minutes, simply add the following term to the above equation:

$$
+ 10 \ \{\text{if RUSH}\}
$$

FIGURE 2-3

Building the Time Equation for Inside Sales Process

Activity	Key Drivers	Time per Step
Enter order	• Receive order	2 minutes (β_0)
	• Set up new account	5 minutes (β_1)
	• Enter order	2 minutes per line item (LI) (β_2)
	• Confirm order	1 minute (β_3)
Prepare quote	• Identify need for quote	1 minute (β_4)
	• Contact vendor about nonstocked items (NS)	5 minutes (β_5)
	• Quote price	6 minutes per line item (β_6)

In this way, analysts adjust the model's time equations as they learn more about the systematic factors that cause process variation, or as the company adds new features, channels, and services.

One final, perhaps obvious and trivial, observation is to keep the time units consistent within an equation. We have found that "minutes" works better than "hours" for measuring most repetitive processes. Working with integers seems to be easier for employees than thinking in terms of decimals or fractions of hours.

TRANSACTIONS AS UNIT OF ANALYSIS

Standard ABC software packages treat products, services, and customers as the ultimate cost object, the fundamental driver of costs. But, as just shown, even for a standard product shipped to an existing customer, considerable variation arises at the order level, not the product or customer level. TDABC software, while capable of driving costs directly to products, services, and customers, calculates many costs at a deeper and more fundamental level by using time equations based on actual transactions. At Citigroup, having this level of granularity was important for organizational buy-in, says Jeff Nachowitz, chief financial officer of Citigroup Technology Infrastructure Division:

> *Transparency of costs is an elusive concept and in a large, complex organization there will be "winners and losers," creating a political element to any chargeback methodology. As such, dealing with facts and data that are reliable and recognizable is key in building integrity and trust with internal customers . . . A typical comment is "I don't understand what you're charging me for or how to manage the cost."*

No information is lost by performing calculations at the order or transaction level, since it is simple to aggregate these up to the higher level of products and customers.

As a vivid example, Hunter Corporation (disguised), a large distributor of scientific supplies, initially developed a conventional ABC model to trace costs and profits only to its 880 customer segments, even though it had more than 350,000 total customers. The conventional ABC model and associated software could not handle the complexity of driving costs down to individual customers. The ABC model reported that one customer segment was unprofitable, but the model could not provide cost or profit granularity beneath this large category. Only after migrating to a time-driven model that accurately assigned costs down to individual orders and transactions did Hunter learn that most customers in this segment were, in fact, quite profitable. The overall segment loss was caused by one large but demanding customer. This insight led to a 180-degree change in strategy. Instead of dropping the entire customer segment, the company renegotiated with the large customer, transforming it and the entire segment into profitability.

BUILDING THE TIME EQUATION

Any company that has already mapped its processes, as in the inside sales process of Wilson-Mohr, can build its time equations directly. Those without process maps can start at a simpler level by estimating the minimum time to perform the process, calling this β_0 in the time equation:

$$\text{Basic process time} = \beta_0$$

Next, add the principal factor that increases this basic process time. For example, the basic time to locate an item in a warehouse for picking could be 2 minutes. Additional time is required to pick the quantity of items. Letting β_1 equal the picking time per item, and X_1 the number of items to be picked for shipment:

$$\text{Process time} = \beta_0 + \beta_1 X_1 = 2 + 0.5 \times (\text{number of items to be picked})$$

For low-cost or low-variability processes, a single driver will usually be sufficient. For higher-cost processes, and for those with considerable variability, the time equation is expanded. Departmental personnel are usually the best source of information about the required complexity.

They know the impact of special orders, complex products, and demanding customers. This variation can be the difference between whether an order is profitable or unprofitable, so it is essential for the cost system to capture the factors that cause variation in resource demands. The Sanac Logistics case study (chapter 9) provides a good example of developing time equations when many transaction contingencies can occur.

Our experiences based on dozens of TDABC implementations suggest that project teams use the following sequence to estimate time equations.

1. *Begin with the most costly processes.* Start the TDABC model where most of the time is spent and cost is incurred. The accurate cost modeling of these processes will have more potential impact on the bottom line than focusing on a department with only a single employee and costing, in aggregate, $60,000 per year. For example, Compton Financial's technology costs exceed 25 percent of total spending. Compton sensibly started with a model that measured how the different customer segments used the company's expensive computing and telecommunication resources. Many companies have process models that can be used as a starting point.

2. *Define the scope of the process.* Be clear about what initiates the process and when it concludes. For example, for outside sales, the main activity could be the time the salesperson spends at a client visit, but the process time could also include the time to set up the appointment, prepare for the meeting, drive to and from the customer's location, and follow up with the customer after the meeting.

3. *Determine the key drivers of time.* For each activity, identify the most significant, influential factor that consumes resource time (capacity). In the previous example, the time to visit and return from a customer's location could be most influenced by travel distance.

4. *Use readily available driver variables.* Companies should not install new data-collection technologies solely to feed a TDABC model. If, for example, the company does not already track within its CRM system how much time a salesperson spends with a customer, it can use other factors on which it does have data—new customer or not, account type, sales volume, number of orders, number of returns, or number of phone calls—to estimate salesperson contact time. However, if key processes that consume a large percentage of total costs have data gaps, such gaps can and do provide ample justification for new data-collection systems. If

an information gap is critical for managing the process, the investment is justified.

5. *Start simple.* Initially, use a single driver variable for an equation. For example, customer delivery time may initially be estimated from the number of orders delivered. If more accuracy is required, then consider what data are available to increase accuracy, for example, customer distance, quantity shipped, and whether cash must be collected on delivery (COD).

6. *Engage operational personnel to help build and validate the model.* At the end of the day, a cost model is only as good as the organization perceives it to be. Ignoring departmental input will limit buy-in and ultimately jeopardize impact. The project team needs to explain the purpose of the project to employees in operations and sales. Next, explain how their department is involved. Work with them in building the initial, albeit simple, time equations. From there, complexity can more easily be understood and added. At Denman & Davis, a steel service center in New Jersey, department managers had to sign off on their process time equations. At Kemps LLC, a manufacturer and marketer of dairy products, the project team used a longtime employee from operations to validate each time equation. He went through each one in exquisite detail, insisting on small modifications, until he was satisfied about its accuracy. Only then would he sign off on it. Operations people, knowing how meticulous this individual was, accepted his sign-off as a guarantee of model accuracy.

ASSIGNING COSTS DIRECTLY ON THE BASIS OF PERCENTAGE OF TIME CONSUMED

Many of the early implementations of TDABC, including several case studies described in part II of this book, used an expedited and simplified approach when the companies built their models. These companies assigned actual monthly departmental costs directly to transactions, products, and customers on the basis of the proportion of actual time used by each transaction. They skipped the estimation of practical capacity and capacity cost rates, to be described in the next chapter, for several reasons.

First, assigning actual monthly costs directly via time equations is extremely simple and quick. Once the company knows its monthly departmental expenses and has estimates of the time used in the department, it can assign costs to objects directly without estimating practical capacity in each department or process. Second, many managers and financial executives value having all the expenses of a department assigned each month to the actual transactions performed, products produced, and customers served. A controller can add up the costs assigned to all the cost objects and verify that these reconcile with the total of departmental expenses recorded in the general ledger. Third, since no unused-capacity cost is recorded, tricky questions of how to assign such costs do not arise.

The process of allocating actual monthly costs to actual monthly transactions can be illustrated with the following simple example. Suppose a department has actual monthly costs of $200,000. The TDABC model for the month uses the department's time equations to estimate all the time demands in the department during the month. Suppose the total time demands add up to 125,000 minutes. The company calculates the cost per actual minute used:

$$\text{Cost per actual minute used} = \$200,000/125,000 \text{ minutes}$$
$$= \$1.60 \text{ per minute}$$

The model assigns this actual cost rate to all transactions performed during the month. For example, a transaction requiring 30 minutes in the department during the month would be assigned a cost of $48, and a customer that used 175 minutes of time during the month would be assigned a cost of $280. The same result would be obtained, of course, by assigning the costs using the ratio of time used to total time worked in the department. For the first transaction, the calculation is (30 divided by 125,000) multiplied by $200,000, which equals $48, and the customer cost calculation is (175 divided by 125,000) multiplied by $200,000, which equals $280.

The advantages of assigning departmental costs proportional to time consumed, however, have some corresponding disadvantages. By skipping the step of estimating practical capacity, the TDABC model does not signal when current operations are either over capacity or under. Also, if it does not calculate capacity cost rates, the company cannot fully exploit the powerful what-if dynamic simulation and activity-based budgeting analyses that will be described in chapter 5. Most important, when the company is operating with considerable excess capacity, the costs assigned to transactions and other cost objects will include not only the cost of resources they actually used but also the cost of unused capacity. If the company makes pricing and order acceptance or rejection decisions using product and customer costs inflated by excess capacity, it risks losing profitable orders and launching a death spiral. The company drops apparently unprofitable orders, products, and customers, and the operating expenses—which inevitably decline much slower than does sales volume—are spread over a smaller and smaller production and sales base.[8]

Conceptually, we prefer to apply time equations to the capacity cost rates that will be described in chapter 3. But we acknowledge that some companies, including many of our case studies in part II, prefer to bypass this step and assign costs on the basis of relative times used by transactions so that all departmental expenses are assigned down to orders handled, products produced, and customer served. Ultimately, companies must decide which approach to use. The decision is based on a trade-off between having a simple, low-cost calculation and one that requires more estimation (capacity cost rates) but that yields a more accurate assignment of the cost of using departmental resources and that reveals explicitly the cost of unused or overused capacity.

SUMMARY

Companies can implement time equations simply, rapidly, and powerfully. On the basis of these experiences, we identify the following benefits from employing this methodology.

Smaller and more scalable models: Time-Driven ABC models are smaller, simpler, and more flexible than conventional ABC models. Process complexity causes only linear increases in model size as analysts add terms to existing time equations.

Greater accuracy: Time-Driven ABC achieves greater accuracy by modeling process variation with additional terms in the process time equation. TDABC is also more accurate since the model is fed by data from a variety of systems, such as ERP, CRM, and the general ledger, which include the actual incidence of transactions and activities performed. People do not have to supply subjective, frequently inaccurate guesstimates of the proportion of their time spent on activities. The closer linkage of time equations to actual operating, distribution, and sales activities generates greater credibility for the model and acceptance among employees about the validity of the reported results.

Ease in building and maintaining models: To estimate time equations, fewer people need to be interviewed, and surveys of time allocations are eliminated. The time consumption data can be estimated or observed directly. The time equations allow the model to automatically incorporate actual variation in process intensity and mix, so the model does not need to be updated every month. As previously noted, the system is generally automated since it can be fed directly by transaction data from ERP and other systems. Analysis of reported results is facilitated because cost data are calculated at the transactional level—orders, line items, and SKUs. This facilitates both highly granular, detailed analysis as well as aggregate analysis at the product line, customer segment, or channel level.

Ease in rollout: Many processes are common across multiple industries. Most companies perform processes such as selling, order processing, purchasing, order fulfillment, order delivery, billing, and collection. Therefore, once a process equation is built at one facility, the equation can often be replicated for all other facilities across that company. Sometimes, a company can benefit by starting from an industry template or by using a process template developed in other industries. How different is the warehouse-picking process between Sysco Foods and Cisco Systems? Both companies trigger the process with a picking ticket derived from a shipping order, both have standard systems to optimize the picking process, and both use automated material-handling equipment to expedite the picking.

Ability to do capacity and predictive analysis: We will illustrate in chapter 5 how to embed a TDABC model into a comprehensive system to link planning to budgeting. The key insight is to use time equations to predict the resource capacity required to fulfill a sales and production plan. This enables a company to anticipate likely shortages or surpluses of resource capacity in future periods. A company can then take immediate actions either to modify the sales and production plans or to adjust future capacity so that the expected future demands can be met with minimal excess capacity or minimal capacity bottlenecks.

Identification of process improvement opportunities: In building the time equation, companies often identify activity steps that are wasteful and inefficient. These provide immediate guidance for process improvement initiatives. Companies with multiple facilities can compare time equations across facilities to identify best practices and transfer these practices to underperforming units. We discuss this benchmarking application in chapter 7.

The concept of modeling business processes is not new, nor is the notion of allocating cost on the basis of time. But using process-based time equations to assign resource costs is novel and powerful. Time equations, simple and intuitive, increase model accuracy and flexibility while reducing model size. They are easily adaptable. Even if the volume and mix of business activity changes, or if cost structures change, the time equations remain valid, without additional surveys or model changes. Their use enables an ABC team to build a model that dynamically reflects the variability and complexity inherent in any business and its processes.

More importantly, because the time equations represent a process model of the business, getting organizational buy-in is dramatically easier than it is with a solution that tries to "simplify the business through a modeling exercise." And the good news is that today, setting up a time equation or obtaining the data to implement it is simple.

NOTES

1. The key role for capacity in an ABC model was explicated in Kaplan and Cooper, *Cost & Effect: Using Integrated Cost Systems to Drive Profitability and Performance* (Boston: Harvard Business School Press, 1998).
2. Enterprise resource planning (ERP) systems provide a means of tracking financials, sales, and operational information. There are a multitude of vendors, the most recognized of which are those primarily designed to run in large companies, such as SAP and Oracle. Some vendors focus on middle-market companies while others target small to medium-sized companies within a specific industry. For example, AFS and IDS serve food distributors. Metalware, Stelplan, and Metalworld serve steel service centers.
3. See S. Anderson, "Should More Distributors and Wholesalers Practice Their ABCs?" Acorn Systems white paper (Houston: Acorn Systems, 1997).
4. R. S. Kaplan and R. Cooper, "ABC Activity and Process Dictionary," in R. S. Kaplan and R. Cooper, *Cost & Effect,* 108–110.
5. Database size is proportional to the number of records in the lowest-cost-object level, multiplied by the number of processes or activities, multiplied by the number of periods tracked in the model, multiplied by 3. Let us suppose we have a company that does 1 million line items and has 1,000 activities across 10 facilities and tracks 24 months of data in the model. Adding one more activity, a seemingly insignificant change, adds to the database 72 million records, a quantity comparable to all the records in a Microsoft Excel worksheet.
6. This example is of more than passing interest since we believe that Wilson-Mohr's inside sales department was, in 1996, the first instance of deriving a time equation to model a department's resource consumption.
7. Each of the fields in the equation is captured in the company's order-entry system, which supports the inside sales process.
8. The death spiral was described in R. Cooper and R. S. Kaplan, "Measure Costs Right; Make the Right Decisions," *Harvard Business Review*, September–October 1988, 96.

## CHAPTER THREE

CAPACITY COST RATES

The Practical Issues

MEASURING THE COST of supplying a department's resource capacity is the second principal calculation in a Time-Driven Activity-Based Cost model. We use capacity cost rates, calculated as the ratio of departmental costs to practical capacity, to drive resource costs down to orders, products, and customers. The numerator aggregates all the costs associated with a department, including the compensation of frontline employees and their supervisors; occupancy, technology, and other equipment costs; and the costs of corporate staff functions that support the work performed in the department. In the customer service department example used in chapter 1, these costs totaled $567,000 per quarter.

The denominator in the capacity cost rate calculation represents the practical capacity of the resources that perform work in the department. For a department whose output is paced by the work of employees, such as in the customer service department, the practical capacity is measured by the quantity of minutes or hours that employees are available to perform the actual work, such as to process customer orders, handle customer inquiries, and perform credit checks on customers. Recall that the customer service department in the example had 28 full-time equivalent frontline employees, each of whom supplied 22,500 minutes of capacity each quarter, leading to a departmental total capacity of 630,000 minutes per quarter. In automated departments, the pace of work is determined by equipment capacity, in which case the practical capacity is measured by the quantity of machine time available for work, after subtracting downtime for, say, maintenance and repair.

With numerator and denominator determined, we calculate the capacity cost rate by dividing the department's costs by the department's practical capacity. For our numerical example, the customer service department's capacity cost rate equals $0.90 per minute ($567,000 divided by 630,000 minutes). This rate is applied to the work performed in the department during the quarter and is based on the time equation for each transaction.

In this chapter, we go into more depth about the practical issues that arise in calculating capacity cost rates. We start with the numerator by discussing how to aggregate costs within a department. We consider when to measure the capacity cost rate at the departmental level or at a process level within the department. We then turn to measuring practical capacity, the denominator, including the treatment of peak and seasonal capacity and the assignment of capacity supplied for particular customers segments. Finally, we discuss the trade-offs between budgeted and actual costs in a period, and the role of variance analysis when a company uses budgeted (standard) cost rates.

ESTIMATING TOTAL DEPARTMENTAL COSTS

The cost of resources supplied to an operating department consists of several elements:

- *Employees:* salaries and fully accrued fringe benefits such as payroll taxes, medical insurance, and earned pension benefits[1]
- *Supervision:* salaries and fully accrued fringe benefits of frontline employees' supervisors
- *Indirect labor:* salaries, fringe benefits, and supervision of support personnel in the department, such as those performing quality assurance and scheduling
- *Equipment and technology:* cost of equipment, including computing and telecommunication resources, used by employees and their supervisors
- *Occupancy:* cost of supplying space for employees, and their equipment and supervisors
- *Other indirect and support resources:* assigned expenses from company support departments, such as human resources, finance, and information technology

Most of these categories are straightforward. A few deserve elaboration.

[handwritten margin notes: "replacement cost = depreciation", "price level index into our depreciation schedule"]

Equipment Costs: Replacement Cost Depreciation and Cost of Capital

Equipment and technology costs include operating expenses, such as utilities and consumable supplies, and the equipment's depreciation expense or equivalent rental payment. Companies that own their equipment usually prefer to use the depreciation expense recorded in their financial statements so that the cost numbers from the ABC system can reconcile with their periodic financial statements. Some companies, however, introduce two optional features to make the calculation more accurate. The first feature recognizes that for long-lived assets, the price level at which the equipment was acquired is likely to be well below the price level at which it will be replaced. Even with a moderate inflation rate of 4 percent per year, the price level increases by nearly 50 percent over a ten-year period. To reflect changes in equipment prices, a company can incorporate a specific price level index into its depreciation schedule. German companies have a long history of using such replacement cost depreciation in their calculation of machine costing rates. Railroad companies, with long-lived assets, such as track, locomotives, and freight cars, often prepare two cost estimates: one based on the historical cost of assets, and one based on their replacement cost.

The second optional feature incorporates the opportunity cost of the investment in the equipment. After all, depreciation assigns only the original cost of the asset over its useful life. The method fails to recover the forgone interest on the original investment in the capital asset. Residual income or economic-value-added calculations add the cost of capital on the unrecovered value of the asset to the periodic capital charge.

Some managers question whether the cost of capital for plant and equipment isn't already reflected in the depreciation charge. The answer is no. Depreciation reflects the return *of* capital; it recognizes, over time, the cash originally spent to acquire the asset. The interest or capital charge against the asset's book value measures the return *on* capital, the additional return the asset must generate to compensate owners for the length of time their capital has been invested in the asset. Think about a mortgage. Depreciation is analogous to the repayment of principal in the monthly payment. The cost of capital is analogous to the interest expense in the monthly payment. All bankers want to get their money back (depreciation) and earn a return on the money advanced for the mortgage loan (the cost of capital).[2]

A simple example illustrates the cost-of-capital calculation. Assume an asset costs $100 with a five-year life and no salvage value. Using

[handwritten margin notes: "cost of capital"; "cash over time to buy the asset = opportunity cost"]

straight-line depreciation, the annual depreciation expense is $20. With a cost of capital of 10 percent per year, the annual capital cost of the equipment is shown in the following table:

Year	Book Value, Start of Year	Depreciation Expense	Capital Charge at 10 Percent	Annual Capital Cost
1	$100	$20	$10	$30
2	80	20	8	28
3	60	20	6	26
4	40	20	4	24
5	20	20	2	22

Recall, however, that the inclusion of replacement cost depreciation and the cost of capital in product and customer costs is an advanced step that does not have to be taken in a company's initial TDABC model. Unless the company is already using residual income or replacement cost depreciation internally, go with the flow and use historical cost depreciation when calculating the cost of using long-lived physical assets. You can keep the economic and replacement-cost depreciation as options to be considered for model updates, once familiarity and comfort with the basic model have been established.

Occupancy Costs

The occupancy costs reflect the cost of supplying space for employees and equipment. The occupancy cost per square meter includes the pro rata share of building depreciation, utilities, maintenance, housekeeping, and insurance costs of the space occupied by employees, equipment, and supervisors. Alternatively, the occupancy cost can be calculated from the equivalent rental cost per square meter multiplied by the space (square meters) occupied in the department. Departments that use more expensive space, such as the clean rooms used to produce semiconductor wafers or refrigerated rooms that store perishable items, should obviously have the higher costs of their utilities and equipment assigned directly to them. In other words, the higher capital and energy costs of these departments should not be imbedded in an average occupancy cost for the entire facility.

Corporate Staff and Support Expenses

Many departments in a company do not directly touch a product, service, or customer. They provide the infrastructure required for frontline people or equipment to perform their work. For example, the human resources department hires and trains employees; maintains records on vacation, medical benefits, and sick leave; and operates the annual performance management system for each employee. The information technology department supplies computers, databases, networks, and other systems that enable employees to be more productive in their activities. And the finance department processes employee paychecks, pays vendors, collects from customers, and prepares periodic financial reports for departments and business units. All these activities are essential for the company to function, and the demand for most if not all of these services comes from the operating departments that produce products, deliver services, and support customers (figure 3-1).

If the operating department costs do not incorporate the cost of corporate staff and support departments, the cost model will not include all the resources required to produce, service, sell, and deliver. And, more important, as will be discussed in chapter 5, if the model does not incorporate the cost of staff and support resources, managers cannot scale the size of these departments as they adjust to the resource capacity in the frontline production and sales departments.

Many companies, however, assign the cost of their support units arbitrarily, using convenient allocation bases, such as percentage of direct labor hours, direct labor dollars, head count, sales revenue, or units of production. While some support costs may be sensibly assigned to departments

FIGURE 3-1

Resource Expenses Flow to Support and Operating Departments

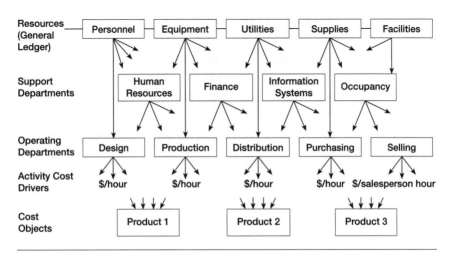

on the basis of one or more of these measures, the convenient allocation bases rarely reflect the demands for services from support departments to operating departments. The goal in assigning support department costs should be economic reality, not simplicity. Percentage allocations rarely, if ever, represent underlying causal relationships. Companies can and should use a TDABC model, using the same principles as applied in building TDABC models for operating departments, to assign staff and support department costs, on the basis of the actual work these departments perform, down to the operating departments they support and service.

Some critics question the assignment of corporate or staff costs to operating departments. First, we must acknowledge that not all corporate staff costs should be charged back to operating divisions. For example, certain corporate activities relate to operating the headquarters office, such as the preparation of external financial statements for shareholders, regulators, and tax authorities and the operations of the corporate governance system and the board of directors. These corporate-level activities have to be performed, independent of the number of operating divisions or the volume and mix of business done in the operating divisions. The costs of these activities should be considered *corporate-sustaining expenses*, costs that must be incurred, independent of the size and mix of business done in the firm. These costs can be differentiated from those caused by specific audit, internal controls, and tax work conducted for individual business units, which can be causally traced to the volume and complexity of work done by these business units. Such business-unit-related costs should therefore be assigned to the units.

The skeptics, however, also believe that corporate expenses are fixed and any allocation to operating units would be arbitrary and not meaningful. There are two fallacies with the skeptics' claim. First, the assignments should be rational, not an arbitrary allocation. The cost assignment should be based on an underlying cause-and-effect relationship between how the corporate resources are supplied and the demands for work by the operating units. Second, such cost assignments are meaningful because support department costs are not fixed; they can vary either up or down, depending upon how much work needs to be done. We invoke the "Rule of 1." If a staff department consists of only one person or one unit of any resource, then we agree that its assignment to operating departments may not be meaningful. But any support department that contains more than one person reveals a large demand for work from that department, which one person alone cannot handle. In analyzing what creates work for the resources in the department, leading to violation of the Rule

of 1, the analyst will be able to determine an appropriate basis and destination for assigning the resource costs of the department.

Consider a support department with twelve people and $500,000 per
year in computing expenses. The relevant question is why the work of this
department could not be done with a single person and a $2,000 personal
computer. The answer to this question establishes an explanation, typically a numerical driver for the magnitude of work demanded from this
department. This driver establishes a cause-and-effect linkage from operating department demands for services to the quantity of work performed by the support department. This driver can then be used to assign
the costs of performing work at the corporate staff department to operating
departments. Over time, if operating departments reduce their demands
for the services provided by the support department, the organization can
shrink the size of its support departments by reducing the resources supplied (e.g., people, computers, and space) for it.

Take, for example, the cost analysis of an accounts receivable (A/R)
department. First, identify the cost of operating the department, say, $8
million per year. Next, identify the practical capacity of the department.
Suppose that the A/R department has 64 clerks, each of whom works
about 130 hours per month, or 1,560 hours per year, net of time off for
vacations, holidays, sick leave, personal leave, work breaks during the day,
and time consumed in meetings, training, and education. The practical
capacity for the department is, therefore, about 100,000 hours per year,
and its capacity cost rate can be easily calculated:

$$\text{A/R capacity cost rate} = \frac{\$8,000,000}{100,000 \text{ hours}} = \$80 \text{ per hour}$$

Next, build the time equation for work performed in the department.
The A/R clerks perform the following tasks:

1. Send invoices to customers each month
2. Receive, record, and deposit cash receipts
3. Maintain customer files (name, address, credit rating, payment
   history, outstanding invoices)

The TDABC project team, through direct observation, obtains the
following data:

Manual processing of invoice and cash receipt   1.0 hour

| Electronic processing of invoice and cash receipt | 0.1 hours |
| Maintain customer credit file (annual) | 0.5 hours |

The departmental time equation is

A/R processing time (hours) = 1.0 × number of manual invoices
+ 0.1 × number of electronic invoices
+ 0.5 × number of customers

Two divisions in the company each have $50 million in annual sales. Under a traditional cost-allocation system, corporate overhead would be allocated (arbitrarily) by the relative percentages of sales in the two divisions. In this case, with equal sales revenue, both divisions receive the same allocation of A/R costs (and of every other corporate-supplied service).

The TDABC team learns, however, that Division 1 generates about 1,000 electronic invoices per year for its 100 large wholesale customers (an average customer does about $500,000 of business per year), and all the customers pay electronically. Division 2, in contrast, has 6,000 small to medium-sized retail customers, requiring 20,000 manual invoices to be prepared annually. All of Division 2's customers pay by mailing in paper checks for each invoice.

Applying the time equation to each division's customers yields the following estimate of A/R time:

Division 1 A/R time = (0.1 × 1,000) + (0.5 × 100)   = 150 hours
Division 2 A/R time = (1.0 × 20,000) + (0.5 × 6,000) = 23,000 hours

The assignments of A/R costs to the two divisions are $12,000 and $1,840,000, respectively. The costs differ by a factor of more than 150, despite the two divisions' having the same level of sales. The assignment is simple to calculate and even easier to justify and defend. Rather than receiving an arbitrary allocation of corporate overhead, each division can readily see how its actions trigger a demand for specific corporate resources. Division 2 can now build the cost of invoicing and collecting into its reference prices and can attempt to reduce its demand for A/R services by shifting its customer mix to larger customers and migrating its customer base to electronic invoicing and payment. If, over time, Division 2 has fewer and larger customers, with most of them paying electronically, the company will realize a lower demand for services for its account receivables department (as estimated through the department's time equation) and can then reduce the number of clerks (and associated support staff and resources) below the current number of 64.

This is the general principle for how to make a resource cost variable. First, through process improvements and shifts in product and customer mix, reduce the demand for the services provided by the resources. Second, adjust the supply of the resource down to the new level required once the process has been improved and the product and customer mix shifted. But these actions are not so obvious, or the consequences from the actions so quantifiable, until an accurate cost model has been used to explain the demand and the supply of resources.

This simple example can be extended to virtually all corporate support departments. To assign the cost of a support department's capacity to operating departments, analysts quantify the demands that each operating unit makes on the support department's resources as we illustrated with the assignment of accounts receivable expenses to the two operating divisions.

CAPACITY COST RATES: DEPARTMENTS OR PROCESSES

The examples in this chapter have so far accumulated costs in the organization's existing organizational units and responsibility centers. Calculating costs at the department level is, in our experience, the simplest and fastest way to build a TDABC model. But a departmental cost rate is valid only if the mix of resources supplied is about the same for each activity and transaction performed within the department. This assumption is violated if the activities and transactions done within the department use different resources.

For example, consider a surgical operating room in a hospital, and suppose that the room contains some specialized equipment that is used only in one type of operation, say, complex cardiac surgery. Then the cost rate for noncardiac procedures should exclude the cost of this equipment, while the cost rate for cardiac procedures should incorporate the cost of this expensive, specialized equipment. In this case, the department needs separate capacity cost rates for the two quite different processes performed within it: cardiac surgery and noncardiac surgery. In general, if one set of departmental transactions uses labor and capital resources that are less expensive while another set of transactions demands costlier labor and capital resources, then separate cost rates must be estimated for the resource group.

In addition, sometimes the capacity of resources within a department will be measured differently, in which case a single capacity cost rate will be inadequate. Consider the warehouse department in a distribution company. The departmental expenses include $2.3 million for warehouse labor and supervision and $2 million of operating expenses for the warehouse itself. The operating expenses include depreciation expenses for the building, fixtures, and equipment, plus the cost of insurance, property taxes, and utilities. For calculating only a single capacity cost rate for the warehouse, the analyst would have to decide whether to base it on the space provided by the warehouse (cubic meters of storage provided per day) or the time available for performing work by warehouse personnel (minutes of personnel capacity available per day). As a first pass, either calculation might be fine. The capacity cost rate based on either warehouse space or personnel time can be estimated rapidly and will probably give an approximately correct answer about the cost of processing cartons through the warehouse. But a calculation based solely on the cost of warehouse space per day of storage consumed, or minutes of personnel processing time used, does not capture the actual cost drivers of warehouse expenses.

Variability in the use of warehouse resources arises from several sources:

1. Cartons have different sizes and therefore occupy different amounts of cubic storage space.
2. Cartons stay in storage for various amounts of time.
3. Warehouse personnel must spend different amounts of time on different sizes of orders. A customer order for a standard carton requires only that a warehouse person locate the carton, pick the carton, and transport it to the shipping area. In contrast, a customer order for a less-than-carton quantity requires the warehouse person to locate the carton, break it open, pick the desired quantity of materials, and then package up the material to be shipped to the customer. Such break-pack quantities are far more expensive to process per unit than carton-sized quantities.

The TDABC model should represent warehouse operations by deconstructing the department into two processes: storing cartons and handling cartons. The resources for *storing cartons* include the building, fixtures, and personnel performing building maintenance, housekeeping, and security functions. The associated resource costs are depreciation, financing, insurance, and taxes on the building and equipment, and the compensation costs of the related personnel. The resources used for *handling cartons* include warehouse personnel, supervisors, and the equipment they use to move cartons into and out of the warehouse—equipment such as forklifts and automated materials-movement machinery.

Once resources and their costs have been assigned to the two processes, the TDABC analyst calculates the practical capacity for each process. For the storage process, capacity is measured by cubic meters of space available for carton storage. This is a good example of when time is not used to measure resource capacity or consumption in a "time-driven" ABC model. The capacity of the handling-cartons process would be measured, as usual, by the time available each month from the frontline warehouse personnel who do the actual work of processing items into and out of the warehouse. The results of this calculation are two different capacity cost rates. The first is the cost per cubic meter per day, a rate that has, in the numerator, the annual building cost divided by 365, and, in the denominator, the total space (cubic meters) available for storage. This rate assigns higher costs to products that take up much space and stay in storage a longer time than it does to the products packaged in small cartons that turn over quickly in the warehouse.

In the second capacity cost rate, the numerator is the warehouse employee expenses in a period, and the denominator is the number of minutes the employees have available for work during the period. The resulting ratio yields a cost rate per minute of warehouse personnel time. Standard storage and shipment of cartons, in efficient, pallet-sized quantities, will use a small amount of warehouse personnel time. But items that require special handling, such as the processing of break-pack quantities, will have much higher times and therefore higher costs assigned to them per unit.

The experience in the warehouse department at a beverage manufacturer provides a more extended example of breaking down the personnel costs of a warehouse department into five subprocesses performed (figure 3-2).

Each of the five processes had different resource intensities of personnel and equipment and different triggers for the work the personnel performed. In developing the TDABC model for this department, the project team mapped personnel resources to the five tasks performed; this task did not involve interviewing or personnel surveys, since the employees were already dedicated to each subprocess. The team then developed the time equation for work in each subprocess on the basis of the variety and complexity of items handled.

In summary, a TDABC model can be constructed quickly at the departmental level. First, the project team accumulates all the relevant departmental costs, selects a single capacity measure for the department (the measure is usually time but can be space, as illustrated by the warehouse department), and calculates the departmental capacity cost rate.

FIGURE 3-2

Warehouse Processes at American Beverage

Process	Personnel (FTEs)*	Core Process	Cost Object	Drivers in the Subprocess Time Equation
Receiving	2	Receiving	Product	# purchase orders, # line items, quantity received, returns
Put-away	3	Put-away	Product	Quantity, bin location
Papercraft	13	Papercraft handling	Product	Quantity, packaging code, product type
Picking stock	7	Picking	Line item	Quantity, packaging code, straightload, bin location
Picking cooler	7	Picking cooler	Line item	Quantity, packaging code, product ID, bin location

*Full-time equivalents

Second, the team develops the equation explaining the consumption of capacity by the transactions and orders handled by the department. After the initial model has been built, the team should reexamine the department's operations to determine whether sufficient resource consumption variation occurs by activities or transaction types to warrant the construction of a more accurate model that decomposes departmental operations into two or more processes. The separate processes can differ by resource intensity (capital- versus labor-intense, or varying use of equipment resources) or by different measurements of capacity, such as time supplied and space supplied.

Now that we have looked at how to measure and accumulate departmental costs, we are ready to calculate practical capacity. Once we have both these numbers, we can calculate a capacity cost rate, which we will use to drive resource costs down to orders, products, and customers.

ESTIMATING PRACTICAL CAPACITY

Practical capacity can be estimated somewhat arbitrarily or studied analytically. The arbitrary approach assumes that practical capacity is a specified percentage, say, 80 or 85 percent, of theoretical capacity. That is, if an employee can normally work forty hours per week, the practical capacity could be assumed to be thirty-two hours per week, allowing 20 percent of personnel time for breaks, arrival and departure, training,

practical capacity

meetings, and employee chitchat that is unrelated to direct work performed. For machines, an allowance of 15 to 20 percent can be made for downtime due to maintenance, repair, and scheduling fluctuations.

While assuming a fixed ratio of practical to theoretical capacity may be adequate for a quick, first-pass model, companies will generally want to study practical capacity more analytically. The analytic approach starts with theoretical capacity and then subtracts explicit quantities for the time that employees or machines are unavailable for doing productive work. For example, machine downtime is the sum of the actual time required for maintenance, repairs, start-ups, and shutdowns. The unavailable time can also incorporate an amount that is held in reserve for protective or surge capacity, which allows the equipment to respond to short-term fluctuations in demand, or disruptions within the factory, without sacrificing output. Having some amount of protective capacity allows the facility to continue to meet customers' demands despite short-term, unexpected delays of materials (either from external vendors or from prior production processes), or when short-term surges in demand occur.

For employee capacity, start with 365 days per year, and subtract time for weekends and other days not worked. Assuming two weekend days (or other nonworking days) per week, this leaves 261 days per year. From this, subtract holidays (e.g., 10 days per year), vacation time (e.g., 20 days per year), and expected days not worked for personal and sick leave (3 days). This leaves about 228 days per year, or 19 days per month, that the typical employee shows up for work. (Obviously, each company in each country should do its own customized calculation of the average number of days its employees work per year and per month.) Suppose further that employees show up for a 7.5-hour workday, or 450 minutes per day. Of this quantity, if 70 minutes are used for breaks, meetings, training, and education, then 380 minutes remain available for performing actual work. Thus, the practical capacity for each employee is 19 multiplied by 380, or 7,220 minutes per month.

The particular parameters must be based on the actual workday for employees at each facility, the different employee work types, and the average quantity of time each employee type is not available for actual work each day. In some European countries, with strict rules on the quantity of hours that can be worked each week, and with extensive holidays and vacations, the quantity of time available for work will be significantly less than 7,000 minutes per month. In developing countries with longer workweeks and workdays, and with limited time off for vacations or holidays, the quantity of employee practical capacity supplied each month could be 150 hours (9,000 minutes) or more.

Various other factors arise when one calculates the practical capacity of equipment or people. These factors can generally be handled, but they do require conceptual thinking and more detailed analysis. We will discuss, in turn, the following issues in estimating practical capacity for a TDABC model:

- Lumpiness in acquiring capacity
- Seasonal and peak-load capacity
- Capacity that enhances service quality
- Assignment of unused capacity costs

Lumpiness in Acquiring Capacity

Some unused capacity arises from the lumpiness of asset acquisition. Consider a company that wants a machine to produce 800,000 units per year. The smallest machine with this minimum capacity, operating 2 shifts (16 hours) per day, could produce 1,000,000 units per year when operating at its practical capacity of 5,000 hours per year and its production rate of 200 units per hour. The company acquires this machine, anticipating that, because of demand constraints or constraining resources elsewhere in production, the machine will operate for only 4,000 hours per year to produce the maximum output of 800,000 units. If the decision to acquire the machine anticipates this maximum usage, then the practical capacity should be measured as 4,000, not 5,000, hours. Should external demand subsequently be higher than anticipated, or if internal bottlenecks elsewhere in the plant get relieved, so that output climbs unexpectedly to 900,000 units per year, then, of course, the denominator volume can be reset to the new normal capacity of 4,500 hours per year.

The basic principle underlying the calculation is to identify the decision that led to the capacity acquisition. In the preceding example, the company's capital budgeting analysis justified the acquisition of the machine with the knowledge that the machine would be used for only 4,000 hours per year. This provides a reasonable basis for estimating the cost per hour for the machine.

A variation of this theme occurs when a company acquires a machine whose annual cost (rental or amortization of purchase cost plus operating cost) is, say, $120,000 per year and demand is expected to build over time. In year 1, the machine is expected to operate for only 2,500 hours, but then increase to 5,000 hours in year 2 and 6,000 hours in year 3 and thereafter. The naive approach would estimate a machine cost rate of $48 per hour in year 1, $28 per hour in year 2, and $20 per unit in year 3 and thereafter. These calculations suggest that the machine is more than twice as costly, or inefficient, in year 1 as it is in year 3. In fact, the machine's efficiency is identical in all three years. Only the volume of business it processes each year is changing, not its efficiency. Two approaches seem plausible to handle this ramp-up in capacity utilization. The first uses the practical capacity (6,000 hours per year) as the denominator volume so that the machine cost rate would be $20 per hour, independent of which year a unit was produced. The unused capacity of 3,500 hours, equivalent to $70,000 in unused capacity cost in year 1, was anticipated in the capital budgeting decision. It could be either charged to the investment account or written off as unused capacity, but it should not affect the signal about the cost of the resources used (slightly more than 40 percent of capacity) by year 1 production.

Alternatively, a company could estimate the total useful hours expected to be supplied over the lifetime of the equipment (the sum of the productive hours in years 1, 2, 3, and so on, up through the maximum economic life of the equipment). This approach also produces a constant cost per hour worked, independent of which year production occurs, but does not lead to an unused capacity amount in any year (unless actual productive hours are less than anticipated). Under either approach, the denominator volume is linked back to the capacity acquisition decision.

Seasonal and Peak-Load Capacity

The next extension is how to handle seasonal or peak-load demands. Suppose the company has demand for people or machines supplying 5,000 hours of work in months 1 through 4 of the year, and demand for only 2,500 hours of work for months 5 through 12 (solid line in figure 3-3). One can think of selling ice cream or soda pop, with peak demand in the four warmest months, and low demand in the cool months; audit services—where peak demand occurs in January through April because most companies have fiscal year-ends on December 31; or phone companies that supply peak demand during the eight hours of the normal business day and lower (consumer) demand in the other 16 hours. Suppose also that it would cost the company $400,000 per month to meet the low demand of 2,500 hours of work per month and $600,000 per month to meet the peak demand of 5,000 hours per month. Note the company enjoys economies of scale in acquiring capacity. But the capacity has to be acquired for the entire year; the company cannot gear up for the peak period and then scale back the resources during the slack-demand period.

FIGURE 3-3

Seasonal Capacity

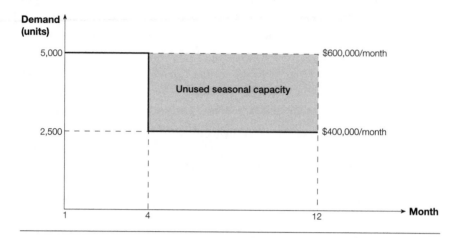

The company decides to meet the peak demand and commits to resources costing $600,000 per month for the entire year. How should the $7.2 million cost be assigned to the annual actual time worked of 40,000 hours (4 months at 5,000 hours and 8 months at 2,500 hours)? Two simple but incorrect approaches would assign the cost without considering the seasonal economics of the business. The first incorrect approach calculates an annual average capacity cost rate:

$$\text{Annual capacity cost rate} = \$7,200,000/40,000 \text{ hours}$$
$$= \$180 \text{ per hour worked}$$

The second incorrect approach calculates a monthly capacity cost rate:

1. Peak period cost rate = $600,000/5,000 hours = $120 per hour worked
2. Slack period cost rate = $600,000/2,500 hours = $240 per hour worked

In the monthly calculation, the cost rate in the peak period is half the cost rate in the slack period. This makes no economic sense, since the peak period requires more resources to be acquired and any additional production in the peak-period months will require even more (costly) capacity to be added. The annual calculation does not distinguish between costs in slack periods and costs in peak periods. Nor does the annual method show that peak-period production is more expensive (requires more capacity resources) than slack-period production.

The preferred calculation recognizes that production in the peak period requires not only the capacity resources used during this period but also the cost of the resources acquired but remaining unused during the slack period. The cost of capacity in the slack period should just be the capacity that would be required if only the slack-period demand were to be met:

$$\text{Cost rate in months } 5\text{–}12 = \$400,000 \text{ per month}/2,500 \text{ hours}$$
$$= \$160 \text{ per hour}$$

The capacity cost rate in the peak months calculates the costs of supplying capacity during these busy months as well as the cost of supplying capacity not needed in the slack months.

$$\text{Cost rate in months } 1 \text{ through } 4 = \frac{(\$600,000 \times 4) + [(\$600,000 - \$400,000) \times 8]}{5,000 \text{ hours} \times 4}$$
$$= \$200 \text{ per hour}$$

As the preceding equation shows, the total cost of supplying peak capacity in the peak months 1 through 4 is the monthly cost of peak capacity ($600,000 per month for four months, or $2.4 million) plus the cost of unused capacity ($600,000 minus $400,000, or $200,000 per month for the eight slack-demand months, for a total of $1.6 million). The total capacity cost of $4 million for these four months is divided by the total hours worked in the peak months (20,000 hours) to obtain the peak capacity cost rate of $200 per hour.

These calculations conform better to the economic reality. The cost rate in peak periods is more expensive ($200 versus $160 per hour) because production in the peak-demand period must pay not only for the costs of capacity resources it uses but also for the cost of capacity resources supplied, but not used, during the slack-demand period.

Capacity That Enhances Service Quality

Suppose a communications company has two types of customers. The first type would be satisfied with low-speed, moderate-quality voice transmission. The second type requires high-speed, very high-quality communication capable of not only excellent voice communications but also high-speed data or video transmission. Rather than supply two different and parallel communications channels, the company finds it cheaper to build the higher-quality, but more expensive, channel required to attract the second type of customer. Both customer types use the same communications system, but if an average unit cost rate is assigned to the time used to service both types of customers, the first type is being charged with costs for a higher-quality service than it was willing to pay for. The decision to invest in the more expensive channel was justified by the preferences of the second type of customer. The communications company made a conscious decision to invest in more expensive equipment so that it could offer the high-quality, high-bandwidth communications channel to that customer type.

In this case, one could estimate the cost rate to be applied to the demand of the first customer type by a simple mental or modeling experiment. How much would it have cost to construct a low-speed, low-bandwidth communication network assuming that all customers were of type 1? The hourly cost rate of providing such a basic network is a reasonable cost assignment to type 1 customers. This calculation is analogous to calculating the cost of supplying capacity only in the slack period (months 5–12) in the previous numerical example.

The extra cost to build the network with high-speed, high-quality features and service can all be attributed to type 2 customers. So even though both customers use the same network, the less demanding (type 1) customers are assigned a cost rate that reflects only the resources required to deliver the desired value proposition to them. The transactions from the more demanding, type 2 customers are assigned a higher rate that includes all the incremental costs of providing the extra resources to deliver the more complex value proposition to them. The ability to assign costs differentially to different types of customers depends critically on being able to distinguish between the different service levels required by diverse customer segments. Because such knowledge is frequently available, the distinctions can be made in practice and used as the basis for assigning differential resource costs to the different segments.

A similar situation arises when surge or protective capacity must be supplied for one set of customers but not another. For example, the department may want to serve one customer segment that provides steady, predictable demand and a second segment, whose demands are erratic and unpredictable. The department chooses to hold protective capacity to meet, without delays, the demands of the second customer segment. The cost of the additional capacity, which provides protective and surge capacity, should be assigned to the second customer segment since this group is the one that creates the demand for that capacity. The costs of the additional capacity should not be included in the capacity cost rate calculation for the predictable customers in the first segment.

Capacity Other Than Time

We have generally assumed that capacity is measured by the time available from people and equipment. But our earlier example of a warehouse illustrated that not all capacity is measured in minutes or hours supplied. The capacity of the warehouse is measured by space supplied; for a truck or railroad freight car, the capacity could also be measured by space supplied (cubic meters or cubic feet of space), though the capacity of transport could also be constrained by weight, such as the maximum number of kilograms that can be carried. For digital storage devices, the capacity would be measured as gigabytes of storage.

Regardless of the units in which capacity is measured—whether time, space, weight, or gigabytes—the principle for measuring the cost of the capacity remains the same. Estimate the cost of all the resources that are involved in supplying the capacity, and divide by the practical capacity that has been supplied. This yields a capacity cost rate measured as dollars per minute, per cubic meter, per kilogram, or per gigabyte. The rate assigns the costs of supplying capacity to the various products, orders, services, and customers that consume portions of this capacity. If we were more precise, we would have used the phrase *Capacity-Driven ABC* rather than *Time-Driven ABC,* but we opted for the easier phrase, which still represents the great majority of resources costed under the approach.

Assignment of Unused Capacity Costs

Using cost rates based on practical capacity leads to a situation in which not all capacity costs are assigned to individual products, orders, services, or customers. Coca-Cola Enterprises Belgium found this feature of TDABC particularly attractive, since the use of practical capacity made under- or overcapacity situations in its facilities more visible, which stimulated discussions about desired staffing levels. The unassigned capacity costs should not be ignored; they remain someone's or some department's responsibility. If the capacity were acquired to meet anticipated demands from a particular customer or a particular market segment, then the costs of unused capacity due to lower-than-expected demands can be assigned to the person or organizational unit responsible for that customer or segment. If the unused capacity relates to a product line, say, when certain production resources are dedicated to individual product lines, then the cost of unused capacity is assigned to the individual in charge of the product line whose demand failed to materialize. Unused capacity should not be treated as a general cost, to be shared across all product lines. Nor should the product line's unused capacity be allocated down to individual products. Such an allocation could cause some products to appear unprofitable, making companies risk the launch of a death spiral by repricing or dropping products.

Consider our original customer service department example, with 28 clerks and a total departmental cost of $567,000 per period. Suppose the rationale for supplying this level of resource capacity came from aggregating the demands from three divisions, which forecasted the following levels of customer service activity:

	Customer Orders	Customer Inquiries	Customer Credit Checks	Total Minutes Demanded (Forecast)
Division A	24,000	600	1,100	273,400
Division B	18,000	500	400	186,000
Division C	13,000	400	900	166,600
Total	55,000	1,500	2,400	626,000
Minutes per unit	8	44	50	
Total time (minutes)	440,000	66,000	120,000	626,000

The demands from the three divisions total 626,000 minutes of processing time per quarter. With each customer service person capable of supplying 22,500 minutes per quarter, the company decides to supply 28 customer service representatives (626,000 minutes needed, divided by 22,500 minutes per representative, which equals 27.82 representatives).

During the period, the actual transactions from the three divisions were the following:

	Customer Orders	Customer Inquiries	Customer Credit Checks	Total Minutes Demanded (Actual)
Division A	23,500	700	1,120	274,800
Division B	13,000	400	440	143,600
Division C	12,500	300	940	160,200
Total	49,000	1,400	2,500	578,600
Total unused capacity				51,400
Budgeted unused				4,000
Variance unused capacity				47,400

Division A, by 1,400 minutes, slightly exceeded its forecasted demand for customer service processing time. Division C used slightly less time

(6,400 minutes) than forecasted, but Division B used much less (42,400 minutes) than forecasted and accounted for almost all the variance in excess capacity supplied (47,400 minutes) in the customer service department. The total unused capacity of $46,260 (51,400 minutes multiplied by $0.90 per minute) can be analyzed (and assigned) as follows:

	Minutes	Cost
Budgeted unused	4,000	$3,600
Division A	(1,400)	(126)
Division B	42,400	38,160
Division C	6,400	5,760
Total unused capacity	51,400	$46,260

The preceding method is not the only way to assign unused capacity costs to operating units, but it is directionally and approximately correct. It assigns most of the unused capacity costs to Division B, whose erroneous forecast most contributed to the excess capacity during the period. The analysis assumed a worst-case situation by our simplification of not considering how the company could have downsized the department's resources during the period as the lower demands from Divisions B and C were being realized.

Consider another situation in which the company knew in advance that resource supply would exceed resource demand, but wanted to retain its existing resources for future growth and expansion. Then the cost of unused capacity could be company-sustaining, assigned at the company level, where the decision to retain unused capacity was made. In assigning unused capacity costs, the general principle is to trace the costs to the unit or level whose decisions affect the supply of capacity resources and the demand for those resources. The assignment of unused capacity costs provides valuable feedback to managers on their demand forecasts and capacity supply decisions.

ACTUAL VERSUS BUDGETED
MONTHLY COSTS

Most companies, at least in their pilot or version 1.0 TDABC system, opt to feed their model with actual costs, as downloaded from their general-ledger system. Thus, the numerator in the capacity cost rate calculation represents actual expenses incurred in the most recent one-, three-, or six-month period. This practice has several desirable characteristics. First, the general-ledger data have already been recorded and can be easily accessed and downloaded. This accessibility is not an unimportant consideration. Second, by using general-ledger data, the company is apparently assigning "actual" departmental and process costs, not some hypothetical ideal cost, and thereby contributes to the credibility of the data. The controller can state, with confidence, "This is what we spent last period; the order, product, and customer costs have been calculated with *real* data." Third, when actual expenses are used, the product and customer costs can be reconciled back to general-ledger expenses. Conceptually, the sum of costs applied to all cost objects (plus any calculated unused capacity costs) will contribute to the amounts recorded in the company's official, audited accounting system. This ability to reconcile TDABC product and customer costs back to audited financial data gives great credibility to the calculated numbers. And fourth, many companies are now operating without fixed budgets, so the only financial numbers they have are historical actuals. These companies may not have budgeted data to use in the model.

But using actual general-ledger expense data in TDABC calculations is not an ideal solution. Actual expenses recorded in a period often reflect timing differentials relating to when bills are paid. Reported expenses for a department or process may be high in a month because a batch of supplies was either paid for or received during the period, but these may not have been used until a subsequent period.[3] Conversely, expenses may be low in a period when supplies are used, but not replenished. These timing differences create a discrepancy between actual spending levels and the actual levels of resources consumed during the period. This problem arises more with monthly data than for semiannual or annual data, for which the timing differences represent a much smaller proportion of total costs.

As a second concern, actual general-ledger expenses will incorporate a department's spending variances, whose causes may be nonrecurring. We believe it is preferable to calculate order, product, and customer costs at an expected, sustainable level of efficiency, and not have expense fluctuations and temporary departmental inefficiencies driven down into product and customer costs. The spending variances may be best dealt with by holding them at the departmental level and using them to evaluate departmental and managers' performance, but not by passing them through into product and customer profit and losses. Managerial decisions are rarely improved by including random cost fluctuations into the calculation of product and customer profitability.

Actual expenses in a period also reflect nonsystematic variation in resource spending. Suppose a machine broke down unexpectedly and unusual repair expenses were incurred. This would raise the costs assigned to the products made in that period. Conversely, in a period when no breakdowns occurred so that no major maintenance or repairs had to be performed, the department would have unexpectedly lower expenses.

Extending this example to a more predictable situation, consider planned maintenance. Suppose, on the basis of past experience and engineering studies, managers estimate that a maintenance and overhaul must be performed after a machine has operated for 1,400 hours.[4] Assume also that the machine is operated an average of 70 hours per week. Therefore, scheduled maintenance on the machine is performed every 20 weeks, or once every 4 months. Working directly from the actual recorded expenses, the financial system would report no maintenance expense for three months, leading to low capacity cost rates during these months. In the fourth month, when the actual maintenance is performed, the department records a heavy expense and the capacity cost rate would increase sharply.

Is the machine efficiency high in the three months when no maintenance is performed and low in the month when the maintenance occurs? Are products produced during the three months when no maintenance is performed less expensive than products produced during the one month when maintenance is performed? Of course not. Basically, the cost of maintaining the machine after 1,400 hours of use is a cost of operating the machine in every period, and for every hour, regardless of the period in which the actual maintenance is performed. Every product processed on the machine, regardless of when it is produced, creates a little more demand for maintenance—a demand that must eventually be satisfied. Consequently, a normalized monthly maintenance cost is a more accurate reflection of product cost than a system that accounts for such costs only when maintenance is actually performed and the actual expense gets recorded in the general ledger.

Managers need to think about the trade-offs between using actual general-ledger expenses and using budgeted or normalized expenses when calculating capacity cost rates. To reduce the distortions due to fluctuations in bill paying, spending variances, and even actual operations, managers may choose to calculate capacity cost rates on the basis of budgeted or normalized departmental expenses.

When the company does use budgeted or normalized expenses in calculating departmental capacity costing rates, its actual period expenses will differ from those driven down to transactions, products, and customers during that period. In this case, the discrepancy can be handled by a traditional spending analysis variance that reconciles the actual and the budgeted departmental expenses. The variance is assigned at the departmental or process level, where it can be managed and controlled, and not driven down to the transactions, products, and customers handled during the period.

SUMMARY

Capacity cost rates are the second element in a time-driven activity-based costing model. The numerator in a capacity cost rate calculation should include the costs of all resources required to prepare an employee or the equipment to perform productive work. These resource costs include the total compensation of employees and their supervisors, the cost of equipment, occupancy costs, and the costs of indirect support departments that can be traced to the department or process and its employees. Companies have the option of modifying the cost of equipment recorded in the official financial statements by adjusting for replacement cost and the cost of capital. If the department performs several processes, each requiring a different mix of resources, then the department must first assign its expenses to the principal processes before calculating separate capacity cost rates for each process.

The denominator in a capacity cost rate calculation for a department or process should be the practical capacity of the resources performing the work. Practical capacity can be estimated by subtracting from the theoretical capacity (the number of hours or minutes per month that employees and machines are available for work) the time for breaks, training, education, and repairs and maintenance. Adjustments can be made to reflect capacity that is supplied just to handle peak and seasonal demands.

Within these general principles, companies can choose to use either actual departmental costs or budgeted ones. As discussed, each approach has advantages and disadvantages.

NOTES

1. Not all fringe benefits need to be included in the employee compensation calculation. The cost of vacations and holidays will be picked up in the denominator of the calculation when employees' monthly costs are divided by the number of days per month the employees actually show up for work. Thus, their compensation for days not worked is already in the numerator, and the cost of vacation days and holidays is captured by subtracting these days from the total number of days available each month.

2. If it wants to go all the way and simultaneously use both replacement cost depreciation and cost of capital, a company should not use the nominal interest rate or cost of capital, as in the above example, but what economists call the real cost of capital, in which inflation expectations are stripped out. This subtle but valid

point was made in F. Modigliani and R. Cohn, "Inflation, Rational Valuation, and the Market," *Financial Analysts Journal* 3 (1979): 24–44.

3. Whether the expenses are recognized when supplies are received or when the invoice is paid will vary depending on the company's financial accounting conventions. Such variation, due to a financial accounting judgment, just reinforces our point about not wanting such fluctuations to impact the measurement of capacity cost driver rates.

4. For example, by looking at the gross ton miles and the speed of loads carried over the track, railroad companies can estimate reliably when track must be replaced and its roadbed repaired. Similarly, airline companies must perform scheduled maintenance on engines after a specified number of miles have been flown.

## CHAPTER FOUR

IMPLEMENTING TIME-DRIVEN ABC MODELS

Launching a Project

NOW THAT WE HAVE LEARNED how to build time equations and to estimate capacity cost rates, we consider how to organize a project to implement a Time-Driven ABC model. Figure 4-1 shows the typical sequence of steps to implement an enterprisewide TDABC model.

PHASE I: PREPARATION

At the launch of the project, an executive sponsor and steering committee should specify the model's objectives. TDABC models can be used for diverse purposes, such as to focus process improvement activities, provide an analytic basis for charging out the costs of information technology (IT) and other support departments, facilitate a product and SKU rationalization process, and, most typically, enhance profitability by transforming unprofitable customer relationships into profitable ones. Having specific objectives for the model focuses the effort and guides the selection of a project champion. A project to measure and manage customer profitability should have the head of marketing or sales as the project champion. The vice president of manufacturing or operations is an ideal champion if the project's primary goal is to identify opportunities for process improvements and cost reductions.

FIGURE 4-1

Typical Time-Driven ABC Implementation

Phase	I. Preparation	II. Analysis	III. Pilot Model	IV. Rollout
Purpose	Develop a game plan and team for the TDABC study	Gather data and conduct department interviews	Build TDABC model template and validate	Roll out template and customize across organization
Actions	• Formulate game plan • Develop model structure • Estimate project cost • Determine data requirements and availability • Select team composition	• Perform time studies • Estimate time equations and capacity cost rates • Finalize data requirements • Finalize pilot model	• Embed time equations into software • Import cost object data • Run model • Validate model	• Develop rollout schedule • Educate facility team members • Gather data and build model by facility • Review findings with facility management and ABC steering committee

Phase I also determines the scope of the model. The initial ABC implementation is generally done as a pilot study, in one facility or branch, rarely for the entire enterprise. The pilot study provides an opportunity for the benefits and implementation cost of the model to be revealed relatively quickly, avoiding, at the outset, the high cost, risk, and time required to build an enterprisewide model. With the scope specified, the project team estimates start and completion dates, cost, and the sources for the data that need to be collected.

Even during the pilot project, the project team should envisage the migration of the model to an enterprise. Given the highly scalable capabilities of TDABC, an enterprisewide model would be a logical next step once the concept had been proven in the pilot study. In one example, a large retailer with over twelve hundred stores conducted a Phase I pilot that included distribution centers and stores. Following the success of this first phase, the model was extended to the enterprise, encompassing all the distribution centers and stores. In another example, at Jackson State University (JSU), the initial study built a model to perform the charge-out of the IT department to administrative and academic departments. During this limited application, the project team thought about the entire hierarchy of cost objects and responsibility centers that might eventually be included in a universitywide model. The team defined data fields that would be flexible enough to accommodate the assignment of

FIGURE 4-2

Scope Expansion with Time-Driven ABC at JSU

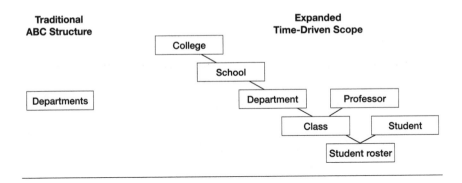

costs down to all university operating units, academic departments, courses, majors, and individual students (figure 4-2).

The composition of the project team also gets determined in Phase I. Figure 4-3 shows a typical TDABC project team. A TDABC project needs active senior management involvement to launch and sustain the project, since an enterprisewide model encompasses many divisions and departments. IT personnel on the project team provide expertise on how to access data and establish automated data feeds into the model. Operational personnel need to be actively engaged to contribute expertise and credibility to the model, particularly the detailed time equations. At Kemps, the vice president of operations spent several months working closely with a department manager to ensure that every time equation represented the actual manufacturing process well. His commitment and assurance proved invaluable in gaining acceptance for the model throughout the company.

PHASE II: DATA DEFINITION, ACCESS, AND ANALYSIS

The TDABC model requires access to detailed transaction and order-level data if it is to realize its potential for greater accuracy. Otherwise, the varying resource demands by different types of orders, SKUs, and customer transactions will not be reflected in cost and profitability calculations.

Consider the data in figure 4-4, collected for a conventional ABC model, at a dairy distributor. These aggregate data are not sufficiently detailed to capture all the economics of each SKU. The product could be

FIGURE 4-3

Typical Project Team

Team Member	Background	Role	Effort
Executive sponsor	• Management or finance	• Gain executive support • Set vision • Implement actions based on model insights	• Infrequent • Present at key meetings (2 days/ month)
Team leader	• ABC experience • Consulting or project management	• Define model structure • Manage schedule • Lead meetings	• Active member • 3–5 days/week
Systems support	• Information technology	• Collect data • Integrate systems	• Infrequent • 5–10 days up front
Model building	• Operations • Consulting • Accounting	• Build model • Build equations • Validate	• Active • 2–5 days/week

delivered as single units, in cases, or in pallet-sized quantities. Each option makes different resource demands on the company. The conventional ABC model, which captures data only at the SKU level, as in figure 4-4, loses the different economics when some customers request standard pallet shipping while others want deliveries of individual cartons or special packaging sizes.

The cost model for a distributor or retailer should incorporate data about an SKU's bin location, weight, package type, frequency of order and replenishment, and shipment method. This allows the model to capture variations from order to order and customer to customer. Figure 4-5 shows a data file directly from a cable company's enterprise resource planning (ERP) system. Note the extensive data fields for each order, including the customer ID, the sales rep who sold the job, the date the work was completed, the type of work done (wip), discounts applied (disc_r), who did the work (opr_id), what node was impacted (fiber_node), the reasons for the work (ord_rsn and sales_rsn), order date, and other comments. These data describe the unique characteristics of the individual order and are directly fed into the TDABC system. With such detailed data, the company can estimate—for each customer, order, and line item— the cost of performing the fulfillment, maintenance, network operations, and check-in processes.

FIGURE 4-4

Conventional ABC Data File

Product (SKU) ID	Product Name	Vendor	Average Price	Average Cost	Total Quantity Sold	Typical Package Type	Number of Orders
101	1 gallon skim milk	Hood	$2.45	$1.25	10,000	4-gallon case	3,600
102	1/2 gallon skim milk	Hood	$1.40	$0.60	6,000	6-gallon case	1,200

The direct data feed, while reducing the time and cost to operate the system on an ongoing basis, requires additional time in the project phase to identify the data characteristics from all the company's information systems, and to install the uploads from the transaction files into the ABC software. Not all the data may be in the production control system or customer order file. Some data may exist in a dispatch system or freight system, and these systems must also be linked to the model.

Furthermore, some relevant data may not be readily available on an automated basis. At Citigroup Technology Infrastructure Division (CTI), the TDABC team knew its total number of servers available, but it did not have the ability to extract data from a single source that tracked:

- Which applications were installed on which servers
- Which operating unit used each application
- The quantity of server time associated with a given application
- Customer services levels

CTI planned to automate the capture and validation of these basic data to eliminate data errors and minimize manual data entry.

During Phase II, the TDABC team, with the help of finance and IT personnel, extracts the general ledger and appropriate transaction files from the ERP and other relevant systems. If the initial project is a pilot, the team gathers only the data required for that location or application. Initially, to keep the model simple, the assignment of corporate staff department costs, such as HR and IT, can be excluded or allocated without the use of time-driven algorithms. These indirect and support costs will be incorporated more accurately when the team scales the model to the entire enterprise.

FIGURE 4-5

Work Order Data for a Time-Driven Model

OrderID	account	sales_id	work_done	wip	fa	wpcnt	disc_r	camp	opr_id	opr_name	fiber_node	tech	ord_rsn	sales_rsn	wip_cmt	ord_date
2064264096	555694-5	309	22-Jan-05	X/CH	50	8	M	VIP	AK	KEITA A	RW16	136	2	C	upgrade to pref. (MA1)	19-Nov-04
2064264100	57890-1	842	22-Jan-05	C/CH	50	9		RETAIL	AQT	NOT ON FILE	WN11	999		R	SUB GOT OVER CHARGE (AQT)	22-Jan-05
2064264103	435144-1	319	22-Jan-05	C/CH	50	4	C	NO CAMP	CJC	COOPER C	BW19	999		5	sub never ordered starz promo (CJC)	05-Jan-05
2064265289	362731-5	798	22-Jan-05	C/DS	51	0	C		DKO	OLIVER D	GB14	1100			DISC SERV@tAP (DKO)	09-Jan-05
2064265854	1961-3	262	22-Jan-05	C/DS	51	6	M		NMT	TWYMAN N	GB10	1100	Q		DISCO AT TAP (NMT)	10-Jan-05

To capture transactions data, the team needs, from IT, the field definitions of the data sources that will be accessed by the TDABC model. Actual data requirements will, naturally, vary from industry to industry. For example, in manufacturing, the data sources include the customer account master, the order or header table, the order or invoice detail file, the product master file, the bill of materials, and the work order file (figure 4-6). The model works with complete cost object files, which greatly simplifies the task of the IT department to respond to the data requests.

Financial and Operational Data Capture

The project team collaborates with the finance department to identify the costs of the departments and processes to be included in the model. The project scope determines the departments and processes to be analyzed.

FIGURE 4-6

Typical Time-Driven ABC Data Files

File	Source	Typical Size	Typical Number of Fields	Sample Fields
General Ledger	Financial system	200+ accounts	3	• Account number • Description • Amount
Customer File	ERP Customer Master Table	1,000+ records	10–20	• Customer ID • Address • Sales rep ID • Terms • Start date
Order File	ERP Order Header Table	50,000+ records	10–20	• Order ID • Customer ID • Order date • Delivery date • Shipment method • Freight charges
Line Item File	ERP Order Detail File	200,000+ records	10–30	• Product ID • Order ID • Price • Quantity • Cost • Package type
Product File	ERP Product Master	5,000+ records	10–20	• Product ID • Bin location ID • Package type • Inventory on hand • Vendor ID

For example, a pilot model for a distributor to measure vendor profitability requires cost data from the departments and the processes that interact with vendors and their products.

Since most general ledgers are already department based, the data capture for costing departments in a time-driven model should be relatively straightforward. Once all department costs have been captured, they can be decomposed further if there are multiple processes within the department. The more complicated situation occurs when a process cuts across multiple departments. In this case, the project team must structure the assignment so that the process costs can be loaded from the departmental cost database.

Within each defined department and process in the model, the project team then conducts the critical step of estimating the *process time equation*. This step requires departmental interviews and perhaps direct observation. As described in chapter 2, the project team interviews two or three employees in each department to determine the key process and activity steps, the drivers that cause variation in the capacity (typically, time) used by cost objects, and the average time per step.

PHASE III: BUILDING THE PILOT MODEL

Building the initial pilot model is the culmination of all the work up to this point. In this phase, the project team uses the time equations to drive department and process costs data down to the cost objects, such as line items, orders, SKUs, and customers. The team learns how to perform the following steps, which will then be generalized to the enterprise model:

1. Drive the general-ledger financial data to departments
2. Drive fully loaded department costs to one or more processes
3. Load transaction data
4. Embed the time estimates and time equations for each process
5. Drive fully loaded process costs to cost objects via time equations
6. Calculate cost and profitability by orders, SKUs, vendors, or customers

Some companies attempt to build their initial model with off-the-shelf spreadsheet software or within their ERP system. While this may be possible, the model becomes complex to build, difficult to troubleshoot, and impossible to scale. One of the principal outcomes from building the pilot model should be to learn how to automate data feeds from ERP and other systems into software specifically designed to perform TDABC calculations and produce management reports. This step sets the stage for scaling to an enterprise model and gives the team familiarity with the capabilities of the TDABC software and assurance that the model can do the following:

- Treat orders and line items as cost objects
- Capture transaction data
- Incorporate time equations with multiple drivers
- Drive general-ledger expenses to departments
- Access and process large corporate databases
- Incorporate resource capacity when calculating cost driver rates and assessing capacity utilization
- Model the complexity of a business in a way that is simple to maintain

Building an enterprise model encompassing all departments, across all facilities, and with thousands of SKUs and customers and perhaps hundreds of thousands or millions of transactions is not a casual endeavor. The pilot project develops experience and expertise on a small-scale model so that extending to an enterprise TDABC model becomes simpler and less risky.

Model Validation

Once the model is built and run, the project team must validate it, financially and operationally. For the financial validation, the costs assigned by the model should reconcile with the general-ledger financial data. Many TDABC models initially suppress the capacity cost calculation and just drive monthly or quarterly general-ledger expenses to cost object records on the basis of the relative percentages of time taken by all the transactions or cost objects. In this way, if the fully loaded general-ledger expense is $1.2 million, then the fully loaded cost per department is $1.2 million, the fully loaded process costs are $1.2 million, and the fully loaded indirect expenses assigned to all cost objects add up to $1.2 million (figure 4-7 shows the flow of expenses for a steel distributor). Since the transaction data for the time equations come directly from the line-item file, the model should also validate revenue, product cost, and discount or rebate information.

Once the arithmetic of the model has been demonstrated by tracking the same expense data through multiple classifications, the company can

FIGURE 4-7

Time-Driven Process and Validation

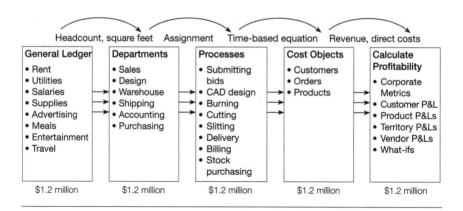

run the model with capacity-based costing rates. The sum of both the costs assigned to the objects and the cost of unused capacity should now equal the general-ledger expenses. The final modification would be to substitute budgeted for actual expenses in those categories in which the company does not want timing issues and spending variances allocated down to cost objects to distort product and customer profitability calculations. For example, the company might choose budgeted maintenance expenses when calculating machine-hour rates, rather than actual maintenance expenses, to avoid month-to-month fluctuations caused by the timing pattern of maintenance activities.

The operational validation checks the accuracy of the time equation estimates. The project team attempts to reconcile the total process or departmental times calculated by the model against the available time, estimated by, say, the number of employees or machines in the department. Consider the data in figure 4-8, from a chemicals distributor, which shows a summary report produced by TDABC software, after the initial run of the system, prevalidation stage.

The calculated model time for shipping pallets is more than twice the rated capacity, suggesting that an error has been made in the units used, the coefficient in the shipping-pallets time equation, or the estimate of capacity. Similarly, the model time for packing refrigerated items is only half the rated capacity. Either the people performing this activity were not busy during the month, or the team might have made an error in the time equation for this process. The project team compares the model and actual

FIGURE 4-8

Summary Process Report for Chemicals Company

Process	MODEL TIME Total	ACTUAL (FTE) Head Count	Capacity (hours)	Utilization
Shipping fluids	145,124	3.3	198,000	73%
Consolidation	190,447	3.0	180,000	106%
Packing small parts	543,878	14.2	852,000	64%
Packing chemicals	91,539	2.4	144,000	64%
Packing refrigerated items	179,429	5.7	342,000	52%
Packing hazardous materials	205,273	2.4	144,000	143%
Shipping pallets	1,620,100	11.7	702,000	231%

times, process by process, and investigates those that indicate large amounts of underused or overused capacity by asking the following questions:

- If the process is apparently working much over practical capacity, could some of the time estimates be too high? Does the department have additional resources and time available that have not yet been incorporated into the model?
- If the model is predicting that the process is operating well below capacity, is the process doing more activities than those attributed to it by the time equation?
- Review the historical trend. Has the process or department been consistently under- or overutilized?

By performing these data validation steps, the project team checks on the parameter estimates used in calculating capacity for departmental cost rates and in estimating the various time equations. Major errors in either will be revealed over time through comparisons of actual and calculated results.

Prepare Tentative Action Plans for Management

When the project team becomes confident in the numbers, it can analyze the data in more depth to generate ideas for profit enhancements.[1] It can identify the characteristics of profitable versus unprofitable orders, contracts, SKUs, and customers and suggest actions for transforming unprofitable elements into profitable ones. Possibilities include targeting customer discounts much more closely to the actual cost-to-serve on individual orders; dropping low-volume, unprofitable products and SKUs; imposing minimum order sizes or standard packaging and delivery for small orders; and renegotiating customer relationships. The team also has a much better view into process inefficiencies. It can raise questions about why a particular transaction, such as setting up an international customer, takes so long. From this analysis, the team can direct process-improvement groups to investigate high-cost, frequently used, and apparently inefficient processes. As discussed in the previous section, the team also has detailed information on capacity utilization, process by process and department by department. With this information, the team can suggest opportunities to shift resources to eliminate both unused capacity and to relieve constraints where process capacity is consistently exceeded. In addition, the project team can look ahead, using forecasts of future sales and production, to anticipate where resource shortages are likely to arise. Team members can also identify for management where capacity can be increased to avoid bottlenecks that otherwise would choke off targeted increases in sales and services. Figure 4-9 summarizes some strategic and operational actions that companies have taken using the data from their TDABC models.

FIGURE 4-9

How Time-Driven ABC Models Have Been Used

Strategic	Operational
• Customer profitability	• Negotiations (customer)
• Product/service profitability	• Menu-based pricing
• Supplier profitability	• Pricing value-added services
• Facility profitability	• Shareholder value reporting
• Cost to serve	• Order optimization
• Stockkeeping unit (SKU) rationalization	• Costing (shared services)
• Process and strategic benchmarking	• Internal controls
• KPIs*/key metrics and trending	• Policy changes (minimum order)
• Compensation (sales reps)	• IT value management
• Balanced Scorecard	• Capacity analysis

*Key performance indicators

We describe some of these actions in more detail in appendix A at the end of this book. Ultimately, decisions on redeploying, eliminating, or adding resources; dropping products; changing terms of sales; and redefining customer relationships are the province of line management, not the ABC project team. But the team can set the agenda for management meetings that discuss how to capture the low-hanging fruit that has been revealed by the cost and profitability analysis. In the case studies in chapters 8 through 14, we will describe the wide range of actions that companies have taken to generate large profit improvements in less than a year by acting decisively on the output from their TDABC models.

PHASE IV: ENTERPRISE ROLLOUT

The easiest enterprise rollout occurs when a Time-Driven ABC model is initially built at a single site of a multifacility company, such as a distributor with essentially identical distribution centers around the country, or a retail bank, with many homogenous branches. The model structure at the pilot site serves as a template for all other facilities since the definition of departments and processes and the time equations for activities will be similar across the company. Consider TW Metals, a steel distributor with forty service center locations across the United States (figure 4-10). It built pilot models at three facilities and saw that the work performed within each location—purchasing, receiving, put-away, picking, cutting, bending, grinding, loading, delivery, and invoicing and collecting—was the same at all three sites. The company applied the time equation templates from the pilot facilities—which had been validated against actual financial and head-count data—across the rest of the sites in a rapid enterprise rollout. Operational personnel simply and rapidly customized the equations to the particular parameters of each company's facility. Company CIO, Aldo Miscelli, reflected on the benefits, "The Time-Driven ABC models helped benchmark our equipment utilization and costs across all our processes and facilities. This helped us focus our efforts on where the opportunities were greatest."

In more heterogeneous companies, the pilot project team becomes the corporate consulting group for the enterprise rollout. It trains and advises project teams at each of the company's facilities. The centralized group standardizes data and process definitions, coordinates the data feeds from centralized IT resources, and monitors the projects at the decentralized business units. For example, at financial institution HSBC, personnel from different operating divisions and geographies were trained

FIGURE 4-10

Rollout of Template at TW Metals

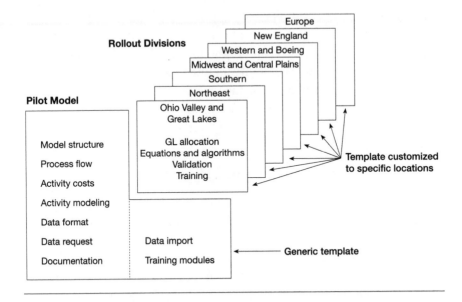

centrally on TDABC concepts, along with other business frameworks, such as Lean Six Sigma. A corporate team of trainers provided the basic fundamentals and then became corporate advisers and consultants for division projects.

COMPARISON OF TIME-DRIVEN AND CONVENTIONAL ABC MODELS

So far in this book, we have discussed many advantages of Time-Driven ABC over conventional ABC models:

- Ease of building, maintaining, and rolling out
- Tighter integration with existing systems
- Greater accuracy through enhanced drill-down and financial and operational reconciliation
- Increased modeling flexibility to handle numerous cost objects
- Dramatically enhanced scalability
- Ability to perform capacity analysis
- Predictive capabilities

But for many companies that have already implemented ABC, these benefits may not apply. Companies and other organizations may be using ABC to answer a specific question. For example, Washington State University was eager to learn whether online courses were more costly to provide than the traditional on-site versions. Having a time-driven model would be overkill, especially in the short term. On the other hand, Comcast Cable had a variety of immediate needs for better cost, profitability, and capacity information. The marketing department wanted to understand the profitability by customer, node, and region, and to quantify the total cost of customer churn. Managers in operations needed accurate information on the capacity utilization of field personnel so that they could assign their employees more effectively and efficiently. And the technology group needed accurate cost information to estimate the return on investment from prospective capital projects. A Time-Driven ABC model offered a feasible approach to meet these diverse enterprisewide informational needs.

We have prepared a matrix to compare conventional ABC and TDABC models for different situations, on the basis of assumptions representing typical situations that might be encountered in practice:

- All departments whose costs are driven directly to cost objects are functional.
- There are five activities per department.
- Each facility has twenty-five departments.
- Model runs are made monthly.
- A small enterprise has twenty facilities.
- A large enterprise has one thousand facilities.

For single-department and single-facility models, the difference between the two methods may not be significant enough to justify converting a conventional ABC model to a time-driven one. But as we extend to enterprisewide models, the sheer volume of transactions and effort makes the investment in time-driven models worthwhile. An additional 100,000 activities or processes run twelve times per year for a company with 1 million transactions per period would translate into an additional 3.6 trillion data fields. This may seem unrealistically large, but actual models in production in *Fortune* 100 companies are even larger, especially for retail operations with more than 1,000 sites. A single, integrated Time-Driven ABC model, which can leverage time equation templates and eliminate the need for routine interviews or surveys, has significant advantages over a

FIGURE 4-11

Conventional Versus Time-Driven Models

(a) Department Model

Dimension	Conventional	TDABC
# models	1	1
# departments	1	1
# activities	5	1
# initial interviews	1	1
# interviews/year	12	0

(b) Facility Model

Dimension	Conventional	TDABC
# models	1	1
# departments	25	25
# activities	125	25
# initial interviews	25	25
# interviews/year	300	0

(c) Small Enterprise

Dimension	Conventional	TDABC
# models	20	1
# departments	500	500
# activities	2,500	500
# initial interviews	500	25–500
# interviews/year	6,000	0

(d) Large Enterprise (high volume of transactions)

Dimension	Conventional	TDABC
# models	1,000	1
# departments	25,000	25,000
# activities	125,000	25,000
# initial interviews	25,000	25–25,000
# interviews/year	300,000	0

large collection of conventional ABC models for enterprise performance measurement.

SUMMARY

Building a Time-Driven ABC model involves a sequence of well-defined steps. Perhaps the most important occurs at the outset, when the project receives executive sponsorship and support. The goals for the project should be established early so that executives are prepared to take action based on the improved cost and profitability information that the TDABC model will generate. An individual with strong analytic and project management skills should head the project team. Other members of the team should be drawn from operations, finance, and IT. If the focus of the project is to measure and manage customer profitability, a representative from marketing and sales should also be a member of the team. If the project will affect product design and development, a representative from engineering and the R&D community will also be helpful. During Phase I, the executive sponsors and project team members decide on a pilot site, where the model will be built and first applied. The site should be representative of company's operations so that the experience can be generalized elsewhere. In addition, the general manager of the pilot site should be a strong supporter for the TDABC implementation.

In Phase II, the project team defines data fields and identifies the data sources from the company's IT systems. The team works with finance to access the general ledger for departmental and process cost information. Working closely with employees in operations, the team members develop the process time equations and the estimates of the time equation parameters.

In Phase III, the project team brings the cost and time data together in the specialized software package to generate preliminary cost and profitability information. The team does various tests to establish the validity of the data and explores the reasons for anomalous and unexpected results. After the data have been validated, the team takes the information to management with suggestions for actions to enhance the profitability of the pilot site.

Once the TDABC model has been developed and validated in the pilot site, the project team, in Phase IV, leads the rollout to an enterprise model. If the company consists of a set of homogenous units, the enterprise rollout is easy and rapid since the pilot model can be used at each facility, with only minor modifications to capture the unique cost structure and time equation parameter estimates for each site. For heterogeneous companies, a separate project team will probably be required at each business unit. In this case, the project team for the original pilot usually serves as centralized trainers, corporate consultants, and enterprise project managers.

NOTES

1. For more information on creating value, see S. Anderson, "He Who Has It on Paper Wins: How to Maximize Your ROI from Profit Management," Acorn Systems white paper (Houston: Acorn Systems, October 2001).

## CHAPTER FIVE

WHAT-IF ANALYSIS AND ACTIVITY-BASED BUDGETING

Forecasting Resource Demands

COMPANIES REAP the full benefits from Time-Driven ABC only if they adjust the *supply* of their resources to the *demands* from products and customers. Companies can improve processes, rationalize their product mix, and modify customer ordering and delivery patterns to eliminate transactions that make excessive demands on resources. None of these actions, however, produce profit improvements by themselves. The actions free up considerable amounts of capacity throughout the enterprise. But companies capture the bottom-line benefits from their newly released capacity only if they can sell more or spend less.

If a company can increase sales when it has excess capacity, its profits will increase sharply since spending, other than on short-term variable costs (such as for direct materials), will remain flat while revenues increase, a sure path for large profit increases. But if the company, with excess capacity, does not increase its quantity of output, then it must turn to the less attractive alternative of reducing the supply of excess capacity so that it is spending less to supply resources.

Activity-based budgeting (ABB) enables companies to forecast the changes in resource demands from projected process efficiencies and changes in the volume and mix of transactions. For example, managers at Lewis-Goetz, a hose and belt fabricator in Pittsburgh, learned from the company's TDABC model that certain products were much more profitable than previously reported. They contemplated lowering prices on these products to capture additional market share, a tactic that might lead to a surge in volume and revenue. But could the company handle the increased volume with existing resources, or would bottlenecks start to appear across the enterprise? Lewis-Goetz used its TDABC model to forecast the capacity utilizations with the higher expected sales volumes.

Executives can use their Time-Driven ABC model as an analytic core to forecast the demands for resources. These forecasts give executives the information to adjust future resource supply and, therefore, the associated spending, to meet those demands. Activity-based budgeting eliminates much of the negotiations and haggling associated with the traditional line-item budgeting process. It replaces negotiations with a rigorous, defensible, and transparent analytic model in which executives authorize spending on personnel and equipment resources to bring the supply of capacity, throughout the enterprise, in line with work needed to be performed to meet sales and production forecasts.

Activity-based budgeting existed before the TDABC innovation. What is new is how much simpler and more transparent the process becomes with TDABC. The supply, cost, and consumption of resource capacity are central features of a TDABC model. It becomes a simple task to exploit the structure of a TDABC model to forecast the change in supply and cost of resources required to meet future periods' demands for work.

MAKING FIXED COSTS VARIABLE

The theory behind activity-based budgeting is straightforward. We recognize that the supply of most of a company's resources—personnel, equipment, and buildings—is committed in advance of a period, before the demand for them is known exactly. A company pays for these committed resources, whether or not they are used during the period. That is why many economists and accountants refer to them as *fixed costs*. While this name is, in a narrow sense, technically correct, it is also misleading; the term *fixed costs* has confused generations of managers and accountants. The costs are fixed only because managers do not act to change them. In this chapter, we show how to connect a company's actions on pricing, order size, and customer service to revised estimates about the demands for resources. These revised demands can reveal unused resource capacity and—should production and sales volumes be projected to increase—some shortages of resource capacity as well. The company can then act to adjust the supply of resources to meet the projected demands. It is through this adjustment of resource supply that the cost of virtually all an enterprise's resources becomes "variable" and not fixed. The only truly fixed costs, in practice, are those for which the spending or commitments have already occurred and are irreversible, such as research and development spending or commitments for pensions based on prior years of employee service.

The sequence of steps to perform what-if or activity-based budgeting is remarkably simple:

1. Build a Time-Driven ABC model based on most recent experience.
2. Calculate product, service, and customer profitability.
3. Make managerial decisions on process improvements, pricing, product and customer mix, product design, and customer relationships.
4. Forecast next period's process capabilities and the volume and mix of sales and production on the basis of the decisions taken to improve profitability.
5. Calculate the next period's demand for resource capacities to meet the sales and production forecasts.
6. Authorize spending (either increases or decreases from current period's levels) to supply the desired resource capacities in future periods.

We illustrate what-if analysis and the activity-based budgeting sequence through an extended numerical example, the Sippican Corporation.

SIPPICAN CORPORATION: A CASE STUDY

Consider the plight of the Sippican Corporation (a fictitious company), a manufacturer of hydraulic control devices—valves, pumps, and flow controllers.[1] Its recent monthly financial results reveal the severe economic impact from price cutting in pumps, one of its major product lines (figure 5-1). The company's overall gross margin of 21 percent is well below its targeted 35 percent level, and the 1.8 percent pretax return on sales is far below the targeted 15–20 percent level that the company has realized in the past. The poor financial performance has occurred despite a recent 10 percent price increase in its new flow controller product line, which met little sales resistance in the marketplace.

Sippican operates with a simple cost accounting system that directly charges each unit of product for its direct materials and labor costs. Materials cost is based on the prices paid for components under annual

FIGURE 5-1

Sippican Corporation: Monthly Operating Results

Sales	**$1,847,500**	**100%**
Direct labor expense	351,000	
Direct materials expense	458,000	
Contribution margin	$1,038,500	56
Manufacturing overhead		
Machine-related expenses	$334,800	
Setup labor	117,000	
Receiving and production control	15,600	
Engineering	78,000	
Packaging and shipping	109,200	
Total manufacturing overhead	654,600	35
Gross margin	**$383,900**	**21%**
General, selling, and administrative expenses	350,000	19
Operating income (pretax)	**$ 33,900**	**1.8%**

purchasing agreements. Labor rates, including fringe benefits, are $32.50 per hour and are charged to products on the basis of the standard run times for each product (figure 5-2).[2]

The company has only one producing department, which machines and assembles components into finished products. The cost system allocates factory overhead costs—including setup, receiving, production control, packaging, shipping, and engineering—to products as a percentage, currently 185 percent, of production-run direct labor cost. Since direct labor is recorded anyway to prepare factory payroll, allocation via direct labor cost is an inexpensive way to assign overhead costs to products. Figure 5-3 shows the standard unit costs, planned gross margins, and actual gross margins for Sippican's three product lines.

FIGURE 5-2

Standard Cost Data

Product Lines	Valves	Pumps	Flow Controllers
Materials per unit	4 components	5 components	10 components
	2 @ $2 = $4	3 @ $2 = $6	4 @ $1 = $4
	2 @ 6 = 12	2 @ 7 = 14	5 @ 2 = 10
			1 @ 8 = 8
Materials cost per unit	$16	$20	$22
Direct labor per unit (hours)	0.38	0.50	0.40
Machine hours per unit	0.5	0.5	0.3
Setup hours per run	5	6	12

FIGURE 5-3

Product Profitability Analysis (Standard Costs)

	Valves	Pumps	Flow Controllers
Direct labor cost	$12.35	$16.25	$13.00
Direct materials cost	16.00	20.00	22.00
Overhead (@185% × DL$)	22.85	30.06	24.05
Standard unit costs	$51.20	$66.31	$59.05
Planned gross margin (%)	35%	35%	35%
Target selling price	$78.77	$102.02	$90.85
Actual selling price	$79.00	$70.00	$95.00
Actual gross margin	$27.80	$3.69	$35.95
Actual gross margin (%)	35%	5%	38%

Sippican's controller, Peggy Knight, realizes that overhead has been increasing significantly in recent years, particularly for setup labor, indirect labor for packaging and shipping, and process engineers. These increases were necessary to handle the small production runs and many shipments now requested by customers, and for developing the process routines used to build newly introduced flow controller models. Knight queries the manufacturing control system and collects data about the number of production runs, shipments, and distribution of engineering personnel during the past month (figure 5-4).

FIGURE 5-4

Monthly Production and Operating Statistics

	Valves	Pumps	Flow Controllers	Total
Production (units)	7,500	12,500	4,000	24,000
Materials cost per unit	$16	$20	$22	
Direct labor per unit	0.38	0.50	0.40	
Machine hours per unit	0.5	0.5	0.3	
Setup hours per run	5	6	12	
Machine hours (run time)	3,750	6,250	1,200	11,200
Production runs	20	100	225	345
Setup hours	100	600	2,700	3,400
Number of shipments	40	100	500	640
Hours of engineering work	60	240	600	900

The differences between the product lines surprise Knight. The average production run for valves is 375 units (7,500 units divided by 20, the number of production runs), while the average production run for flow controllers is less than 18 units. Also, the average valve shipment is 188 units (7,500 units divided by 40, the number of shipments), while for flow controllers it is 8 units. As Knight fears, the flow controller product line is using indirect resources disproportionately from its shares of company revenues and units sold.

Sippican has the two classic symptoms of a company desperately needing a more accurate cost system. First, the company is spending more on overhead than on either direct labor or direct materials (figure 5-3). Second, the company has considerable diversity in its product mix. Valves, a standard product that requires little technical support, are produced and shipped in large batch sizes, while flow controllers, a newer product line, are produced and shipped in small batch sizes and require extensive technical support. The combination of high spending on indirect and support resources and high variety in product and customer characteristics is an unfailing recipe for heavily distorted costs in a traditional standard cost system.

With this in mind, Knight initiates a TDABC project in the hopes that the more accurate costing of present resources will enable Sippican to project its future resource demands more effectively. Knight takes a step-by-step approach, outlined in the next sections, to develop an activity-based budgeting model for her company's situation.

ABB Step 1: Build a Time-Driven ABC model

Knight launches a project to build a Time-Driven ABC model of Sippican's manufacturing operations. She wants an accurate cost model to quantify financially the impact of each product line's use of indirect resources. The project team spends about a week in the factory and collects the following information:

1. A setup is performed whenever a batch of components must be machined in a production run. Each component in a product requires a separate production run to machine the raw material or purchased part to the specifications for the product. Because of the large number of setups, currently about 25 percent of the production employees just perform setups. Some other production workers do not operate any machines, but perform only manual

assembly work. Their assembly time per product is already included in the direct-labor-hour estimates for each product.

2. Sippican operates two 7.5-hour shifts each weekday. Each shift employs 45 production and assembly workers, plus 15 setup workers. These workers receive two 15-minute breaks each day. They also receive an average of 30 minutes per day for training and education activities, and all the workers—production, assembly, and setup—spend 30 minutes each shift for preventive maintenance and minor repair of the machines.

3. The company has 62 machines for component processing. These machines are generally available for the 6 hours per shift that production workers are actively engaged in production or setup activities on the machines. Sippican leases the machines. Machine operating expenses are about $5,400 per month; this amount includes lease payments, supplies, utilities, and maintenance and repairs.

4. The receiving and production control departments employ 4 people over the two shifts. These personnel order, process, inspect, and move each batch of components for a production run. It takes 75 minutes for all the activities required to get one batch of components ordered, received, and moved to a machine for processing. This time is independent of whether the components are for a long or a short production run, or whether the components are expensive or inexpensive.

5. The work in the packaging and shipping area has increased during the past couple of years as Sippican increased the number of customers it served. Each shipment takes 50 minutes to prepare the packages and labels, independent of the number or types of items in the shipment, plus 8 minutes per item to bubble wrap and pack in the carton, whether the item is a valve, a pump, or a flow controller. The packaging and shipping area employs 15 people in each of the two shifts (30 in total).

6. Employees in the receiving, production control, packaging, and shipping departments work a 7.5-hour shift that includes two 15-minute breaks per day, and 30 minutes, on average, for training and education.

7. Sippican employs 8 engineers for designing and developing new product varieties. The engineers' total compensation is $9,750 per month. Much of their time is spent modifying flow-control products to conform to customer requests. Engineers work 7.5-hour

shifts. After breaks, training, education, and professional activities, engineers supply about 6 hours of productive work per shift.

With this information, Knight's project team starts by estimating the
capacity cost rates for each major production process: fabrication and assembly, setup, receiving and production control, packaging and shipping,
and engineering. Figure 5-5 summarizes the calculations of capacity cost
rates, and figure 5-6 shows the aggregate supply, cost, and utilization of
Sippican's production resources.

The data reveal that the company has sensibly expanded its supply of
people and equipment resources to meet the demands for work. All the
resources are currently being used to near their available capacity. Sippican's low profitability cannot be attributed to excess capacity or poor capacity utilization. Its problems must lie with the existing economics of its
products and processes.

ABB Step 2: Calculate product cost and profitability

The project team brings all the data together into an integrated Time-
Driven ABC model that assigns production costs to the three product
lines on the basis of the cost of the resources the products use. It matches
these costs to revenues (figure 5-7). Valves are now seen to be even more
profitable than previously thought. Pumps, while not earning the targeted
35 percent gross margin, are still strong profit contributors. Flow controllers—previously thought to be the most profitable product line—
actually lose money because of the high costs for their setups, engineering support, and packaging and shipping.

FIGURE 5-5

Capacity Cost Rates for Resources

	Employed Days/ Month	Monthly Cost	Paid Hours per Day	Productive Hours per Day	Hours per Month	Cost per Hour
Production workers	20	$3,900	7.5	6	120	$32.50
Indirect workers	20	3,900	7.5	6.5	130	30.00
Engineers	20	9,750	7.5	6	120	81.25
Machines	20	5,400		12	240	22.50

FIGURE 5-6

Monthly Resource Cost and Utilization

	# Units	Monthly Cost/Unit	Total Cost	# Hours Available	# Hours Used	Capacity Used (%)
Direct labor	90	$3,900	$351,000	10,800	10,700	99
Machines	62	5,400	334,800	14,880	14,600	98
Setup	30	3,900	117,000	3,600	3,400	94
Receiving and production control	4	3,900	5,600	520	431	83
Engineers	8	9,750	78,000	960	900	94
Packing and shipping	30	3,900	117,000	3,900	3,733	96

This phase of work illustrates in more detail the fundamental TDABC concepts introduced in chapter 1. It shows how a company works from readily available data to build an accurate model of the cost of resources used by individual products or product lines. Extending the analysis in a subsequent phase would enable many of the marketing, selling, and administrative resource costs (the $350,000 "below-the-line" expenses in figure 5-1) to be driven down to individual orders and customers. Of course, the most important question comes after the model has revealed the actual profit and losses of the products. How will Sippican's management team react to the report on the actual economics of their product lines shown in figure 5-7?

WHAT-IF ANALYSIS

The TDABC model has stimulated the management team to explore several action possibilities. The team immediately notices the high cost of labor and machine time for flow controller setups. Sippican is spending more on setting up to produce flow controllers ($148,500) than it spends on materials and direct labor ($140,000) to produce the product. One possible remedy would be to impose a minimum order size for flow controllers. Managers may ask, "What if we impose a minimum acceptable order size of fifty units? How would this policy affect costs?" The answer can be easily obtained with the TDABC model.

FIGURE 5-7

Sippican Corporation Time-Driven ABC Product Cost and Profitability

	Valves	Pumps	Flow Controllers	Total	Unused Capacity	Actual
Sales revenue	$592,500	$875,000	$380,000	$1,847,500		$1,847,500
DL expenses	92,625	203,125	52,000	347,750	3,250	351,000
Material expenses	120,000	250,000	88,000	458,000	—	458,000
Contribution margin	379,875	421,875	240,000	1,041,750	(3,250)	1,038,500
Machine run-time	84,375	140,625	27,000	252,000	6,300	258,300
Set-up labor	3,250	19,500	87,750	110,500	6,500	117,000
Machine setup	2,250	13,500	60,750	76,500	—	76,500
Receiving and production control	750	3,750	8,438	12,938	2,663	15,600
Engineering	4,875	19,500	48,750	73,125	4,875	78,000
Package and ship	31,000	52,500	21,000	104,500	4,700	109,200
Manufacturing overhead	126,500	249,375	253,688	629,563	25,038	654,600
Total costs	$339,125	$702,500	$393,688	$1,435,313	$28,288	$1,463,600
Gross margin	$253,375	$172,500	$(13,688)	$412,188	$(28,288)	$383,900
Gross margin %	42%	20%	–6%	22%		21%
Selling and administrative						350,000
Operating profit						$33,900
Return on sales						1.8%

The project team could simulate the impact of producing the same quantity of flow controllers with the proposed minimum-order size constraint. If every order were for exactly 50 units, then the 4,000 total sales of flow controllers would require 80 production runs (down from the 225 actually experienced in the previous month). But some orders might be for more than 50 units. So the project team assumes 60 production runs for flow controllers, an average batch size of 67. Reducing the number of production runs from 225 to 60 yields a savings of 165 setups, whose impact can be calculated as follows:

Setup labor reduction: 165 × 12 hours/setup   = 1,980 hours

Machine time savings: 1,980 hours

Receiving and production control: 165 × 1.25 hours/setup = 206.25 hours

The monthly capacity of each resource, from figure 5-5, is as follows:

Setup (production) workers: 120 hours

Machines: 240 hours

Indirect labor: 130 hours

If the average batch size of flow controllers increases to 67, with nothing else changing, Sippican could meet its production commitments with 165 fewer production runs, and enjoy the potential savings below:

16	fewer setup employees at $3,900 per month	$62,400
8	fewer machines at $5,400 per month	43,200
1	less receiving-and-production-control person at $3,900	3,900
	Total monthly savings	$109,500

This is a simple example of what-if analysis. Managers perform sensitivity analysis around the current operating plan to assess easily and accurately the resource and cost impact from proposed actions.

As another example of what-if analysis, the TDABC model has revealed, for the first time, the very high costs associated with setup activities. Suppose Sippican's managers explore the benefits of launching a new initiative to focus its process engineers on reducing setup times for all products. Under this scenario, the company would accept the current volume and mix of orders as given and not change any pricing or order terms with customers until it first tried to improve its own internal processes. "What if," the managers wondered, "setup times could be reduced by 40 percent across the board? What would the impact be?"

The project team can run quickly through a scenario in which setup times are reduced to the following times:

Valves: 3.0 hours

Pumps: 3.6 hours

Flow controllers: 7.2 hours

All other production and sales parameters are assumed to remain the same. Under this scenario the total setup times are the following:

	Before (Hours)	After (Hours)
Valves	100	60
Pumps	600	360
Flow controllers	2,700	1,620
Total setup	3,400	2,040

The setup time savings of 1,360 hours would allow Sippican to maintain the same sales and production schedule as before but with 11 fewer setup people (1,360 hours divided by 120 hours per setup employee) and 5 fewer machines (1,360 hours divided by 240 hours per machine) for a potential cost savings of $78,900 per month. Thus, Sippican can see the potential benefits and rapid payback from starting an initiative focused on setup time reduction. Since the TDABC model has already estimated the resource capacity for every category of resource, any contemplated reduction in resource demand can be immediately translated into the quantity of resources that can be saved.

These two examples of what-if analysis show how managers use their Time-Driven ABC models to explore the resource supply implications of decisions about products, customers, and operating processes. The ABC model of current operations, including resource capacities and resource demands, provides the starting point for analysis. The what-if analysis enables managers to perform simple, inexpensive studies that translate contemplated changes in product mix, processes, order parameters, and customer service into the implications for changes in resource supply and spending. The forecasted spending changes provide the fact-based benefits case for proposed changes in products, customers, and processes.

ACTIVITY-BASED BUDGETING

What-if analysis assesses the impact of incremental changes to operations and sales. It studies these effects when one or a few parameters vary at a time. The most extensive analysis occurs when the company makes comprehensive plans for changes in product mix, processes, and customer relationships. Such comprehensive planning occurs at least annually when the company conducts strategic planning and translates the updated strategy into detailed sales and operating plans for the upcoming year. Some companies now forecast and plan even more frequently as they migrate from an annual planning exercise to quarterly rolling forecasts, looking ahead five or six periods into the future.

Whether the planning is done annually or quarterly, imbedding the company's TDABC model into the process enables the forecasted sales and production plan to be translated into the specific resources that must be available to meet forecasted targets. After all, if a company forecasts a 10 percent sales increase, it must know whether such an increase can be handled with existing production and support resources, or whether bottlenecks will arise in resources already being used at or near capacity. Alternatively, if the company forecasts an 8 percent productivity improvement, management needs to know which resources presently supplied will no longer be needed if the targeted productivity gains are to be translated into actual cash savings. Otherwise, the productivity improvements just produce unused capacity in future periods. The TDABC model provides a powerful analytic tool for translating aggregate plans into detailed resource requirements.

Few of an organization's resources adjust automatically to short-run changes in operating and sales levels. Perhaps only the energy to operate machines, and the direct materials used in production, are truly short-term variable costs that fluctuate with changes in operating levels and mix. The resources that are most variable or flexible within short periods are typically the resources the organization purchases from outside suppliers. Outside suppliers include vendors from which an organization purchases materials; utility companies from which it purchases energy; manpower agencies from which it leases temporary, part-time workers; and individual labor suppliers from which it purchases labor hours as needed or pays for on a piecework basis.

Much of a company's cost base consists of organizational infrastructure, including the following:

1. Personnel—frontline and support employees, engineers, salespersons, and managers—with whom the organization has a long-term contractual commitment, either explicit or implicit
2. Equipment and facilities
3. Information systems supplying computing and telecommunications

Decisions to acquire new resources or to continue to maintain the current level of these committed resources are typically made during the budgeting process. Once the authorization to acquire and maintain organizational resources has been made, the expenses of these resources appear to be fixed and unrelated to local, short-term decisions about product mix and customer expansion or contraction. The time to make spending on these resources variable is during budgeting. A TDABC model gives managers the information they need during the budgeting process to acquire, supply, and maintain only those resources needed to perform the activities expected in upcoming periods.

Activity-based budgeting is simply Time-Driven ABC performed in reverse. A TDABC model drives costs, via time equations and capacity cost rates, from resources to orders, products, and customers on the basis of the capacity they use. In contrast, activity-based budgeting starts by forecasting the volume and mix of products, orders, services, and customers. Then it estimates the quantity of capacity that must be supplied to meet the forecasted demand, and, finally, calculates the cost—that is, the budget—authorized to supply the needed resource capacities. The process is iterative. Using the first run through the model as a basis, the company varies the assumptions, continually testing different scenarios, until it reaches a targeted profitability scenario.

ABB Step 3: Take managerial decisions on process improvements, pricing, and product and customer mix

The Sippican Corporation, after reviewing the TDABC calculations of product-line profitability, makes the following decisions to improve profitability. It plans to refocus on its core product lines of valves and pumps. It wants to increase market share in valves, which are now seen as the company's most profitable product line, by offering discounts for large orders, an action that the TDABC model has revealed to be highly profitable. In an attempt to stabilize and perhaps reverse the pricing pressure on pumps, Sippican will stop discounting small orders of pumps; it will meet price competition in this product line only for large production orders. It also plans to continue to raise prices aggressively for its flow controllers, especially for small orders, and will establish a minimum order size policy of 50 units.

For productivity improvements, Sippican will direct its engineers to launch a six sigma study of the setup process and will set a target to dramatically decrease setup times so that small-lot production will not be so costly to offer in the future. Sippican recognizes that its new policy may lead to lower sales of pumps and flow controllers, but it is prepared to make that trade-off now that it sees the full costs and losses associated with small-lot production.

ABB Step 4: Forecast the next period's process capabilities and the volume and mix of sales and production

Peggy Knight, working from the forecast for the next period, develops the specific sales and production plan shown in figure 5-8. The estimates of expected production and sales volumes and mix for an ABB model need to be more detailed than in a traditional aggregate production plan. The estimates must include the quantity of products and services that will be sold, as well as the individual customers (or customer types) expected to buy the products and services. The estimates also include details on the production and sales ordering process. For example, the budget should include the number of production runs for each product, the frequency of materials orders and receipts, the number of customer orders, and the method of shipment. Technology has made forecasting at this level of detail easier. Companies can now use their ERP systems to extract information from the order and production schedule files and the master customer and SKU files to generate typical production and customer order patterns.

Sippican's sales and production plan shows how the new focus on larger orders leads to far fewer production runs and shipments. Knight forecasts that the six sigma initiative for setup time reduction will yield 20 percent improvements next period for all three product lines. The new production plan requires more direct labor and machine hours since the

FIGURE 5-8

Forecasted Sales and Production Plan

	Valves	Pumps	Flow Controllers	Total
Price	$75	$80	$110	
Previous price	$78	$70	$90	
Sales (units)	12,000	12,000	2,500	26,500
Previous sales units	7,500	12,500	4,000	24,000
# production runs	40	40	60	140
# shipments	40	70	100	210
Total DL hours	4,800	6,000	1,000	11,800
Setup labor hours/run	4.0	4.8	9.6	
Total setup hours	160	192	576	928
Machine hours (run and setup)	6,160	6,192	1,326	13,678
Engineering hours	60	240	400	700

increased volume of valves more than compensates for the anticipated sales reductions in pumps and flow controllers caused by the elimination of price discounts and small orders.

The detailed production plan shown in Figure 5-8 is the key step for time-driven activity-based budgeting. Once such a credible production plan has been created and approved, the remaining steps to construct an activity-based budget are easy to implement.

ABB Step 5: Calculate the next period's demand for resource capacities to meet the sales and production forecasts

Working from the detailed forecast of volume and mix of products, services, and customers in the production plan, Knight can now forecast the demand for resource capacity in each production department and process. She can use modified time equations to reflect process improvements and changes, such as the reduction in setup times. The forecast of resource demands is identical to that used in calculating conventional budgets for the purchasing of materials, the utilization of machines, and the supply of direct labor. Both conventional budgeting and activity-based budgeting are based on the forecasted production mix for the upcoming year. Activity-based budgeting extends the conventional budgeting exercise by forecasting the demands for all the indirect and support processes: ordering, receiving, and handling materials; processing customer orders; handling customer complaints and requests for technical support; scheduling production; and setting up for production runs.

Figure 5-9 shows the demand for resource capacity in Sippican's various departments to meet the production plan in figure 5-8. The critical calculation, simple to perform, given all the data collected and available, appears in the third column, Estimated Resource Demand (hours). To illustrate, the demand for setup hours comes directly from the production plan in figure 5-8 and already incorporates the benefits of fewer production runs and the 20 percent forecasted reduction in setup times per run. The demand for receiving and production control capacity is calculated by multiplying the number of production runs (140) by the time required per production run (75 minutes, or 1.25 hours, per run). The demand for packaging and shipping is calculated from the simple time equation:

$$
\begin{aligned}
\text{Packaging and shipping time} &= (50 \text{ minutes} \times \text{number of shipments}) \\
&\quad + (8 \text{ minutes} \times \text{number of items shipped}) \\
&= (50 \times 210) + (8 \times 26{,}500) \\
&= 222{,}500 \text{ minutes} = 3{,}708 \text{ hours}
\end{aligned}
$$

FIGURE 5-9

Estimated: Resource Demands from Sales and Production Plan

Resource	Monthly Productive Hours per Unit	Estimated Resource Demand (hours)	Calculated Resource Supply	Budgeted Resource Supply	Previous Resource Supply
Labor (direct)	120	11,800	98.33	100	90
Labor (setup)	120	928	7.73	8	30
Machines	240	13,678	56.99	57	62
Labor (receiving and production control)	130	175	1.35	2	4
Labor (packing and shipping)	130	3,708	28.53	29	30
Engineers	120	700	5.83	6	8

The data for engineering hours comes from discussions with the head of engineering regarding the quantity of effort required for the six sigma initiative for setup time reduction and for supporting the three product lines at forecasted sales volumes and mix.

The activity-based budgeting team calculates the required resource supply by dividing the resource demands by the capacity of each resource unit. The capacity per resource unit has already been estimated in the original TDABC model. For example, in the Sippican Corporation, each production worker (either direct or setup) and engineer supplies 120 hours of work per month, and each machine can supply 240 hours of available time per month. Column 4 in figure 5-9, Calculated Resource Supply, shows the exact quantity of resources required to meet the next period's production and sales plan. Recognizing that most resources do not come in fractional quantities, the activity-based budgeting team (or computer program used to implement this step) rounds the actual calculated quantity to the next highest integer (column 5). The budgeted resource supply may also include some extra resource units to handle peak or surge demands or provide a buffer in case actual sales and production exceed forecasted levels. This is a judgment call that managers can make during the activity-based budgeting process. The numerical calculations reveal the minimum resource supply required—at anticipated productivity levels—to meet the production plan. Managers can adjust this figure up to provide a protective buffer, or adjust it down to be conservative in contracting with resource supply, expecting to use overtime or reductions in planned downtime (for training, education, and maintenance) to accommodate higher demands for productive work.

Companies may discover that their current resource supply is well above that anticipated for future operations. This is when companies have the opportunity to make the costs of these resources "variable," by redeploying, eliminating, or—in the case of plant, property, and equipment—selling the resources no longer needed. Alternatively, companies may learn that they cannot meet all the resource demands in their production plan with existing resources. They have three options at this point. They can acquire the resources needed to meet the production plan, they can revise the production plan downwards so that it can be fulfilled with existing resources, or they can attempt to increase the productivity of their existing resources so that the increased demand for work can be met through efficiency gains. None of these options is a trivial decision. Activity-based budgeting does not make these decisions automatically; it simply signals to managers the consequences from their new production and sales forecasts. It identifies where excess capacity or capacity shortages will exist, department by department and process by process, if no adjustments are made to current resource supply. It is up to the company's managers to make the hard decisions about changes in production and sales forecasts and how to accomplish the required resource reduction or acquisition to match the revised plans.

ABB Step 6: Authorize spending (either increases or decreases from the current period's levels) to supply the desired resource capacities in future periods

The final step is simple, once management has made the critical decisions on the quantity of resources to be supplied next period. Knight estimates the budget for resource spending when she multiplies the quantity of authorized resources by the cost per unit of each resource. The right-hand column, Budgeted, in figure 5-10 is the authorized (budgeted) quantity of each resource multiplied by its per-unit cost ("Monthly Cost/Unit" column in either figure 5-5 or figure 5-6). The remaining columns in figure 5-10 reflect the product costs associated with the sales and production plan in figure 5-8. The costs attributed to each product are based on the resource costs incurred to meet each product's forecasted production plan. The difference between the costs attributed to the products, summarized in the Total column, which represents the sum of costs attributed to the three product lines, and the budgeted cost (the Budgeted column)

FIGURE 5-10

Sippican Corporation: Projected Sales and Product Profit Analysis

	Valves	Pumps	Flow Controllers	Total	Unused Capacity	Budgeted
Sales (units)	12,000	12,000	2,500	29,500		
Sales revenue	**$900,000**	**$960,000**	**$275,000**	**$2,135,000**		**$2,135,000**
DL expenses	156,000	195,000	32,500	383,500	6,500	390,000
Material expenses	192,000	240,000	55,000	487,000	—	487,000
Contribution margin	552,000	525,000	187,500	1,264,500	(6,500)	1,258,000
Machine run-time	135,000	135,000	16,875	286,875	45	307,800
Set-up labor	5,200	6,240	18,720	30,160	1,040	31,200
Machine setup	3,600	4,320	12,960	20,880		
Receiving and production control	1,200	1,200	1,800	4,200	3,600	7,800
Engineering	4,875	19,500	32,500	56,875	1,625	58,500
Package and ship	49,000	49,750	12,500	111,250	1,850	113,100
Manufacturing overhead	198,875	216,010	95,355	510,240	8,160	$518,400
Total costs	$546,875	$651,010	$182,855	$1,380,740	$14,660	$1,395,400
Gross margin	$353,125	$308,990	$92,145	$754,260	$(14,660)	$739,600
Gross margin %	**39%**	**32%**	**34%**	**35%**		**35%**
Selling and administrative						350,000
Operating profit						380,600
Return on sales						**18%**

equals the cost of unused capacity that has been planned or authorized for the period.

The cost of planned unused capacity is not associated with any particular product line (or customer). It arises from the lumpiness with which most resources are acquired, from managers' conscious decisions to supply some buffer capacity for the period, or because managers are unable or unwilling, in the short run, to reduce available resource capacity to that required for next period's production. The column Unused Capacity shows the economics associated with decisions to supply capacity beyond the anticipated needs for the production plan.

The calculations in figures 5-9 and 5-10 illustrate the analytic approach in which budgeted (authorized) spending on resources arises endogenously, from within the model. The analytic budgeting process highlights the spending that must be incurred if the company's sales and production forecasts for the subsequent period are to be realized. For Sippican, the company is likely to be delighted with the budget forecast since it reveals the opportunity to improve gross margins to 35 percent and operating margins to 18 percent, dramatic improvements over performance in recent months. If, however, the forecasted spending and profits are not acceptable to management, then the activity-based budgeting team must go back to the drawing board; develop alternative scenarios for pricing, product and customer mix, and productivity improvements; feed the new scenarios into the TDABC resource demand model; and reestimate resource spending, margins, and profitability. The process should be iterative and even exploratory. The existence of an accurate analytic model of company operations at the core of the budgeting process enables managers to explore several scenarios for the future and then commit to resource capacities that give the best opportunities for profit enhancements for the upcoming period.

BUDGETING FOR DISCRETIONARY RESOURCES

Activity-based budgeting, as illustrated in the Sippican Company example, is most useful for resources that perform repetitive activities, especially for processes triggered by demands from orders, products, services, and customers. Managers must also budget for discretionary spending for the upcoming year. This spending includes advertising, product marketing and promotion, research and development, employee training, and general customer support. The outcomes from spending on advertising, R&D, and market promotions are, for most companies, not as predictable as the capacity acquired when they spend on operating and support people, equipment, technology, and space. The amount to spend on intangible assets can rarely be derived directly from the sales and production forecast. Authorizations to spend on branding or enhancing the image of a company or a product, on R&D, and on the improvement of employees' capabilities must still be done judiciously, through the experience and wisdom embedded in the senior management team.

SUMMARY

Activity-based budgeting, based on Time-Driven ABC models, does not solve all the problems associated with budgeting. But it can replace a great deal of the judgment, negotiation, and subjectivity currently required to implement line-item budgeting processes. It provides an analytic approach for deciding on the quantity of resources that needs to be supplied to meet future periods' forecasts of production and sales. Rather than negotiate about fixed line-item budgets, activity-based budgeting provides an objective, rigorous process to forecast the level of spending on resource capacity required to implement the company's strategic plan.

Activity-based budgeting does require the company to specify, in far greater detail than conventional methods demand, how production and sales demands will be met and the available supply, acquisition cost, and efficiency of company resources. With effective activity-based budgeting, however, managers will have much greater spending control over their cost structure, particularly over what they previously considered their fixed costs.

NOTES

1. This discussion is derived from R. S. Kaplan, "Sippican Corporation (A)," Case 9-106-060 (Boston: Harvard Business School, 2006).
2. The full compensation, including fringe benefits, for direct and indirect employees (other than engineers) is $3,900 per month. Employees work an average of twenty days per month (holidays and vacations accounted for the remaining two to three days per month).

## CHAPTER SIX

FAST-TRACK PROFIT MODEL

Creating the New Due-Diligence Process for Mergers and Acquistions

IN THIS CHAPTER, we push the limits of Time-Driven Activity-Based Costing by introducing a new capability for fast-track profit modeling.[1] We demonstrate how to quickly build a simple TDABC model for assessing the attractiveness of a company being considered for an acquisition. By using such a model during the due-diligence process, a prospective buyer can identify where profit opportunities exist, how they can be captured, their cost and impact, and whether the organization has the capacity to execute. While it may seem difficult to build an ABC profitability model of a company not yet owned, acquirers can often start from an existing profit model in the industry and feed actual transaction data from the prospective target into the model template. This practice enables the potential purchaser to identify profit opportunities in advance of an acquisition.

RATIONALE FOR A FAST-TRACK PROFIT MODEL DURING DUE DILIGENCE

Fast-track profit modeling considerably extends the value of the traditional due-diligence process, which today relies on high-level financial statements, market comparables, and qualitative reviews to assess valuation, risk, cultural fit, and organizational capabilities. Due diligence must occur within a short time window, typically one to two months, for the potential buyer to negotiate a letter of intent. Beyond this time constraint, buyers have limited access to acquisition targets and don't want an expensive investigation process for a transaction that, five times out of six, is not consummated.[2] But such a high-level, imprecise due-diligence process cannot identify where opportunities exist for rapid profit turnarounds. Acquirers typically do not have the time or resources to dissect the performance of the business by individual SKUs and individual customers.

These obstacles can be overcome by building a fast-track TDABC model that gives visibility to the approximate profit performance of the target's individual SKUs, customers, market segments, and channels. The model also enables the potential buyer to stand out from other potential acquirers. Acquisition teams today assemble pitch books to boast prominent industry veterans, industry partnerships and alliances, prior deal track record, deal structure, and financing arrangements. But this traditional private equity pitch has become increasingly commoditized as competition intensifies over fewer deals and distinctions between acquirers fade.[3] From the perspective of the acquiree, whoever pays the highest multiple of earnings before interest, taxes, depreciation, and amortization (EBITDA) or cash flow typically wins. From the perspective of the acquirer, however, six things matter: (1) a good management team, (2) favorable industry dynamics, (3) easy cost-cutting, (4) image makeover, (5) low acquisition multiple, and (6) opportunities for up-sell or cross-sell of the new entity. According to the Boston Consulting Group, "the acquirer needs to take an all-encompassing view of the value that might be created or lost in a prospective transaction."[4] Having a deeper understanding of profitability drivers expands the analysis from how high a multiple of existing EBITDA to pay, to how much the acquirer can quickly increase the target's EBITDA by taking actions to transform unprofitable operations into profitable ones. In this way, profit enhancements become a stronger driver of value than changes in multiples, though the profit enhancement does not rule out an increase in the EBITDA multiple in the eventual resale of the company.

The feasibility of building a fast-track profit model of a target, in advance of an actual acquisition, is facilitated by the following factors:

1. Enterprisewide profit-model templates already exist for a variety of industries. These templates, which can be easily customized to represent the actual processes performed by a business, from sales to assembly to delivery, provide the framework for estimating the

revenue, cost, and profitability of individual product lines, SKUs, and customers.

2. Transaction data on existing operations are readily available. Most companies run their business with ERP systems and have staff experienced with downloading data from order header, order detail, customer, and product files.

3. Activity-based software can integrate the potential acquiree's order, product, and customer data into the cost and profitability templates. Accurate and detailed profitability models can now be built in days or weeks instead of months or years. The models highlight which specific customers, sales representatives, contracts, products, services, and vendors are losing money. The result is the ability to quantify the profit opportunities from transforming unprofitable products, vendors, and customers into profitable ones.

In the remainder of the chapter, we present three case studies that document the development of the methodology for applying TDABC models to private equity transactions.

CASE STUDY NUMBER 1: DEVELOPING A FAST-TRACK PROFIT MODEL AT PIONEER CONTROLS

In 2002, the Pioneer Controls Company (disguised), a distributor of industrial controls devices, was in deep trouble. An overly aggressive acquisition strategy in the 1990s had left the company with plummeting net income and $14 million of debt. The company was defaulting on its loan covenants and in serious jeopardy of losing key vendors. The company approached Oak Forest Ventures, a boutique private equity firm focused on distribution turnarounds, about a potential buyout.

The private equity team soon realized that Pioneer Controls' leadership had focused too narrowly on growing top-line revenue in anticipation of an initial public offering. The company had overpaid for its seven recent acquisitions, without regard to the strategic fit of any, and now had operational redundancies and inadequate controls. By not properly managing the integration process, Pioneer Controls had not realized any synergies from its larger scale. It now had too many branches, too many sales representatives, too much overservicing of customers and vendors, and too much autonomy at the branch level. The outcome from the flawed acquisition and integration processes had primarily been increased debt and decreased profitability.

As part of its due diligence, Oak Forest met with Pioneer Controls' management team. The equity firm decided to build a TDABC model of Pioneer Controls' operations—a model that it could use to assess the potential for profit enhancements.

Step 1: Build the profit model

Oak Forest gained access, from Acorn Systems, to an existing activity template for an industrial controls company. The project team matched the template to each department of Pioneer Controls' thirty dispersed facilities. The team gathered readily available information from the company about head count, square footage, and salaries. It then studied the standard time equations from the industry template and validated that they made sense, adapting them when necessary. The team completed this initial model setup and validation in two days.

Step 2: Load the data

The team downloaded one month's general-ledger data from Pioneer Controls' JD Edwards system. It also prepared three critical transaction files—customer master, order header, and order detail file—for the same monthly period. This data access and setup took three days to perform.

Step 3: Review the findings

The team ran Pioneer Controls' monthly data on the Acorn Time-Driven ABC software system. The run time was six minutes. After validating the data, and encouraged with the ease and speed of running the model, the project team requested, received, and ran five more periods of monthly data. The team then spent two days analyzing the six months of cost and profitability data, exploring the specific areas of profit opportunity among Pioneer Controls' seven operating divisions, thirty-seven branches, ninety-eight sales representatives, four thousand five hundred customers, four hundred vendors, and various business policies.

The Oak Forest due-diligence team wanted to quickly identify the biggest profit opportunities up front and determine which could be quickly executed to reverse the profit decline and start to pay off the debt. For example, figure 6-1 shows the distribution of profits earned across the core company and its recent acquisitions. Each of the newly acquired companies was unprofitable. Figure 6-2 shows the current losses and profit opportunities in branches, sales representatives, customers, processes, and policies.

The detailed profit-model approach not only identified the buckets of opportunity, but also highlighted the specific root causes of losses. It gave

FIGURE 6-1

Pioneer Controls' Monthly Postacquisition Performance

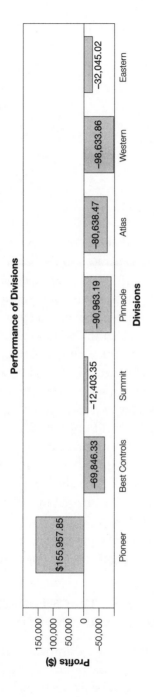

Company Profitability Master

Performance of Divisions

ID	Name	Revenue	Direct Cost	Gross Profit	Indirect Cost	Profit
160	Pioneer	$4,192,263.11	$3,290,491.35	$901,771.76	$745,813.91	$155,957.85
200	Best Controls	1,029,504.60	849,140.91	180,363.69	250,210.02	(69,846.33)
400	Summit	759,287.96	602,441.37	156,846.59	169,249.94	(12,403.35)
700	Pinnacle	702,804.48	524,606.35	178,198.13	269,161.32	(90,963.19)
300	Atlas	557,603.36	406,425.26	151,178.08	231,816.55	(80,638.47)
800	Western	473,576.34	323,715.10	149,861.24	248,495.10	(98,633.86)
500	Eastern	53,092.22	42,211.40	10,880.82	42,925.84	(32,045.02)

FIGURE 6-2

Value Identified at Pioneer Controls

Area	Key Findings	Annual Profit Impact
Branches	50% unprofitable	$2.6 million increase
Sales force	70% unprofitable	$1 million increase
Customers	60% unprofitable	$1 million increase
Redundant processes	Inside sales, customer service, inventory	$1 million increase
Business policies	Minimum order size, rush orders, restocking, intercompany transfers	$0.8 million increase
Total		$6.4 million increase

Oak Forest an action plan to consolidate the branches, sales force, and departments to eliminate losses and generate profits, actions that collectively would boost Pioneer Controls' EBITDA from $1 million to $7 million quite quickly. On the basis of this analysis, Oak Ventures offered a purchase price higher than other potential acquirers and won the business. The profit turnaround model also enabled the private equity team to attract lenders, such as GE Capital, and other equity partners, to participate in the financing. The forecasted increase in EBITDA would lead to higher interest coverage, increase the amount of debt that the new Pioneer Controls could support, and thereby reduce the equity that Oak Forest would have to contribute. Finally, the profit opportunities also attracted management candidates to help lead the turnaround.

The Oak Forest team beat the competition to acquire Pioneer Controls. The company implemented many of the changes identified during the due-diligence process. EBITDA soon increased by more than $4 million, and Pioneer Controls' management now believes that more can be captured. In the summer of 2006, Pioneer Controls launched a project to update the original TDABC model to highlight new opportunities.

CASE STUDY NUMBER 2: THE FAST-TRACK PROFIT MODEL APPROACH VALIDATED AT FAIRMONT COMPANY

In May 2005, Questor Management Company, a private equity firm, approached Acorn Systems about analyzing the profitability of a large retail company, Fairmont (disguised), that was being auctioned off by a leading investment bank. Fairmont was one of the world's oldest retail companies, with several well-known brands and hundreds of stores. After a period of declining profitability triggered by global competition, an American conglomerate had acquired Fairmont in the late 1980s. The conglomerate, now faced with declining profitability in its other businesses, decided to shed its nonstrategic, underperforming Fairmont division.

Questor Management sought "companies with performance opportunities, ranging from corporate divestitures, to under-performing and troubled companies," and Fairmont was just the type of company it was looking to acquire and turn around. The first cut, which Questor survived, had reduced the number of potential acquirers from twelve to five. The investment bank asked these five finalists to submit their offer price by June 27, 2005.

Fairmont had over 30,000 SKUs, numerous channels, and thousands of customers. Questor was particularly concerned about the explosion in SKUs and product lines at Fairmont. "It seemed that the business was growing out of control . . . Lines were added to achieve revenue growth without regard to profitability," explained Kevin Prokop, a Questor director.

Questor agreed to work with an Acorn consultant to build a fast-track profit model if Questor could acquire the following information:

1. A general ledger
2. Head count and salaries by department
3. Product SKU and customer data
4. General business information such as distribution and sales channels, and operating policies

The information trickled out gradually from the investment bank. Initially, Questor received only a high-level profit-and-loss statement, which listed major expense buckets that were not broken out by departments. Soon, however, the Questor/Acorn team received a file that identified each employee and that included the person's salary, department, and position. The team could now approximate the fully loaded costs of each department. While this information could be used to calculate departmental performance metrics, such as shipping cost per order, the team could still not drive costs down to individual SKUs.

Repeated requests for the product file finally struck gold on June 3, when the investment bank delivered a detailed SKU file that included five years' worth of dollar and unit sales data; price, cost, and category information;

and inventory levels. Upon receiving these data, the team fast-tracked the TDABC model to deliver results by the June 15 deadline.

Step 1: Build the model structure

The team assembled the critical files and data in several days. By June 9, it had built the entire model structure for Fairmont around thirty core departments (figure 6-3), including time equations that could drive departmental process costs down to all SKUs.

Step 2: Load the data

To calculate SKU profitability, only two files needed to be loaded, a general-ledger file and the SKU file. The team loaded the data in one day, on June 10.

Step 3: Run the model and review the findings

Running the model took place on Friday, June 10, and again on June 13, after the team made revisions. The findings (figure 6-4) surprised even the experienced Questor partners. Over 80 percent of the SKUs were unprofitable, losing in aggregate more than $60 million dollars. The losses on these SKUs represented 480 percent of the current profits of $13 million. The team could see immediately that by consolidating inventory, repricing, and changing service levels, it could create at least $15 million in near-term profit improvements.

FIGURE 6-3

Fairmont Departments and Processes

Core Department	Fully Loaded Cost
Product Manufacturing	$64,525,119
Selling	49,810,376
Marketing/Advertising/Creativity	15,602,778
Product Development	13,467,378
Infrastructure Support	9,317,472
Business Technology	9,095,990
Customer Service	6,253,866
Accounting and Finance	5,760,851
Executive	4,471,422
Distribution and Picking	3,743,724

FIGURE 6-4

Cumulative Profitability by SKU at Fairmont

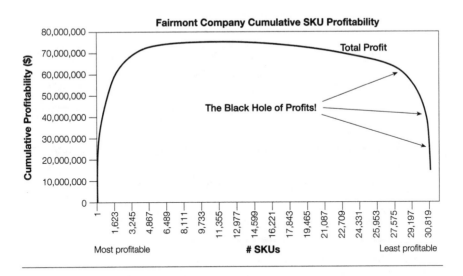

Armed with these findings, Questor increased its offer for Fairmont from $150 million to $180 million. The fast-track model encouraged Questor to bid more because it gave visibility and confidence into future profit potential. Unfortunately, this high offer was not enough to win the deal. Within the field of eight bidders, Questor came in second to a strategic buyer. Without a clear path of profit improvements, as would be provided by the profit model, the winner may have a difficult time justifying the purchase price, which represented a significant premium above the value implied by Fairmont's historical financial results.

CASE STUDY NUMBER 3: OUTPACING
THE COMPETITION AT WAYLAND

Phoenix Capital (disguised), another leading buyout firm, also saw the potential benefits of using a fast-track profit model. Phoenix wanted to sell Wayland, the distribution division of a food manufacturer, Belmont Foods (disguised), that it currently owned. The division had become a noncore asset, and the sale would provide capital to fund additional food acquisitions. Phoenix realized that providing detailed profit improvement information could give a bidder more confidence in raising the price it was willing to pay. Oak Forest and its equity partner, Cardinal Paragon, would build a quick TDABC profit model to evaluate the Wayland opportunity.

Oak Forest used a standardized process:

- Oak Forest sent data requirements for Wayland division in March 2006 (taking 2 hours to prepare and send the requirements).
- Belmont Foods sent the data files for CY2005 in April 2006 (Belmont took 1 day to prepare the files; Acorn took less than 1 day to review them).
- Oak Forest customized an existing grocery distribution template provided by its partner, Acorn Systems (2 days).
- Oak Forest loaded data and ran the TDABC model for 2005 data (1 day).
- Oak Forest reviewed the findings (1 day).

In just five days of actual work, spread over a several-week period, the Oak Forest team had created a detailed analysis of profit improvement opportunities at Wayland. Figure 6-5 shows the expected gains, derived from the fast-track time-driven profit model for the three postacquisition years.

FIGURE 6-5

Opportunities Identified at Wayland

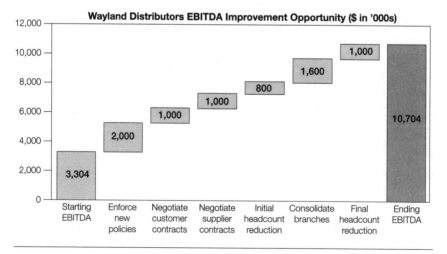

FIGURE 6-6

The Value Capture Roadmap at Wayland

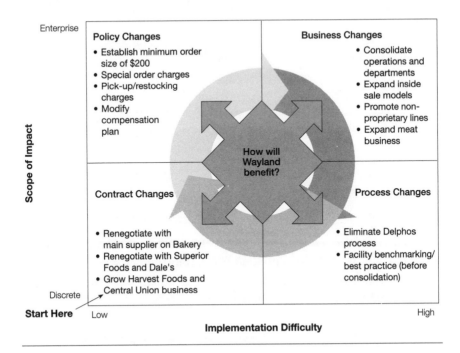

Figure 6-6 shows the specific and detailed actions Oak Forest anticipated to realize the potential $7 million in profit improvements. These actions were based on a model of profitability by customer ship-to, order, vendor, and SKU.

Figure 6-7 illustrates the value of knowing the profit improvement up front. With a minimum profit improvement of $2.5 million, and an EBITDA multiple of 6, $15 million of additional value would be created.

Oak Forest felt confident using this data to raise its bid by $15 million. Beyond the higher price, Phoenix Capital felt that the Oak Forest bid was attractive for several other reasons:

Greater likelihood for long-term success: Wayland was Belmont Foods' largest customer. Therefore Belmont had an interest in the viability and longevity of Wayland. Phoenix wanted any buyer to have a plan for Wayland to grow profitably. It now knew that Oak Forest, through its TDABC model, had developed a plan for immediate postacquisition actions.

FIGURE 6-7

Impact on Deal Economics for Wayland

Current Valuation	Forecasted Improvement	
EBITDA: $3.3 million (FY 2005)	Current EBITDA: $3.3 million	
EBITDA multiple: 6×	1. High improvement:	+ $7.4 million
	2. Medium improvement:	+ $3.5 million
$3.3 million × 6 = $19.8 million	3. Low improvement:	+ $2.5 million
Less project debt = N/A		
Enterprise value = $19.8 million	EBITDA Multiple: 6×	
	1. High value created:	+ $44.4 million
	2. Medium value created:	+ $21.0 million
	3. Low value created:	+ $15.0 million

Profit Enhancement Impact

Operational buy-in: Phoenix also believed that Wayland personnel would buy into the profit-enhancing opportunities since the people could visualize the changes needed and collaborate to implement them and benefit from the changes.

In June 2006, Oak Forest's offer was accepted. The company was acquired in October. Oak Forest immediately set its acquisition team to work on implementing the postacquisition strategy to capture the profit opportunities revealed during due diligence. At the time of the writing of this book, the company had already improved EBITDA by over $2 million.

THE GENERAL TDABC DUE-DILIGENCE PROCESS

The examples of Pioneer Controls, Fairmont, and Wayland illustrate the feasibility and power of building a fast-track profit model during the due-diligence process. Armed with this information, a private equity firm can learn in advance about the profit opportunities in currently unprofitable or breakeven products, customers, facilities, sales representatives, and vendors. The firm can explore whether a particular product could be repriced, an unprofitable regional sales office or distribution center shut down, or an unprofitable customer relationship renegotiated. Large differences in profitability among different SKUs within the same product family lead to questions about the drivers of the cost variation and whether the problem should be solved by process improvements (in handling and producing small orders), repricing, or SKU rationalization. The general approach for building a TDABC model during due diligence and how it affects an acquisition strategy can now be summarized in figure 6-8.

We already covered the first two steps, Scope the Opportunity and Drive the Investment Strategy, in figure 6-8 in our descriptions of the due-diligence processes for acquisition of Pioneer Controls, Fairmont, and Wayland. Companies first screen potential companies for acquisition, then develop a quick TDABC model to assess profit turnaround opportunities and drive the acquisition pricing policy. We now go into more detail about steps 3 and 4.

Implement the Strategy

The third step in figure 6-8, when the acquirer has won the bidding competition for the target company, is the most critical. The acquirer must work with the company management to implement a profit-turnaround strategy. Having already built a high-level profitability model expedites the turnaround process considerably. First, all changes occur within a factual model of underlying causes that have led to losses in operations in

FIGURE 6-8

Fast-Track Profit Model for Acquisition Process

	Scope the Opportunity	Drive the Investment Strategy	Implement the Strategy	Harvest the Returns
Purpose	Target industries and companies that benefit most from the profit enhancement approach:	Leverage team experience to expedite and properly structure acquisition:	Expedite company profit improvements by leveraging expertise:	Accelerate and expand exit opportunity potential to achieve superior investor returns:
Actions	• Screen industries based on market and *investment attractiveness*. • Screen industries based on *strategic* fit with profit model methodology. • *Build a profit model* to identify profit potential in advance of acquisition, leveraging industry template models where possible.	• Perform additional due diligence using the profit model and fund managers' expertise. • Raise and structure capital to effect transaction. • Devise management incentives to drive operational changes. • Align key stakeholder interests around profit enhancement.	• Install Acorn's time-driven ABC software to identify and capture profit improvement. • Actively participate with management team on value capture and improve operations. • Institutionalize profit management across organization. • Document and report performance enhancement.	• Establish company as leader in profitability and operational performance, promoting the company's track record of successful execution. • Cultivate relationships with multiple exit channels—industry consolidators, brokers, banks, and private equity firms.

the past. The acquirer and the acquired company should be on the same page about the economics of current operations, and this should build the buy-in for the needed changes. The data-driven profitability model creates a shared understanding around the need for change and where changes are most urgent, as well as the action steps—process improvements, product rationalization, customer renegotiation—that are most likely to transform unprofitable operations into profitable ones. In this way, both the acquiring group and the management of the operating company own the solution.

Typically, transformations in one or two key areas—products, vendors, processes, regions, or customers—will be truly decisive in the profit turnaround. These one or two areas can then be monitored and measured regularly to track the company's progress and ensure that the company stays focused on meeting its objectives.

Harvest the Returns

In the fourth step, the company develops and installs a detailed TDABC profit model for its operations. The model tracks changes in the profitability of different product lines, segments, channels, customers, and geographies as the company implements the profit-turnaround strategy and as its competitive environment evolves. These dynamic forces create new circumstances for transforming unprofitable operations into profitable ones, and the company needs to continually track the next generation of profit-improvement opportunities. All these contribute to continual EBITDA enhancements, eventually enabling the acquirer to position the company for resale to a more permanent owner or for a public offering.

SUMMARY

A fast-track profit model, exploiting the simplicity and power of Time-Driven ABC, provides acquirers with a powerful new tool for the due-diligence process. Advances in industry templates, information technology, and the TDABC innovation itself now enable an acquirer to quickly identify key issues, questions, and levers for profit turnarounds. All these advances allow the acquirer to develop a holistic value-creation plan based on the profit-improvement opportunity and the ease of capturing that opportunity. If the private equity firm wins the bidding contest, the profit model subsequently becomes a blueprint for managing the turnaround company and aligning company management to the required actions. The model also helps build support for change and facilitates the execution of the strategy, as articulated in the value-creation plan, eventually preparing the company for resale and exit. In short, building, analyzing, and implementing a fast-track profit model becomes a consistent thread running throughout the life cycle of a private equity firm's portfolio company, ensuring real and targeted value creation for the private equity firm and its partners.

NOTES

1. This chapter is derived from S. Anderson and K. Prokop, "Acquiring Profit Opportunities: Rethinking M&A," Acorn Systems white paper (Houston: Acorn Systems, July 2005).
2. The authors surveyed ten private equity firms. On average, 16 percent of the letters of intent resulted in a closed acquisition.
3. According to John Curran of the Corporate Board, since around 1996, over $445 billion of capital has flowed into private equity funds. However, the ratio of uninvested capital to equity invested was more than 15.
4. Kees Cools et al., *Growing Through Acquisitions*, Boston Consulting Group report (Boston: Boston Consulting Group, May 2004).

## CHAPTER SEVEN

ENHANCING BUSINESS PROCESS IMPROVEMENTS

New Applications for Time-Driven ABC

TIME-DRIVEN ACTIVITY-BASED COSTING complements important initiatives in business process improvement, such as lean management, supply-chain optimization, and benchmarking. These applications represent significant potential extensions to the traditional process-costing, product- and customer-profitability management, and budgeting roles for TDABC models described in earlier chapters. But because the application of TDABC in these settings has only recently been applied, its efficacy is less proven. In this chapter, we introduce these promising new extensions of TDABC that enhance companies' continuous improvement projects.

ENHANCING LEAN MANAGEMENT

Lean management evolved out of the original lean manufacturing system developed in the 1980s at Toyota.[1] Lean manufacturing includes continuous improvement techniques, such as just-in-time (JIT), jidoka, and kaizen, whose guiding principle is to eliminate waste. Taiichi Ohno, the Toyota visionary who led the development of this operating philosophy, believed that overproduction, waiting and other idle time, unnecessary movements, inventory, and defects were all examples of waste since they represented unnecessary work and excess resources.[2] Eliminating the root causes of waste would reduce costs, improve quality, and make processes faster and more responsive.

Extending the ideas from manufacturing to the enterprise, lean management teams now focus on delivering exactly what the customer needs (lean consumption) in the most efficient way possible (lean provision). According to a Gartner Group research study, company chief information officers (CIOs) rated business process improvement as their number one priority for 2006.

THREE CORE PRINCIPLES

Before starting the journey toward lean management, a company first educates and trains its lean team. Lean Six Sigma, a variant that integrates lean management and six sigma quality methodologies, uses a formal training regimen called "black belt training." Once trained, the "certified" black belts serve as missionaries throughout the rest of the organization to indoctrinate and train other personnel in other departments.

Lean management consists of three core stages: identify waste, identify the fix, and implement it. In the first step, the lean management team identifies specific waste within a process chain. Lean management addresses not only localized processes within the four walls of its manufacturing plants, but also the processes surrounding how the company procures items from suppliers, how customers buy from the company, and how the product or service is produced and delivered to the customer. The lean management team prepares value stream maps (figure 7-1 shows a typical value stream map, in this case for a small manufacturing plant) that document all the activities or processes currently being performed by a supplier, the company, or a customer. Each block represents a process. In a more detailed level of analysis, each block can represent a specific activity step within a process. For each step or process, the team documents who performs it, how long it takes, the key drivers of process time, and its output. The team interviews department personnel to validate the steps and the process characteristics. It then designates each process or step as value-added (VA) or non-value-added (NVA, or waste), according to whether the process adds value for the customer. Often, the team spends several days collecting data for each process.

The processes in figure 7-1 for the manufacturing plant show the system before the impact of lean management. The company, experiencing difficulties with excess work in process inventory and schedule delays, had hired Dick Barry and several consultants from University of Texas to

FIGURE 7-1

Current Value Stream Map (Pre-lean)

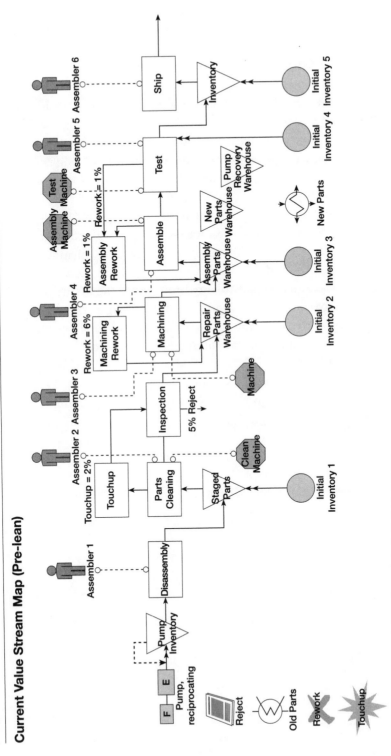

Source: Dick Barry, Manual of Lean Concepts Applied to Process Models.

apply lean management approaches to its processes. Using the value stream map, the team spotted several bottlenecks, or "hot spots," leading to non-value-added time (figure 7-2). The triangular inventory symbol labeled Staged Parts in figure 7-1 ranks number two on the hot spots of figure 7-2, indicating a high source of congestion and delays.

The second step identifies creative ways to eliminate waste and perform the same activities more efficiently. The team brainstorms about potential fixes to inefficient activities and processes. This includes, for each suggestion, estimates of the process impact and ease of implementation. This labor-intensive effort typically takes several days for each business process.

In the third step, the team implements the approved changes. Lean management teams screen the best ideas and work with department managers to convert the ideas into specific project implementation plans.[3] Some lean teams fall down in this most important step. They play a major role in identifying and solving problems in the first two steps, but are less effective in gaining support from operating personnel to ensure that the fixes are actually put into practice. The six sigma black belts require additional training in the interpersonal skills required to gain the confidence and support of the operating people. When well implemented, the results are impressive. For example, figure 7-3 shows the modified plant process flow with no work-in-process inventory buildups (note the absence of inverted triangles).

FIGURE 7-2

Ten "Hot Spots" in Process Stream

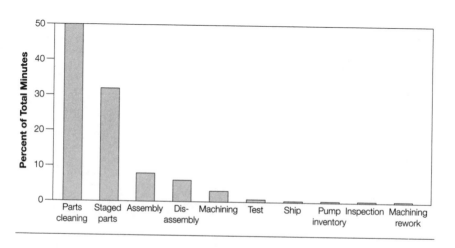

FIGURE 7-3

Future Value Stream Map (Post-lean)

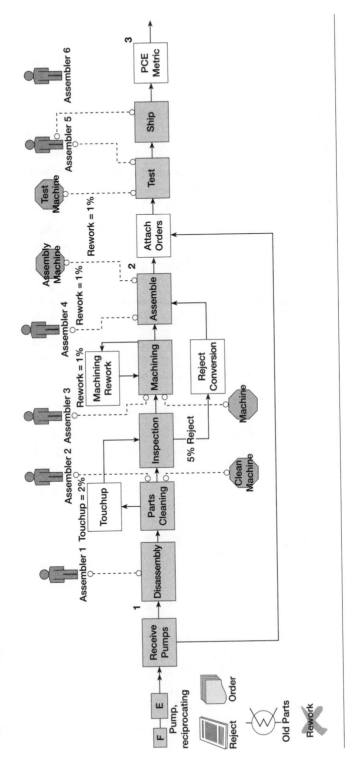

Lean management was originally developed for manufacturing companies but is now being extended to service industries as well. Financial service, government, and health-care enterprises use lean models to streamline their operations and shrink or eliminate unnecessary steps.

Many similarities exist between lean management and TDABC. Both methods start with teams descending on departments to manually gather department data to improve specific department processes. Lean management projects document process quality and cycle times but provide little to no information on process resources and costs. TDABC provides otherwise missing measurements, specifically, process capacity and cost. In short, TDABC will monetize lean projects by determining, for example, the most efficient means of processing orders. A TDABC project could measure the cost of orders processed on the Web, through EDI, by fax, and by phone. The TDABC model could subsequently validate the cost savings from making each ordering channel more efficient or shifting the mix of incoming orders from high-cost to low-cost channels.

The capacity focus of TDABC complements beautifully the lean management philosophy. All the factors that consume resource capacity are identified; teams can work to reduce the capacity required to accomplish value-added work. Moreover, teams have summary financial data to guide their efforts to eliminate or reduce non-value-added work, such as materials movement and setups that currently consume high-cost resource capacity. Using activity-based budgeting, as described in chapter 5, project teams can identify the reduction in resource capacity that can be accomplished through lean management projects. Without the TDABC discipline, lean management teams would be otherwise unable to forecast the resource savings possible from their improvement activities.

Both lean management and TDABC are based on process maps. TDABC adds the new feature of time equations that explain the demands on resource capacity by orders, deliveries, products, services, and customers.

Since both methodologies are data-driven and fact-based, both promote accountability and ownership among operating employees. For lean management, department personnel provide process details and devise creative solutions. With TDABC, departmental personnel identify the resources used by the department's process and help build their department's process time equation.

Some other differences between lean management and TDABC do exist. Lean management projects eliminate waste within departmental processes. TDABC deals with factors that cause complexity within processes. The complexity is not waste; it arises from customizing the process for individual customer demands to create value and differentiation for customers. The efficiency of a process that handles customer-specific variation cannot be measured simply by the average time or cost per setup, per delivery, or per unit produced.

Lean management projects typically collect aggregate data at the customer or product level, such as total number of orders. These aggregate data must often be hand-collected or custom-downloaded. TDABC works off data captured from the company's ERP business system and can thus explicitly incorporate order- and transaction-level details. The TDABC model uses these details to explain the variations in process time and cost caused by specific attributes and differences in a customer's order, request, or attribute.

In addition, a TDABC model integrates process time and cost data across the enterprise. Lean management, in contrast, focuses intensively on eliminating waste at the process level. The time-driven model reveals how individual products, customers, and orders draw on process capacity throughout the company. Its focus on individual products, customers, and transactions gives the TDABC model a hook by which to accumulate total enterprise process time, quality, and cost on the basis of product, customer, and transaction characteristics. Thus, a combined approach—lean management and TDABC—provides benefits that neither technique can achieve on its own (see summary in figure 7-4).

Some lean management advocates, however, with perhaps only a superficial understanding of ABC, claim that ABC's traditional value comes at too high a cost. They claim, erroneously, that the costs analyzed by an ABC model are, in any case, fixed and therefore not of great value to analyze. The critics also complain that ABC assigns unused capacity and therefore overburdens products with excess costs.[4]

These complaints, at best, are about conventional ABC and have all been addressed by the Time-Driven ABC innovation. We described in chapters 1 through 3 how to build inexpensive but complex, comprehensive models that highlight actual process times and capacity utilization. In chapter 5, we demonstrated how virtually all an enterprise's costs can be made variable when resources are authorized via an activity-based budgeting approach. These innovations provide much tighter linkages between the process improvements made under a lean management initiative and the costing and other decisions that reduce the future supply of resource capacity to capture the gains from the process improvements.

FIGURE 7-4

Lean Management and Time-Driven ABC: Summary Comparison

Characteristic	Lean Management	Time-Driven ABC	Benefit from Adding TDABC
Focus on process	• Manually identifies waste in process	• Views process as department-specific, and as an aggregation of activities • Creates time equation for each process that identifies inefficiencies	• Enables predictive analysis, capacity analysis, operational validation, process benchmarking
Define activity steps	• Manually identifies waste in activity steps	• Measures the average time per step	• Enables model templates to be used for rapid model build and rollout
Data collection level	• Collects data at the customer or product level in an aggregated fashion (e.g., number of orders)	• Uses data at transaction and line item level to increase accuracy	• Analyzes all transaction, product, and customer data • Adds accuracy by controlling specific characteristics of individual transactions
	• Performs custom downloads	• Accesses complete transaction files from ERP system	• Expedites model building and maintenance process • Data are easier to extract

INTEGRATING TIME-DRIVEN ABC WITH LEAN SIX SIGMA

Some companies, such as HSBC, are extending their Lean Six Sigma initiative (a variant of lean management) to incorporate TDABC capabilities. The companies train their six-sigma black belts to apply TDABC and integrate it into their methodology using the following sequence of steps:

1. *Define the processes.* Figure 7-5 shows the activity steps identified in the definition phase in a typical process, the checking of customer lines of credit (LOC).
2. *Measure the elapsed time for each process step.* During this measurement phase, the project team interviews department personnel to estimate the average time per step. Industry standard times can also be applied. Figure 7-6 shows a typical data collection sheet.

FIGURE 7-5

A Lean Six-Sigma Process Map

Example: Line of credit application processing

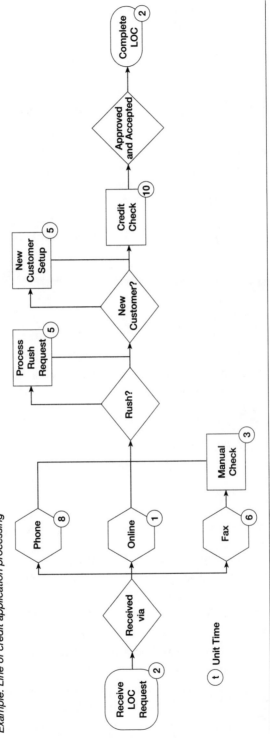

FIGURE 7-6

Time-Driven Process Data

Task	Time	Volume	Minutes	Cost	Unit Cost
Receive LOC request	2	30,000	60,000	$72,396	$2.41
Receive LOC via fax	6	6,000	36,000	43,438	7.24
Receive LOC online	1	15,000	15,000	18,099	1.21
Receive LOC via phone	8	9,000	72,000	86,876	9.65
Manual check	3	6,000	18,000	21,719	3.62
Perform rush request	5	4,500	22,500	27,149	6.03
Perform credit check	10	27,000	270,000	325,784	12.07
Set up new customer	5	9,000	45,000	54,297	6.03
Complete LOC	2	22,500	45,000	54,297	2.41
			583,500	$704,055	
Actual cost				$748,000	
Difference (unused capacity)				**$43,945**	

3. *Build the process time equation.* Once the process equation is defined, the model dynamically updates with little to no intervention. A sample time equation for the credit application process follows:

Credit application time = 2 + 6 {if fax} + 1 {if Web} + 8 {if phone}
+ 3 {if manual} + 5 {if rush} + 10 {if credit check}
+ 5 {if new} + 2

SUMMARY: LEAN MANAGEMENT AND TDABC

Lean management has proven its usefulness many times in many locations. It identifies opportunities for waste reduction and improving the value delivered to customers. TDABC enhances this value delivery since its scope is broader, encompassing an enterprisewide solution instead of a local department or process study. The information gleaned from TDABC is more accurate and complete, since it is based on enterprisewide transaction data rather than a manual download of average customer and process-specific data. Mitch Max, partner at DecisionVu (formerly The Performax Group), who focuses on process improvement projects within the financial services industry, makes the linkage between the two methodologies explicit: "Time-Driven ABC capitalizes on this investment [in documenting processes for Sarbanes-Oxley and Lean Management] by translating process flow documentation into a cost flow model, and in turn by placing reliance on process consistency as the basis for model building."[5]

Dan Stusnick of HSBC also remarked on his company's use of time-driven models with Lean Six Sigma: "The approach taken in our Lean Six Sigma project is completely valid and proven, and we are replicating it in various degrees elsewhere in HSBC. The main difference is that we now use the Time Driven [ABC] methodology, and train our black belts in how to use it."[6]

SUPPLY-CHAIN MANAGEMENT

Companies are not only optimizing their processes within their organizational boundaries, but are also attempting to streamline and optimize processes with external partners, especially suppliers and customers. By extending a TDABC model outside their organization, companies can measure the cost of their relationships with customers and suppliers. A time-driven model of the specific steps on a supply chain usually reveals the inefficiencies between the company and its supply chain and triggers actions to significantly improve the processes and, hence, profits.[7]

Supply-chain transactions involve multiple activities by the seller and include the following:

Selling	Shipping
Quoting	Delivery
Order processing	Installation
Order picking	Billing
Order assembly	Collecting
Quality control	Customer service
Packaging	

Buyers perform a comparable set of activities, such as vendor selection, purchasing, scheduling, receiving, inspecting, moving, and payment. Analyzing all these activities reveals a myriad of costs, as high as 40 percent of revenues, being incurred for transactions between sellers and buyers, costs that are typically invisible to both parties. Apart from their sheer magnitude, supply-chain costs vary substantially by buyer and seller. Calculating an average cost per purchase grossly distorts the economics of a particular vendor-customer relationship. The true economics can only be revealed by a detailed calculation that includes all the costs associated with the activities performed in an actual transaction between an individual supplier and customer.

Companies that understand the transaction costs they incur with external partners can usually find ways to reduce the costs. For example, one company learned that its inspection costs from a supplier were unusually high because of high defect rates. It sought compensation by asking for price discounts. The vendor refused the discount request but agreed to improve its processes so that the items shipped to the company would have zero defects. The cost of the supplier to ensure perfect quality was well below the cost its customer was currently experiencing to detect and remedy defective items from the supplier. To illustrate the range of possibilities from applying TDABC to supply-chain relationships, we employ an extended example.

EXTENDED CASE STUDY

Clairmont Devices (disguised), a semiconductor manufacturer, developed a TDABC model to measure customer profitability. The model revealed that many of its large distributor customers, such as Frontier Electronics (also disguised), were highly unprofitable because of extensive order processing, picking, packaging, and delivery activities.

Independently and at about the same time, Frontier had completed its own TDABC study of supplier profitability and discovered that Clairmont, one of its largest vendors, was unprofitable because of high purchasing, receiving, inspection, and stocking costs. These findings, of course, were not a coincidence. Many activities were linked between the two firms so that inefficiencies and costs created by one firm drove inefficiencies and costs at the other.

Frontier operated with a decentralized structure with each of its fifty distribution sites performing its own purchasing and sales. Semiconductor chips had a short life span, and their usage was highly specialized. Frontier's engineers at each site worked closely with local customers to design custom assemblies that required specialty semiconductor chips from Clairmont. As a consequence, Clairmont received many small orders for customized products from many Frontier sites (figure 7-7). Conversely, Frontier's decentralized structure led to its incurring high purchasing costs because of the inefficient receiving, inspection, and stocking activities performed at each dispersed location.

FIGURE 7-7

Clairmont-Frontier Supply Chain

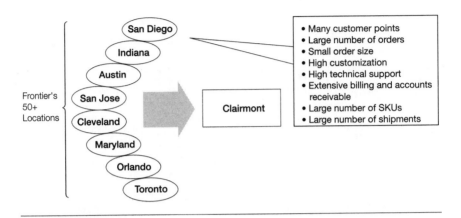

Acorn Systems consultants worked with both companies to develop a process map that showed how actions by one company triggered activities at the other (figure 7-8). The consulting team focused intensively on the purchasing–order linkage because of the large opportunities for process improvement and cost reduction. The TDABC model estimated the fully loaded process cost, the capacity time (in minutes), and the unit time required for each process step (figure 7-9). From these parameters, the model calculated the cost per process unit.

To see the potential magnitude of the inefficiencies, assume that 50 locations of Frontier ordered 5 times every week, for a total of 13,000 orders per year. Each order contained, on average, 10 items, for a total of 130,000 line items. Working through a thought experiment, if Frontier had a centralized purchasing department that aggregated the orders from each location each week, it would order about 2,500 line items annually. Further, Clairmont would ship to one central Frontier warehouse. Figures 7-10 A and B show the potential cost savings from the more centralized, coordinated purchasing pattern. The what-if thought experiment suggested that total supply-chain purchasing and ordering costs of more than $1.8 million could be cut to about $430,000.

Returning to the actual experience of these two companies, we see the cost and profitability of the Clairmont-Frontier relationship in figure 7-11. Before the supply-chain study, Frontier believed that Clairmont was one of its most profitable vendors, as Frontier generated nearly $10 million in revenue and over $2 million in gross profit from selling Clairmont-sourced

FIGURE 7-8

Clairmont-Frontier Supply-Chain Links

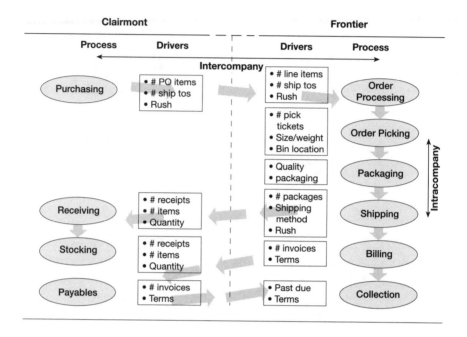

FIGURE 7-9

TDABC Cost of Process Steps

Process	Fully Loaded Process Cost		Capacity Time (minutes)		Unit Time for Process		Cost per Process Unit
	Cp	/	*Tp*	×	*Tpu*	=	*Cpu*
Purchasing	$400,000		500,000		12.5 min		$10 per order
Order processing	$1,000,000		2,000,000		20 min		$10 per order
Picking	$5,000,000		4,000,000		1.67 min		$2 per unit
Packaging	$250,000		500,000		2 min		$1 per unit
Shipping	$2,400,000		600,000		5 min		$20 per order
Receiving	$1,200,000		400,000		5 min		$15 per order
Stocking	$2,000,000		2,000,000		2 min		$2 per item
Billing	$200,000		40,000		2 min		$10 per order
Payables	$100,000		50,000		2.5 min		$5 per order
Collection	$50,000		50,000		20 min		$20 per order

FIGURE 7-10

A. Frontier Process Costs

Process	Current Number of Transactions	Current Process Cost	Total Cost	Ideal Number of Transactions	New Process Cost	Total Cost
Purchasing	13,000 orders	$10 per order	$130,000	52	$100 per order	$5,200
Receiving	13,000 orders	$15 per order	$195,000	52	$100 per order	$5,200
Quality inspection	130,000 units	$1 per unit	$130,000	130,000	$0.5 per unit	$65,000
Stocking	130,000 units	$2 per unit	$260,000	130,000	$1 per unit	$130,000
Payment	13,000 orders	$5 per order	$65,000	52	$50 per order	$2,600
			$780,000			**$208,000**

B. Clairmont Process Costs

Process	Current Number of Transactions	Current Process Cost	Total Cost	Ideal Number of Transactions	New Process Cost	Total Cost
Processing	13,000 orders	$10 per order	$130,000	52	$100 per order	$5,200
Picking	130,000 units	$2 per unit	$260,000	130,000	$1 per unit	$130,000
Packaging	130,000 units	$1 per unit	$130,000	130,000	$0.5 per unit	$65,000
Delivery	13,000	$20 per order	$260,000	52	$100 per order	$5,200
Billing	13,000	$10 per order	$130,000	52	$50 per order	$2,600
Collections	13,000	$10 per order	$130,000	52	$50 per order	$2,600
			$1,040,000			**$211,000**

products. The numbers in figure 7-11 revealed that the frequent purchasing activities performed by Frontier to acquire products from Clairmont had led to significant bottom-line losses. Inside and outside sales departments at each branch were purchasing and ordering products from Clairmont. Accrued interest was high because Clairmont products sat as inventory in all remote branches. Inbound freight was high since Clairmont shipped

FIGURE 7-11

Frontier Vendor Profitability: Clairmont Versus Company Average

	Amount	Clairmont	Company Average
Revenue	$9,684,000	100%	100%
Direct cost	7,620,000	78.69%	82.98%
Gross profit	2,063,172	21.31%	16.74%
ABC indirect costs	2,672,316	27.60%	14.86%
Profit	**−609,144**	**−6.29%**	**+1.87%**
Outside sales	420,000	4.33%	2.20%
Inside sales	300,000	3.10%	1.20%
Accrued interest	245,808	2.54%	0.78%
Inbound freight	169,272	1.75%	0.80%
Picking	77,472	0.80%	0.17%
Packaging	43,578	0.45%	0.06%

thousands of small packages to the branches. Total picking and packaging costs were high, as each branch performed these functions for the small-order quantities it received. Clearly, while decentralized operations enabled fast, flexible response to end-use customers, decentralization also incurred far higher costs than centralized purchasing, warehousing, and distribution would.

The ending to this story, however, was not happy. Neither company had ever seen accurate, detailed data about its supply-chain relationships before. But because both companies were highly oriented to short-term profit measurement and committed to their existing procurement and distribution methods, Frontier and Clairmont were unable to come together to identify changes within the supply-chain relationship that both companies considered acceptable. At the end of the day, neither company acted and both companies continued to believe that the other was the cause of losses between them.

On the other hand, we know many stories with happy endings. For example, a *Fortune* 100 discount retailer used the insight from its TDABC implementation to share supply-chain costs with its top vendor suppliers to successfully renegotiate delivery, merchandise, service, and payment terms. This resulted in significant profit improvement for all parties.

IMPLEMENTATION ISSUES

A principal barrier to ABC modeling of supply chains is obtaining valid data on supplier-customer transactions. For example, a large U.S. retailer attempted to get detailed data from approximately one thousand of its suppliers. Only a dozen of the larger suppliers could provide the data; the rest, constituting the bulk of its midmarket suppliers, could not. After spending over $30 million and many person-months of effort, the retailer canceled the high-profile supply-chain management project. Even when data on supply-chain processes are available, the information is often inaccurate or misleading. Clairmont discovered that its traditional cost system greatly underestimated the cost of outbound freight, a problem that led to $2.4 million in unrecovered costs.

If companies can overcome the barriers to collaboration, the opportunities are high. We recommend starting with a grid plotting gross revenues and operating profits for all supply-chain partners (figure 7-12). The best near-term profit opportunities are in the lower right-hand cell:

FIGURE 7-12

Profit Performance Matrix

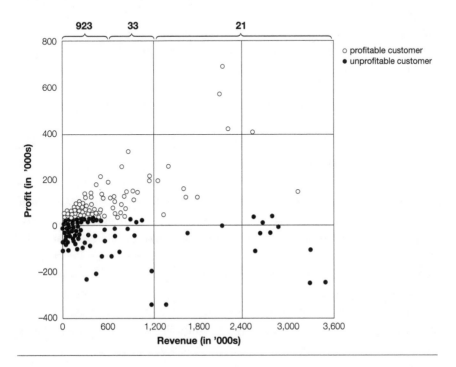

large, unprofitable (or marginally profitable) supply-chain relationships. Higher-volume relationships are likely longer-term, across multiple product lines, and with professionally managed (not family-managed) companies.

These factors facilitate a discussion on how to collaborate to enhance total supply-chain profits. Also, relatively few relationships fall into the lower right-hand corner cell, so management can focus on transforming these key relationships. For example, a leading beverage company learned that it needed to modify its delivery processes with its large, unprofitable accounts. It instituted several new supply-chain policies, such as minimum order size, and soon realized significant profit improvements with these accounts. We also suggest engaging a trusted third party to facilitate safe and effective collaboration while maintaining confidentiality of sensitive company information.

In performing supply-chain profit analyses, companies must drive down into the details of the relationships. High-level, averaged figures cannot identify the root causes of supply-chain problems. We described in chapter 2 how the conventional ABC system at Hunter Corporation forced the company to aggregate data about its 350,000 customers and 100,000 SKUs into 800 customer groupings and a small number of product categories. This average, aggregated data did not provide sufficient levels of credibility and granularity to renegotiate contracts with the company's large, sophisticated vendors and customers. Only after successfully installing a TDABC model, which captured actual transaction data for all vendors, SKUs, and customers, could Hunter begin transforming its supply-chain relationships.

Before sharing cost and profitability data with key vendors and suppliers, companies should focus first on improving their own supply-chain processes. Our prior example revealed the opportunity for enormous cost savings if Frontier could aggregate the purchasing demands from its myriad dispersed locations into a centralized procurement function. As another example, Open Plains Steel, a steel distributor, initially believed that its unprofitable customers were caused by prices that failed to cover the cost of customized services, such as metal slitting. The company's TDABC profit model showed, however, that the actual drivers of losses were the higher costs incurred at two of its distribution centers. Open Plains Steel benchmarked the process cost structure at these two facilities and immediately saw opportunities to lower these centers' costs to company and industry averages, which would eliminate the losses currently being experienced with most of the currently unprofitable customers. Open Plains Steel understood that it couldn't expect customers to pay for its internal inefficiencies.

SUMMARY: SUPPLY-CHAIN OPTIMIZATION
AND TIME-DRIVEN ABC

Using innovations in information technology and process modeling, companies can measure costs and profit by SKU, product, order, customer, and channel. These detailed data enable the enterprises to determine the root causes of costly and unprofitable supply-chain relationships. The information provides the basis for internal process improvements and fact-based discussions with key supply-chain partners that transform unprofitable relationships into profitable ones. Given the large dollars spent in supply chains, the resulting profit improvements can be dramatic.

BENCHMARKING

Companies use benchmarking to compare the current performance of a process with that of comparable internal or external business units. Statistical benchmarks of process costs, especially those provided by outside benchmarking services, are often misleading. The companies being benchmarked may have different definitions of what costs are to be included in the process and experience considerable variation in the nature of the transactions handled by superficially similar processes. For example, processing a customer order for a retail catalog store is quite different from processing a customer order in a business-to-business transaction. For companies that have multiple similar facilities, however, the discipline of creating a TDABC model provides comparable process cost data across facilities. The process time equations give managers a means to benchmark similar processes across different facilities. For example, at Texas Steel, some facilities perform additional quality-assurance steps to achieve ISO certification. As a consequence, an assembly process at an ISO-certified facility takes considerably longer than at noncertified locations. Such a difference would be captured by a TDABC equation, enabling analysts to control for process differences across facilities. The company can compare efficiency and productivity data and identify and share best practices across dispersed units.

As one additional benefit, once several companies within an industry have developed TDABC models from a similar template, the enterprises can compare process efficiencies across them. Industry templates can come from an independent external agency, such as a trade association, or a consulting firm with industry experience. Thus, TDABC facilitates internal and external benchmarking studies, an opportunity that is only beginning to be realized.

CASE STUDY OF TIME-DRIVEN
BENCHMARKS IN DISTRIBUTION

Consider the situation at Nationwide Metals (disguised), a steel service center and distributor. The company adopted TDABC in 2002 to deal with a difficult competitive situation of depressed steel prices and excess capacity in its forty-four semiautonomous facilities, many acquired in a recent merger. Management planned to consolidate to thirty high-performing facilities, but it didn't want to lose the highly profitable customers of the fourteen facilities it would shut down. Also, even within an overall unprofitable facility, several processes could be highly efficient. A regional general manager argued that it would be more effective to consolidate processes: "Let's preserve our most efficient and profitable processes, and merge the least profitable ones into them." But the company needed valid data, comparable across all facilities, before it could identify and transfer best practices.

Knowing that other companies in its steel distribution industry had already successfully implemented TDABC models, Nationwide Metals decided to embark on its own companywide ABC study. The company wanted data within five months, the deadline for making final decisions on consolidating facilities. It decided to leverage Acorn's prior industry experience and industry templates.

The project team started by building a facility template that incorporated all the core processes. Since most of the processes were basically the same at each facility, the team asked managers at each local branch management to drive their general-ledger costs to each process and to provide coefficient estimates for the time equations for their facility. The engagement of local managers increased model accuracy as well as operational buy-in across the forty-four branches. The team then developed a small operating system to download monthly transaction data—the general ledger, customer master file, order file, and product master file—immediately after the end of each month to produce monthly process costs and product and customer profitability reports. Despite the wide scope of operations and the large transactions file, the project was successfully completed within the five-month schedule (figure 7-13).

The company learned that more than 50 percent of its branches were unprofitable. Each unprofitable branch, however, had highly profitable customers and services. Simply closing down an unprofitable branch would jeopardize the profitable customer relationships and potentially lose valuable process capabilities. For example, the unprofitable Atlanta

FIGURE 7-13

Nationwide Metals Model Rollout Schedule

Areas	Sales and Process	Process Only	Sales Only	Rollout Site	MODEL BUILDING		VALUE CAPTURE	
					Session Dates	Completion Dates	Session Dates	Completion Dates
Southwest	3	1		Texas	Complete	Complete	Jun 27	Jul 16
Southeast	3		2	Georgia	Complete	Complete	Jun 27	Jul 16
Central	2	1	2	Missouri	May 22, 23	Jun 8	Jul 2	Jul 27
Western	5		1	California	Jun 5, 6	Jun 22	Jul 17	Jul 27
Midwest	2		1	Indiana	Jun 28, 29	Jul 13	Aug 19	Aug 10
Mid-Atlantic	4		1	Pennsylvania	Jul 10, 11	Jul 27	Sep 25	Sep 25
New England	2		1	Connecticut	Jul 18, 19	Aug 10	Aug 21	Sep 14
Northwest	3			Washington	Jul 31, Aug 1	Aug 17	Sep 27	Oct 1
Corporate model				Texas	Aug 3–17	Sep 1	Sep 21	Oct 1
U.S. integration				Acorn Office	Aug 3–30	Sep 1		
Europe	3			France	Sep 10, 11	Sep 11	Sep 12	Sep 12
Global Integration				Texas	Oct 1	Oct 1	Sep 21	Oct 1
Total	27	2	8	9 sites				

site had the most efficient order-entry process in the southeast region (figure 7-14).

Before closing the Atlanta plant, management considered three potential actions:

1. Move the Atlanta order-entry team and process to a nearby facility.
2. Maintain the team as a freestanding call center in Atlanta.
3. Study the best practices used in Atlanta, and transfer that knowledge to other order-entry processes in the remaining facilities.

The company decided to follow a regional consolidation strategy. For example, the southwest region had six facilities. The San Antonio facility was profitable, but one in Houston, four times the size of the San Antonio branch, was highly unprofitable. The TDABC model showed, however, that the Houston facility had an order-entry cost of $45 per order while San Antonio's cost for the same process was $80. The cost rate at San Antonio was $0.92 per minute versus $0.58 per minute for Houston. The difference was counterintuitive because the Houston site had a much higher overall cost structure. Some of the cost difference was due to different capacity utilization (San Antonio, a relatively new site, had been staffed for a capacity it had yet to reach). The team looked deeper by comparing the time equations between the two sites (figure 7-15).

Returns and credit memos took only five minutes in Houston, versus fifteen minutes in San Antonio. Additional efficiencies in Houston made the average time to process an order much less than in San Antonio. If the Houston business were shifted to San Antonio, the Houston inside-sales process should also be shifted to bring efficiency gains to the San Antonio operation.

FIGURE 7-14

Time-Driven ABC Cost Benchmarks for Order Entry at the Southeast Area Plants

Cost benchmark	Birming-ham	Nashville	Atlanta	Savannah	Jackson-ville	Charlotte
Cost per order taken	$24.92	$26.11	$19.25	$37.22	$48.34	$25.12
Best in class	$19.25	$19.25	$19.25	$19.25	$19.25	$19.25
Variance	$(5.67)	$(6.86)	$(0.00)	$(17.97)	$(29.09)	$(5.87)
Variance	–29%	–36%	0%	–93%	–151%	–31%

FIGURE 7-15

Order Process Cost Differences Between Houston and San Antonio Plants

Location of Plant	Cost per Order	Information for Time Equation
Houston order entry	$45.45	Transforming a quote into an order takes 5 minutes at a minimum. A buyout or direct order takes an additional 5 minutes. Memory purchase orders do not take more time. Credit memos take 5 minutes. If it is a service provider purchase order, add 12.5 minutes. Freight-forwarded items (which are boxed) take 30 minutes.
San Antonio order entry	$79.64	Transforming a quote into an order takes 5 minutes at a minimum. If it is a buyout, a direct order or a memory purchase, it takes an additional 5 minutes. Credit memos take 15 minutes.

Nationwide Metals was able to leverage the TDABC benchmarking data with corporatewide process improvements and facility consolidation. It used the following steps for its benchmarking process:

1. Compare facility profitability.
2. Identify high-cost, inefficient processes.
3. Benchmark these processes to other locations.
   a. Compare cost per minute.
   b. Compare time equations.
4. Identify how to leverage. Examples:
   a. Roll out best-practice processes to other facilities.
   b. Merge poor-performing departments with high performers.
   c. Fix poor performers.

Nationwide used its benchmarking data to decide on the twelve locations to close. It consolidated the operations and processes of the closed facilities into the active ones.

The customer profitability information guided company marketing and sales personnel to key clients to ensure they would not be hurt by the changes. The company also made sure it retained the profitable sales representatives from the closed facilities. A Nationwide executive remarked, "It was equivalent to using a scalpel on our business. We could cut out the fat without hacking the muscle that supported our best customers."

Time-Driven Benchmarks in Retail Operations

A large commercial bank had similar problems with performance across its 160-branch system. The bank had recently expanded its product and service offering, but management was concerned that the branches had not been staffed efficiently for the broadened product mix. Some were overstaffed, leading to excess capacity costs, while others were probably understaffed, contributing to poor customer service. Furthermore, management believed that considerable variation existed in branch efficiency. The bank introduced TDABC to analyze branch efficiency across its network. The model revealed, as suspected, large variation in process efficiencies and capacity utilization that could not be explained by branch type or size.

The bank began to use the model for staffing decisions, transferring personnel from branches with excess capacity to new initiatives within the branch, or to branches with capacity shortages. The bank also focused on the root causes of variations in process costs across branches. For example, taking deposits was a high-cost process, representing 28 percent of all maintenance costs. The TDABC model revealed which branches were more efficient for this key process and enabled the company to transfer the best practices to all branches. As it improved branch processes, the team could predict the impact on process cost and capacity utilization, enabling the bank to capture the gains from the benchmarking effort.

Acorn has worked with several large retailers to help them use their store-level Time-Driven ABC models to simulate the utilization and efficiency of sales consultants and retail sales clerks. The TDABC model captured the time spent by the two classes of store personnel to perform their various activities. The model revealed considerable variation in the capacity utilization and efficiency of store personnel. The model provided the basis for best practice identification and capture, as well as providing a predictive model for the required number of personnel of each type based on the forecasted SKU sales volume and customers served store by store.

SUMMARY: BENCHMARKING AND TIME-DRIVEN ABC

Time-Driven ABC enhances benchmarking studies by standardizing costing definitions in a process and using time equations to control for variations in the demands for process capacity by products and customers. The time-driven model also isolates the effect of variation in capacity utilization when a company is measuring process efficiency. Traditional benchmarking can produce apparent performance differences that on subsequent analysis are revealed to be solely due to variation in capacity utilization. For example, a highly efficient retail or distribution branch may have a higher average unit cost that is caused solely by a lower volume of business. Without the focus on capacity embedded within the TDABC methodology, a traditional benchmarking study may err in its identification of efficient and inefficient branches.

The TDABC benchmarking approach generally enjoys greater organizational buy-in because the process-cost benchmarks are based on actual transactions and local modeling of time equation coefficients. This enables the process-cost numbers to reconcile back to financial and operating results. Benchmarking with a TDABC model will yield the highest payoffs when applied to high-cost processes, for which capacity utilization and demand vary significantly across homogeneous branches of retail and wholesale companies, such as distributors, retailers, and consumer banks.

CHAPTER SUMMARY

In this chapter we introduced some innovative applications of Time-Driven Activity-Based Costing that integrate well with an organization's continuous improvement initiatives. While the applications have, to date, been limited, they offer considerable promise for complementing existing projects involving lean management, supply-chain optimization, and benchmarking. We anticipate that, over the next few years, more companies will begin applying these concepts, along with new ones, to their organization. The underlying premise behind most of these extensions is that better information from TDABC makes existing programs stronger. Most companies will continue to realize value from each of these extensions. This chapter described how to integrate the improvement initiatives with TDABC to make even better decisions and focus the company on the biggest opportunities for process improvements and cost reductions.

NOTES

1. James P. Womack, Daniel T. Jones, and Daniel Roos, *The Machine That Changed the World: The Story of Lean Production* (New York: Harper Perennial, 1991; reprint edition).
2. Ohno, Taiichi, *The Toyota Production System* (Portland, OR: Productivity Press, 1988).
3. Michael George, *Lean Six Sigma* (New York, McGraw-Hill, 2002), 146–148.
4. Ibid.

5. Mitchell Max, "Sox + ABC = Value," The Performax Group white paper (Toronto: The Performax Group, 2005).
6. Private correspondence to authors.
7. S. Anderson and L. Putterman, "Building the Profit-Focused Supply Chain: A Game Plan for Capturing Real Value," Acorn Systems white paper (Houston: Acorn Systems, February 2004).

Time–Driven Activity–Based Costing in Action

## CHAPTER 8

KEMPS LLC

Handling Product, Distribution, and Customer Variety

HISTORY AND BACKGROUND

Kemps, a leading U.S. dairy in the Upper Midwest and Gulf states, produces and distributes a full line of products, including milk, ice cream, sour cream, cottage cheese, and yogurt.[1] During the 1990s, Kemps, like most dairies, saw a major consolidation in its customer base. Small, independent retailers became absorbed or put out of business by giants such as Wal-Mart, SuperValu, Nash Finch, and Roundy's. The buying power from these large distributors and retailers put suppliers' margins under heavy pressure.

Kemps also had to respond to increased demands from its wholesale and retail customers for more specialized packaging, distribution, warehousing, and just-in-time replenishment services. Many large retailers were reducing their refrigerated and frozen warehousing and receiving capacity, pushing the responsibility for managing inventories onto suppliers, such as Kemps. SuperValu began charging its dairy suppliers for handling and storing products in its retail freezers. Target, another large customer, instituted consignment sales so that Kemps would earn revenues only when consumers paid for the product at Target's checkout counters.

To supply the multiple delivery options demanded by its large and diverse customer base, Kemps managed a complex transportation system.

Its trucks delivered full loads to supermarkets and their distribution centers; made direct deliveries of less-than-truckload quantities to convenience stores, small retail stores, and homes; and shipped double-stacked frozen loads of ice cream to distribution centers across the United States.

Kemps plants, responding to customer and consumer demand for high product variety, were now operating complex production processes. Predictable, high-volume production runs produced standard products. Special recipes of ice cream, yogurt, and milk in customized packaging for retailers' private-label brands, however, required small, unpredictable production runs. Recently, Kemps installed a $2.5 million line just to produce a new product line, yogurt in a tube.

Historically, the company had focused on developing a long-term relationship with its retail and wholesale customers. Kemps would provide whatever services its customers requested, under its philosophy of delivering the right products to the customers in the right quantities at the right time. For example, Kemps might bid for a customer contract, assuming deliveries would be made twice a week. If the customer subsequently asked for daily deliveries, Kemps would meet this demand.

CEO Jim Green, realized that Kemps could no longer be "all things to all people." He led an internal effort to redefine the Kemps mission in light of the changed competitive environment. The project concluded with a new mission based on two primary themes:

- Be the best-cost producer in the business.
- Become the best branded-foods company by executing around a passion for the brand.

Green believed that to install and operate the new culture for lower cost, Kemps needed to have a deep and accurate understanding of its costs by product, brand, and, especially, customer.

Limitations of a Traditional Cost System

At Kemps, the existing manufacturing standard-cost system incorporated excellent data about the materials cost and plant-operating expenses at the department level. The system applied overhead costs as a percentage of the direct manufacturing costs. The standard costs did not reflect the effects of run size, since the system did not incorporate information about the setups or tear-downs as machines shifted between flavors, products, and packaging. The unit costs for, say, a twelve-ounce package of cottage cheese were the same, whether the production run lasted for ten minutes or four hours.

Changeovers were costly since some product was lost at the start of each production run until the process stabilized. Product was also lost at the end of each run, when the machine had to be stopped and cleaned in preparation for the next product. In addition to the material losses at the beginning and end of each production run, the company incurred a high opportunity cost during changeovers, as expensive machines were idle and not producing salable product.

Production changeovers and operating complexity could vary even within product type. Chocolate ice cream, for example, could be produced from a number of ice cream mixes by the addition of the necessary chocolate flavorings and other ingredients to the previous run. Other flavors, such as vanilla, required that the previous flavor be completely cleaned out before a production run could start. If an ice cream product contained allergens, such as nuts, eggs, soy, or wheat, the employees had to sterilize the vat before producing a nonallergenic product variety. On the filling line, additional changeover costs were incurred when personnel had to set up a special run for an individual customer's special labels and containers.

Once the finished products were in inventory, warehouse personnel picked them out of the coolers to prepare them for shipment. The average cost to pick a case of products was $0.30, but studies revealed the actual cost to be 20 percent lower when the step involved full pallets of standard cartons, and up to 35 percent higher for a partial case of product for a less-than-truckload (LTL) delivery.

Kemps had many delivery options for its different customers. Supermarkets typically wanted a full-truckload shipment. Even within a full shipment, some supermarkets wanted products delivered on large, wheeled carts (bossies) that carried twenty cases. Others wanted the cartons dropped off with a wheeled dolly that could accommodate only five cases per move. Kemps lowest-cost option arose for customers, such as SuperValu, that supplied their own trucks; for these customers, orders were priced on the basis of FOB (freight on board). For the many locations of a convenience-store chain, Kemps trucks did direct store delivery (DSD). A typical DSD truck route involved ten to fourteen stops per day. LTL deliveries were used for customers wanting a dedicated delivery for orders that did not fill up truck capacity.

Kemps also had considerable diversity in administrative demands among its customer base. Small convenience stores, with low sales volume and high delivery-frequency requirements, involved some of the most complex order handling. Since these outlets did not have electronic ordering capabilities, the administrative staff at Kemps entered orders manually after a phone conversation with the local store manager. These stores also had high turnover among store managers, so order-entry personnel at Kemps were typically dealing with inexperienced and untrained store managers; Kemps employees often had to make two or three calls per day to finalize the terms for a single order. The convenience-store managers' poor ordering and merchandising decisions could lead to stale inventory, which was subsequently returned to Kemps for refund credits and disposal. In contrast, the high-volume Kemps accounts were staffed by experienced, professional dairy-products managers. These accounts used extensive electronic ordering and processing, with little human intervention required. Replenishment was driven by accurate forecasts and real-time point-of-sale data so Kemps experienced little obsolescence and few returns with these accounts.

TIME-DRIVEN ABC PROJECT

Christopher Thorpe, vice president of financial services, had joined Kemps in 1996. In his previous positions, he had been an activity-based costing consultant and had helped install ABC systems in private- and public-sector enterprises. Despite his familiarity with ABC and his awareness of the problems with the existing cost system, Thorpe had concerns about applying Time-Driven ABC at Kemps. The company had spent years perfecting its direct materials and labor cost standards, which were now tightly integrated into the ERP system. Because Kemps was upgrading its ERP system, Thorpe considered delaying a new cost systems project until the modifications had been accomplished and the system stabilized. Furthermore, the director of operations had extremely high standards for accuracy and would have to be convinced that a new costing system would not be less accurate than the existing one. Kemps was also in the process of being sold to a new owner, who might not be interested in making a long-term investment in a more accurate costing system.

In October 2001, Green and Thorpe decided to launch a pilot ABC study in Kemps Northern Division, which consisted of three milk plants, a cottage-cheese plant, and one ice-cream plant with distribution throughout Minnesota, western Wisconsin, and part of Iowa. To ensure buy-in from the organization on the process and the final product, Thorpe formed a multifunctional ABC project team consisting of the following people:

Joe Schmitz (project leader)	Financial Manager, Northern Division
Paul Kunkel	Director, Operations Services
Rod Fenstra	Regional Sales Manager
Mike Young	Distribution Manager
Julie Frana	Business Services Manager
Mark Staub	Information Systems Manager
Mike Roeltgen	Acorn Systems consultant

In the time-driven approach adopted by Kemps, the ABC project team first measured the total costs of a given department, such as the filling line or the order and picking process. The total costs of a production line included (1) equipment depreciation and operating expenses; (2) occupancy costs, including space, heat, and light; and (3) staffing—salaries and fringe benefits for line workers and supervisors. For distribution processes, the costs included truck drivers' salaries and fringes, truck depreciation or lease expense, and truck operating expenses—fuel, other supplies, repairs, and maintenance. The finance and information systems managers on the project team designed the system so that departmental and process costs could be automatically downloaded and accumulated each month from the company's JD Edwards general-ledger system.

The team then obtained estimates of the unit times required to perform any activity associated with producing, storing, and delivering products, and with processing individual customer orders. Knowing that not all mixing and filling changeovers took the same amount of time, the team obtained estimates—either by direct observation or from historical records—of changeover times for each product variety.

In the cooler order and pick process, the team estimated the time required to prepare each type of delivery order: partial cases, a partial stack of cases, and a full stack of cases. The picking and loading times could also vary for each type of product since case size varied across the product line. For distribution activities, the project team decided to equip truck drivers with onboard computers. Drivers would punch in an activity and route code at the start of a route, log in when they arrived at a customer's destination, and log out when they returned to their truck and resumed driving the route. In this way, the ABC model could be fed with accurate data on the time taken to reach each customer's location and the time spent at each drop-off point.

Time equations allowed the team to estimate how the time required to perform an activity changed, depending on the particular characteristics of the order. For example, for the activity of checking the accuracy of a pallet or group of pallets prior to delivery to a customer, an order consisting of one or two pallets (a full pallet is seventy-two cases) required 1 minute per pallet to check. For orders of three or more pallets, however, only 45 seconds was required per pallet. Since each case must be counted, the verification time included an additional allowance of 1 second per case. Finally, an order of more than one pallet required an additional 15 seconds to coordinate the grouping of pallets into a single order and to write down the number of pallets on the order form. This type of complexity would be impossible to reflect in a traditional ABC approach. But the time-driven model estimated the time to check a customer order prior to shipment with a simple time equation:

Order checking time = 1 + 60/72 {if number of pallets < 3}
(in seconds) per case   + 45/72 {if number of pallets ≥ 3}
                         + 15/[72 × (number of pallets − 1)]

For multiple-use product fillers, the TDABC team developed complex calculations that modeled production activity. Within the cultured plant, for example, Kemps used a single product filler to produce multiple sizes of sour cream across different labels. For sour-cream products, the company calculated run time by product size, incorporating the time for label and size changes:

Run time = shipping quantity/200 units per minute {if size = 24 ounces}
            shipping quantity/255 units {if size = 12 ounces}
            + 10 minutes {if size change} + 5 minutes {if label change}

This calculation enabled Kemps to attribute machine changeover times for size and for label changes to the products causing the idle time. The data made visible the production drag from low-run-time, high-setup-time product orders.

The modeling of distribution expense created a unique challenge. Kemps made frequent route changes so that it could continually optimize its truck delivery capacity as service levels changed at existing accounts and as new accounts were added. Consequently, distribution times changed regularly. The implementation team decided to incorporate daily drive and serve times from the onboard computer system directly into an activity equation:

Customer delivery
(in minutes) per case   = (drive time + serve time)/number of cases delivered

Kemps used this information to compute delivery expense across the variety of customer store formats and channels. Managers could then match actual delivery expense to customer pricing, discovering that many customers were not being charged the full cost of the delivery services they required.

Two additional examples of time equations follow, one for picking cases of manufactured milk, and one for preparing boxed products for shipment.

Milk Cooler Line Loading

In the milk plant warehouse, cases of manufactured milk were stored in stacks of 6 cases, with each case containing 4 gallons of milk. When warehouse staff received an order for a certain number of milk gallons, a worker pulled the cases and some individual gallons, and put them on an automatic track to a location where the milk would be assembled with other items into a customer order for delivery. The team found that the time a worker needed to read the order, find the inventory in the stacks, and load the first stack of milk cases or gallons on the line was 20 seconds. Picking any number of cases up to a full stack—orders for 4, 8, 12, 16, 20, and 24 gallons—took the same 20 seconds of time. Additional stacks or full cases took 10 seconds each to pick and load. If a customer ordered 5 gallons of milk, the employee took 20 seconds to pick a case of 4 gallons and then spent an additional 5 seconds to pick the 1 gallon of milk from another case. An 11-gallon order required 20 seconds for 2 complete cases plus an additional 15 seconds to pick the 3 additional gallons (3 gallons multiplied by 5 seconds per gallon). The table below shows the total time, and the time per gallon, required for different quantities of milk gallons.

Number of Gallons	Total Time (seconds)	Seconds per Gallon	Number of Gallons	Total Time (seconds)	Seconds per Gallon
1	25	25	24	20	0.8
2	30	15	25	35	1.4
3	35	11.7	26	40	1.5
4	20	5.0	28	30	1.1
5	25	5.0	44	30	0.7
8	20	2.5	45	35	0.8
12	20	1.7	46	40	0.9
16	20	1.25	47	45	1.0
20	20	1.0	48	30	0.6

This complex relationship can be summarized with the following time equation:

Manufactured-milk picking time = 20 seconds + [5 seconds ×
　　　　　　　　　　　　　　(number of gallons remaining after
　　　　　　　　　　　　　　dividing by 4)] + [10 seconds ×
　　　　　　　　　　　　　　(number of stacks − 1)]

Minneapolis Milk Plant: Warehouse Area for Boxed Products

In the warehouse of the Minneapolis milk plant, employees handpicked boxed products and batched them together for shipment. Two types of products were stored here: items manufactured in the Minneapolis plant and outside-vendor-purchased items that were brought to the plant for Kemps to sell and distribute.

Employees spent 30 seconds preparing each order for shipment, independent of the order's size. The time per unit is calculated as 30 divided by the total number of units in the order. Workers spent an additional 10 seconds finding and picking each line item in the order, plus 5 seconds to pick each full case. If the employee had to retrieve a partial case to pick individual items, it took 4 seconds for the line item plus 1 second per individual piece to pick, up to a maximum of 15 seconds for the line item. Finally, if the product was manufactured in the Minneapolis milk plant, it would first be boxed in this warehouse area.[2] All the above times were multiplied by 2.5 to reflect the time required to do the boxing. The time equation is this:

Handling time (in seconds) = [30/number of units +
per line item　　　　　　　(10 × number of units) + the lesser
　　　　　　　　　　　　　of either (4 + the number of units),
　　　　　　　　　　　　　or 15 {if picking individual units}
　　　　　　　　　　　　　+ (5 × number of cases)] × 2.5
　　　　　　　　　　　　　{if manufactured in plant}

The completed model contained 250 time equations. While each equation could be quite complex, all the order characteristics, such as size, composition, and delivery method already existed in the company's customer-order-entry system. The calculation of the activity times for all the processes used for each customer order could be done via a simple calculation in the ABC software program.

Paul Kunkel, the team's representative from manufacturing, had twenty years of experience in operations. He wanted the time equations to accurately reflect actual operations and drove the team to obtain the details for each product, each type of changeover, and each variation in activity. He took the full activity model of manufacturing, filling, and picking activity times back to plant supervisors for them to review and sign off on. Given his experience and credibility, this manager's endorsement of the model's validity was critical to its acceptance among plant personnel and senior management.

Not all costs were assigned by the time-driven methodology. Salespeople provided an annual estimate of the percentage of time they spent with each of their customers. That way, customers that required little sales maintenance and support, such as food service and schools, would receive low customer support expenses while customers that required extensive support would receive a much higher assignment of selling expenses.

Kemps senior management wanted to assign each month's operating expenses to the products and orders processed for customers. The ABC model assigned each department's monthly costs to all the activities it performed that month, based on each activity's percentage of total time taken in the department. Production line costs would be driven down to each SKU produced, according to the percentage of time that the SKU took—both run time and changeover time—on the line that month. For warehousing operations, if the activity of "picking and loading partial cases" represented 32 percent of the processing times in the cooler department, then 32 percent of that department's monthly costs were assigned to all the partial cases handled during the period. This cost would then be distributed on a pro rata basis to each partial case handled, enabling this cost to be incorporated in the total cost of serving each customer ordering a partial case that month.

WHAT DID NOT GO WELL?

The project, expected to last for six months, evolved into a full-year saga. The operations team took four months to approve the time equations for manufacturing. Some of the equations had dozens of operands that adjusted resource consumption for every transaction variation. Second, the transaction data that fed the model were riddled with errors. Product IDs on invoices did not match product masters. SKU units were measured differently (e.g., pounds or ounces) even within the same product family. Finally, management had numerous distractions, such as the ERP upgrade project and the sale of the business to a new ownership group. Fortunately, the TDABC team persevered and overcame all these problems to produce a working system.

NEAR-TERM BENEFITS

By the spring of 2002, the project team got preliminary results from a simplified model, which was sufficient to stimulate some near-term actions. The team continued to extend and refine the model, finally completing the full customer profitability model the following year. The model contained details on every product produced by Kemps for every customer. It provided the Northern Division general manager with profitability by any route and by any customer, even when the customer had multiple locations and was served by multiple routes.

Process Improvements

Some short-term actions were implemented immediately. Bob Williams, vice president of operations, noticed that many products were being run as customer orders arrived. Typically, he was running a product eight times per month, with thirty-minute changeovers occurring between each run. He encouraged salespeople to modify their customers' behavior so that the customers placed orders weekly, a change that enabled demands to be met with four production runs per month. This order consolidation released two hours of productive capacity per product per month and eliminated the materials losses associated with product and package start-ups and shutdowns.

Williams also saw the costs of the long changeovers on the filling line. For the newly installed tube yogurt line, he recommended that the company shift to a generic label on the individual tubes, with the customized labeling done only on the outside packaging, a change that would greatly improve line efficiency. The capacity gained by these process improvements enabled Williams to reduce overtime and eliminate one shift per week, without any loss in productive output.

Rationalize Product Mix

Kemps launched a key initiative to use the Time-Driven ABC information to reduce its overall cost base by creating a SKU rationalization team, which consisted of the senior managers of operations, sales, marketing, finance, and business services and CEO Green. The team met every three weeks to review the unprofitable SKUs reported in recent periods by the TDABC model and decide which of these should be discontinued and which retained. The combination of process improvements and SKU rationalization allowed the team to shut one plant and bring its volume into the large Minneapolis plant.

The SKU team also looked at a cost-to-serve matrix for each SKU and customer combination. When the SKU team identified any plant's SKUs that underperformed in terms of profitability, the next step was to work with the customer to increase price, reduce complexity by increasing lot production size, or ultimately drop the SKU.

Enhancing Customer Relationships

Greg Kerr, vice president of sales, described how he used the system in a competitive situation with an existing customer:

> We currently served the customer's two existing store chains. He had just purchased a third group of stores and was about to put the new business out for competitive bids. In the past, we would have waited to see what price we had to meet to take on the additional business and make a decision at that point. With the new model, I decided to meet with the customer before the bidding process. We talked about how to lower the total cost of serving him, such as by consolidating the labeling across the three chains and by making higher quantity but fewer deliveries. We described how these changes would lower the prices we would charge him. We won the new business without the customer ever going to competitive bids.

SuperValu, a large Kemps customer, had been using ABC itself for several years. SuperValu appreciated that one of its key suppliers now used the same costing methodology so that both customer and supplier could jointly search for cost-reduction opportunities. A near-term win resulted when Kemps arranged for its shipments to SuperValu to be cross-docked, and to capture some of the savings that SuperValu gained from the new shipping arrangements.[3]

In another situation, Kemps saw that it was losing money with one of its customers, a chain of specialty high-end shops. The problem was due to the low volume and high variety of products ordered and the small, just-in-time deliveries the customer requested. A Kemps senior executive called on the customer, explained the situation, and offered three options:

(1) accept a price increase and a minimum order size; (2) eliminate its private-label ice cream, replacing the product with the Kemps standard branded product that was already being produced in efficient, high volumes; or (3) find another ice-cream supplier. The customer inquired, "Why the change?" to which the executive responded, "For twenty-five years, we didn't understand our true manufacturing costs and the impact that specialty production had on our margins." The customer accepted a price increase of 13 percent, agreed to the elimination of two low-volume products, and agreed to accept full rather than partial truckload orders, thereby eliminating internal storage charges for Kemps. The changes produced immediate benefits of $150,000 per year.

Kemps used its TDABC model proactively to become the leading dairy supplier to a national customer. Kemps demonstrated that it could identify the specific manufacturing, distribution, and order-handling costs associated with serving this customer on the basis of actual order characteristics: DSD (direct store delivery) or shipments to distribution centers, gallon versus pint deliveries, and volume and mix of products. The TDABC model facilitated an open, trusting relationship between supplier and customer that differentiated Kemps from its competitors.

Kemps also became aware that some of its smaller convenience-store customers had been overordering and returning product to it when the date code had expired. To save the high cost of these rebates and returns, Kemps offered these retailers a 2 percent discount if the retailer would manage its own inventory without the return option. In this way, Kemps eliminated 95 percent of out-of-code returns, generating a net saving of $120,000.

Green (Kemps' CEO) commented on the impact of TDABC on the company:

> *Activity-based costing enabled us to reduce complexity across all our operations, especially complexity that customers did not want to pay for. The new cost system gave us an immense insight into the huge costs associated with our operational complexity, especially the number of different product lines and the number and impact of all our diverse customer service requirements. Today, we do not do any new contract with an existing or a new customer without first going through an ABC analysis. The salespeople now understand the importance of accurate and proper costing.*

SUMMARY

The Kemps case is an excellent introduction to TDABC projects. It is a comprehensive, enterprisewide implementation encompassing cost and profitability measurement across manufacturing, warehousing, distribution, and sales. Kemps used an exemplary project management approach. It started with strong leadership from the CEO and CFO, who selected a well-diversified project team. The team members represented the major functions in the company, facilitating buy-in across all organizational units. The pilot study was done at a site where the general manager was feeling competitive pain. He was prepared to act decisively once he had confidence in the measured process costs and the profitability of products and customers.

Technically, the case illustrates the development of complex time equations to capture transaction variation and detail. A critical role was played by the project team's operations management representative, who validated each time equation. His attention to detail provided credibility for the TDABC model for the entire line organization.

Once the TDABC model had been built and validated, top leadership at Kemps acted decisively to improve processes, rationalize product mix and variety, modify unprofitable customer relationships, and establish a new fact-based process that was used successfully to negotiate new customer relationships.

NOTES

1. This case study of Kemps is drawn from R. S. Kaplan, "Kemps LLC: Introducing Time-Driven Activity-Based Costing," Case 106-001 (Boston: Harvard Business School, 2005).
2. A separate time equation (10 minutes per pallet of 72 cases; boxed products take about twice as long) estimates the time for receiving and stocking items purchased from external vendors.
3. Cross-docking eliminates the need to place incoming supplies into warehouse inventory. With cross-docking, the shipments from several suppliers arrive simultaneously at a company's distribution center. The company's distribution personnel on the receiving dock pick and consolidate batches for individual truckload delivery, avoiding moving items into and out of inventory.

## CHAPTER NINE

SANAC LOGISTICS

Time Equations to Capture Complexity in Logistics Processes

SANAC, a family-owned Belgian company, distributes and retails branded plant-care products to four customer groups: farmers, growers, public sector companies and landscapers, and large and small consumer shops. In 2005, it had total revenues of €62 million, generated through sales of 298,000 line items across 7,000 products to 7,000 customers. It operated a 25-truck transportation fleet and a 22,500-pallet warehouse. Of its 129 employees, 40 were sales technicians and 57 worked in the logistics department. Sanac had enjoyed a compound annual growth rate of 10 percent from 1996 to 2005.

COMPETITIVE STRATEGY

Sanac created differentiation by offering customers three key services: advice, marketing and knowledge of the market, and excellent logistics.

- *Advice:* Sanac strived to provide its professional clients with solutions, not just products, so that it could build long-term, reliable, and trusting relationships with its clients. Skilled technicians counseled

This chapter was written by Patricia Everaert (Assistant Professor, Ghent University), Werner Bruggeman (Professor, Ghent University, and Managing Partner, B&M Consulting), Gertjan De Creus (CEO, Sanac), and Kris Moreels (Managing Partner, B&M Consulting).

customers on how to most effectively use the products distributed by the company. For small and medium-sized retail outlets, Sanac provided informational displays since these shops did not have the expertise or time to deal with technical questions or give advice to their customers. Sanac even ran a sales area for one retail client, helping the store to be profitable with little to no investment in time or training for the retailer's employees.

- *Market knowledge:* Sanac gained knowledge of its seasonal and trendy markets from its employees: technicians, salespeople, and truck drivers. The company leveraged this market knowledge to help retail clients stock merchandise and avoid unsold inventory at the end of a planting or growing season.
- *Logistics:* Sanac's logistics expertise was a considerable advantage for its relationships with sophisticated buyers in supermarkets and hypermarkets. For these customers, any delay meant a loss of sales. Logistics was also critical for agricultural professional customers, for whom speed of delivery was essential to avoid problems with their plant products.

MARKET EVOLUTION

In the 1990s, Sanac was sales-driven and had little insight into the profitability of its different customers. At the turn of the twenty-first century, competition increased and profit margins came under pressure as customers asked for more services. Sanac faced strong seasonal fluctuation in its activities and a growing complexity and diversity among its products and customers. These changes in the environment forced the company to change from a growth strategy to a *profitability-enhancing strategy.*

Despite stable gross profit margins and a large increase in sales from €37 million to €62 million in four years, Sanac's overall return on sales had decreased during this period. The company tried to address this apparent paradox through calculating profitability by sector. Marketing had recently focused on the new segment of consumer shops. But managers didn't know the cost of serving this new segment or its working capital requirements for inventory and accounts receivable. Sanac's existing cost-accounting system calculated only contribution margin—gross margin minus logistics and commercial costs—by products and segments (figure 9-1).

Not included in the contribution margin calculations was €2.5 million in unallocated overhead. These costs, considered in principle as fixed,

FIGURE 9-1

Sanac Contribution Margin by Sector (2002)

Customer Sector	Contribution Margin	Sales Increase
Agriculture	17%	+ 3%
Horticulture	20%	+10%
Home and garden	24%	+20%

were increasing each year. Even with rough assignment of the overhead costs, Sanac believed that the agriculture sector was profitable, the horticultural sector was operating at a loss, and the consumer segment was losing lots of money. The company acknowledged the distressing finding that the sector with the most rapid growth and the focus for Sanac's new growth strategy was its least profitable. Sanac was reluctant to shift more of its business to a new sector when it did not understand the sector's underlying economics.

THE FAILURE OF A CONVENTIONAL ABC MODEL AT SANAC

Sanac's previous growth strategy had forced the company to stock large quantities of a wide range of products. The company delivered any order to any client in the shortest possible time and in whatever quantity the client requested at a single posted price. For its new profit-enhancement strategy, Sanac wanted to know the costs of each customer, order, delivery, line item, product, and supplier (figure 9-2 shows the hierarchy of these various cost objects). Sanac was prepared to abandon clients, products, or even markets if they were unprofitable and could not be improved. But before taking such drastic actions, Sanac CEO Gertjan De Creus, wanted to have a valid system for measuring costs and profits at a detailed level.

De Creus hired a local consulting firm to build a conventional ABC model. He soon realized that this approach would not work, for several reasons. First, he wanted monthly profitability data at the level of business unit, products, orders, and customers. Also, Sanac's rapidly growing consumer-shop segment made continual requests for product resupply. Sanac had to respond immediately with decisions about price and delivery. In such a dynamic environment, the cost model would have to be updated

FIGURE 9-2

Sanac Wanted to Measure Profitability at Different Levels

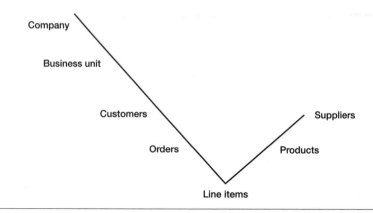

monthly with actual data. This was not possible with the conventional ABC approach without hiring ten new controllers and continually resurveying employees.

Second, because Sanac had strong seasonal sales, it made little sense to define average capacity utilization. The company experienced 80 percent of its sales in four months and had much idle capacity during the winter. De Creus did not want all the unused capacity costs to be charged to the one customer that ordered during November. He did not believe that customers served in the slack period were more expensive than customers served in the peak period, and he thought it foolish to raise prices during slack periods and lower them in peak periods. Average costs would not be adequate. De Creus wanted to know each month the unused and overused capacity in each department.

Third, Sanac had high complexity in activities, and its seven thousand clients made significant and varied demands for services and logistics. This wide diversity in the consumption of resources required that costs be traced to the order level, not averaged at the product or customer level. The cost of serving customers varied by packaging, product, delivery terms, extent of advice, and payment terms. The cost of serving a small farmer was very different from that of a DIY (do-it-yourself) store of a large chain. To capture this complexity and diversity within a conventional ABC system would require an enormous number of activities. When analyzing activities for a conventional ABC model implementation, the Sanac project team learned that it could not capture the details of its diverse logistics activities. Also, the average cost rates, such as the cost per drop and the cost per order, would not be meaningful or credible to the employees, who would interpret and act on the profitability reports.

As Sanac tried to build a complex conventional ABC model to capture the details of its operations, the company decomposed its 106 logistics activities into 330 subactivities (figure 9-3). The proliferation of activities under the conventional ABC model was caused mainly by order-, route-, and drop-off-related activities. The large increase in supplier-related activities was caused by complexities in the contract terms that different suppliers had negotiated.

The Sanac team had difficulty assigning resource costs to the large number of subactivities. For example, for the activity of receiving incoming goods, the team attempted to calculate the unloading cost per pallet received, the checking cost per line item on the pallet received, the loading cost per pallet to return, the loading cost per pallet to return with reusable containers, the storing cost for one homogeneous pallet, and the storing cost for one heterogeneous pallet. For each of these activities, the normal volume of the activity drivers needed to be estimated, which was impossible.

After concluding that a conventional ABC model would be inadequate for its needs, Sanac turned to a time-driven ABC approach, which was just being introduced into the European market.

FIGURE 9-3

Number of Activities in the Time-Driven ABC Model at Sanac

Time Equations for Each ...	Resources in % of Total	Number of Activities in Time-Driven ABC (1)	Number of Activities for Conventional ABC (2)	% Increase in Activities [(2)–(1)]/(1)
Supplier	10	28	133	+375
Product	4	14	20	+43
Customer	10	29	45	+55
Order	48	23	87	+278
Route	11	4	13	+225
Drop-off	10	5	23	+360
Line item	7	3	9	+200
Total	100	106	330	+211

CHALLENGES ENCOUNTERED IN INTRODUCING TIME-DRIVEN ABC

The new processes to install TDABC were not universally welcomed at Sanac. Educating department personnel in this family-run firm on how the time equations worked was often problematic. The salespeople, who were turnover (sales) driven, did not understand the need for accurate costing of each transaction. Several disagreed with De Creus's belief that losses were being incurred in some product lines, customers, and market segments. These skeptics believed that all core product lines and businesses were profitable and that De Creus was being fooled by inaccurate allocations of overhead expenses.

DEVELOPING TIME EQUATIONS AT SANAC

Sanac's project team saw that the time equations in a TDABC model could accurately capture the details of the company's complex and diverse activities without much effort. The team also believed that such details would convince the organization about the significant opportunities for profit improvement right in front of it.

Receiving Incoming Goods

The team built a time equation for the receipt of incoming goods, a seemingly simple process that still had many tasks, each with different time drivers. One interviewee described the different tasks that occurred when a truck with incoming goods arrived at the receiving dock of the warehouse:

When the truck arrives, the warehouse supervisor assigns a dock to the driver (1 minute). Next a warehouse employee enters the delivery voucher into the computer. The input of the general information about the truckload takes about 1 minute to enter, plus an additional 10 seconds for each purchased line item on the truck. Unloading of pallets takes 2.5 minute per pallet. Each arrival also requires 1 minute of administration time to communicate information about reusable containers or to deal with specific problems. After the truck is unloaded, the delivered goods must be checked, prepared, and stored in the warehouse. This operation takes 1 minute per homogeneous pallet and 15 minutes per heterogeneous pallet. If reusable containers are to be returned to the supplier, the employees need to spend 10 minutes per pallet for sorting, counting, and blistering. Sometimes pallets, previously delivered but now empty, have to be returned to the supplier. In this case, the pallets are transported in batches of 15 from the warehouse and loaded onto the truck. This operation needs 3 minutes per batch of 15 pallets. Finally, a warehouse employee takes about a minute to sign the voucher accompanying the order.

The project team subdivided the order receipt process into the different tasks. Each task added a time component to the order-receipt time equation (figure 9-4).

Clearly, the process of receiving incoming goods could not be driven simply by the number of purchase orders, as in a conventional ABC model. The process required multiple drivers to represent all the factors influencing actual processing time for a given order. The TDABC project team derived the following time equation to capture the time drivers in figure 9-4 for the receipt of incoming goods:[1]

FIGURE 9-4

Time Drivers for the Activity "Reception of Incoming Goods"

Subtask	Time Driver	Time Consumption per Unit Time Driver
Dock assignment	Number of deliveries	1 minute per delivery
Input general information	Number of deliveries	1 minute per delivery
Input line item information	Number of line items per delivery	10 minutes per line item
Unloading truck	Number of pallets per delivery	2.5 minute per pallet
Communicating information	Number of deliveries	1 minute per delivery
Returning reusable containers	Number of pallets with containers per delivery	10 minutes per pallet with containers
Returning pallets	Number of staples of returned pallets per delivery	3 minutes per staple pallets to return
Checking and storing	Number of homogeneous pallets per delivery	1 minute per homogeneous pallet
Checking and storing	Number of heterogeneous pallets per delivery	15 minutes per heterogeneous pallet
Signing off the voucher	Number of deliveries	1 minute per delivery

Receiving time per delivery $= 4 + 0.17X_1 + 2.5X_2 + 10X_3 + 3X_4/15$
$+ 1X_5 + 15X_6$

where X_1 = number of line items
X_2 = number of pallets received
X_3 = number of pallets to return with reusable containers
X_4 = number of pallets to return
X_5 = number of homogeneous pallets received
X_6 = number of heterogeneous pallets received

The equation enabled the time per delivery receipt to be calculated on the basis of the specific characteristics of the incoming order. For example, the reception of incoming goods with 10 line items, 10 pallets, and no reusable containers or pallets to be returned requires *31 minutes*. A reception of incoming goods with 10 line items, 10 pallets, 5 pallets with reusable containers, and 2 staples of 15 pallets to be returned requires *87 minutes*. The time equation shows how the receiving time varies, depending on the known parameters associated with each incoming order.

Customer-Related Activities: Drop-off with the Customer

As another example, consider the process of delivering an order to a customer's location. The conventional ABC model had used one activity driver, the number of customer drops, and calculated an average cost per drop. But in reality, the cost per drop depended on many variables. The team recorded the following interview about the dropping activity:

Farmer routing: *An order dropped at a farmer's premises normally takes 5 minutes per order, except when it is a first delivery. In this case, the drop takes 10 minutes. When the truck driver also has to take back returned goods, the driver needs an additional 5 minutes to check the goods and to finish the necessary administration. When reusable containers have to be taken back, the truck driver needs 10 minutes to check the labels. Delivery under cash payment requires an extra 20 minutes per drop delivered to farmers and growers, and 5 minutes for all other customers.*

Nonfarmer routing: *When the customer is not a farmer and the goods are delivered on pallets, the time per drop is 2 minutes per pallet. If delivery is in packs, the time per drop is 1 minute per pack. The waiting time can vary by customer type. In garden centers, the waiting time is typically 15 minutes, while in large distribution companies, the waiting*

*time is 30 minutes per drop. But when the delivery goes to Makro or
Leroy Merlin, the driver has to wait 60 minutes. Nonfarmer customers
also might have goods to take back. When an appointment has been
made, the goods are ready to load and have been assigned a return code.
In this case, the loading of returned goods takes 3 minutes. When no appointment has been made, the driver has to call Sanac to obtain a return
code. This inquiry takes about 30 minutes. Loading and checking empty
pallets takes 2 minutes, and cash payment requires 10 minutes.*

The interview revealed how the time per drop depends on the type of
customer (farmer or nonfarmer), the type of nonfarmer customer (large
distribution company or not, garden center or not, Makro/Leroy Merlin
or not), the type of delivery (first delivery or not), the availability of a return code, the need to take back goods, the need to take back reusable
containers, the mode of payment (cash or noncash), the number of pallets, and the number of packs.

The project team noted that its previous, conventional ABC model
was inaccurate since it used only an average cost per drop-off. This led to
undercosting deliveries that consumed a lot of resources due to long
waiting time, cash payments, and many goods to return; and to overcost-
ing deliveries that consumed fewer resources since they involved no waiting time, no cash payments, and no goods to return.

The team prepared a chart that summarized the data from the interviews (figure 9-5). The time drivers affect the process times for the
drop-off activity in different ways. Some factors determine an additional
subtask during the delivery process (e.g., for a first-time delivery, the
driver needs more time to talk with the farmer); other factors determine
the *type of time driver* (e.g., a farmer drop-off takes 5 minutes per drop, a
nonfarmer drop-off depends on the number of pallets and the number of
packs), and some factors determine the *time per unit time driver* (e.g., return
of goods takes 3 minutes for a nonfarmer and 5 minutes for a farmer).
The example also illustrates how time spent in a certain activity might *de-
pend on the event of other activities*: the subtask of taking back returned
goods requires more time when no appointment has been made. The
team built the following time equation for the delivery activity, which allowed interdependencies between activities.

$$\text{Delivery time per drop} = 5X_1 + 5X_1X_2 + 5X_1X_3 + 10X_1X_4 + 5X_1X_5$$
$$+ 15X_1X_5X_6 + 2X_7X_8 + X_7X_9 + 15X_{10}$$
$$+ 30X_{11} + 60X_{12} + 30X_7X_3X_{13} + 3X_7X_3$$
$$+ 2X_7X_{14} + 10X_7X_5$$

where X_1 = 1 if farmer routing; 0 otherwise
   X_2 = 1 if first delivery; 0 otherwise
   X_3 = 1 if returned goods; 0 otherwise
   X_4 = 1 if returned reusable containers; 0 otherwise
   X_5 = 1 if cash payment; 0 otherwise
   X_6 = 1 if customer is farmer or grower; 0 otherwise
   X_7 = 1 if nonfarmer; 0 otherwise
   X_8 = number of pallets
   X_9 = number of packs
   X_{10} = 1 if garden center; 0 otherwise
   X_{11} = 1 if large distribution center; 0 otherwise
   X_{12} = 1 if hypermarket Makro or Leroy Merlin; 0 otherwise
   X_{13} = 1 if driver has to call the office for return code (no prior
      appointment made); 0 otherwise
   X_{14} = 1 if empty pallets to return; 0 otherwise

The time equation, with its mixture of algebraic and Boolean terms, fully captured the complexity of the activity to drop products off at a customer location. Some variables, such as X_{10}, X_{11}, and X_{12}, have a *main effect* on the activity time (e.g., garden centers, large distribution centers, and the hypermarkets Makro and Leroy Merlin all require large waiting times). Many variables influence the activity time through *interactions* with other variables. This means that the variable does not have a simple effect on drop-off time; its effect depends on the existence of one or more variables. For example, the time of a drop is not always 5 minutes per order in the farmers' routing. When this is a first delivery, an additional 5 minutes of time is needed—a two-way interaction $X_1.X_2$ between "farmer versus nonfarmer routing" (X_1) and "first delivery" (X_2). When no appointment was made for the nonfarmers who have goods to return, the additional time can be modeled by a three-way interaction $X_7.X_3.X_{13}$ between the three indicator variables "nonfarmer versus farmer" (X_7), "goods to return versus no goods to return" (X_3) and "no return code versus return code" (X_{13}).

The equation revealed how the activity time per drop differed significantly across deliveries. An order shipped to a farmer with no return of goods or reusable containers, and no cash payment, requires a drop time of only 5 minutes. An order shipped to a farmer with normal delivery, goods and reusable containers to be returned, and cash payment requires 40 minutes. An order shipped on pallets to a garden center, 10 pallets, goods to be returned but appointment has been made, no pallets to return, and no cash payment, requires a drop time of 38 minutes. An order

FIGURE 9-5

Time Drivers for the Activity "Drop Off Goods to Customers"

Subtask	Time Driver	Time Consumption per Unit Time Driver
Dropping the goods	• Farmer or nonfarmers' routing: ○ Number of *drops*, in case of delivery to farmers ○ Number of *pallets*, in case of delivery on pallets to nonfarmers ○ Number of *collies*, in case of delivery in collies to nonfarmers • First delivery in case of delivery to farmers	• 5 minutes per *drop* for farmers • 2 minutes per *pallet* for drop to nonfarmers • 1 minute per *pack* for drop to nonfarmer • 10 minutes per drop to a *new* farmer.
Take back returned goods	• Returned goods: ○ Number of drops ○ Appointment being made in case of returns from nonfarmers	• 5 minutes per drop for *farmers* • 3 minutes per drop for a *non-farmer* • 30 minutes per drop to nonfarmer if no appointment was made
Take back reusable containers	• Reusable containers to take back: ○ Number of drops, in case of returns from farmers	• 10 minutes per drop to farmer
Waiting	• For nonfarmers: type of customer: ○ Garden center ○ Large distributor ○ Leroy Merlin, Makro	• 15 minutes per drop to garden center • 30 minutes per drop to large distributor • 60 minutes per drop to Makro or Leroy Merlin
Take back pallets	• Pallets to take back: ○ Only for nonfarmers: the number of drops	• 2 minutes per drop to nonfarmer

Cash payment	• Cash payment:
	○ For farmer's routing, type of customer:
	  • Farmer
	  • Grower
	  • Other
	○ For nonfarmer's routing
		
		• 15 minutes per drop
		• 15 minutes per drop
		• 5 minutes per drop
		• 10 minutes per drop

shipped on pallets to a garden center, 10 pallets, goods to be returned, no appointment has been made, no goods to return, cash payment, requires a drop time of 78 minutes.

In the complete Sanac TDABC logistics model, more than half of the resources and activities needed more than one time driver to explain the variation in their use. Remarkable is that more than 10 percent of the time equations required nine or more terms to capture the predictable variation in process times.[2]

FINDINGS AND ACTION STEPS

In March 2004, the company began to generate monthly profitability reports. It soon took actions to reduce the diversity of its client base, narrow its product line, and became more disciplined with its clients on payment terms, service expectations, and the pricing of special services.

The biggest impact came from the customer profitability reports, which showed the surprising result that Sanac's largest customers were its least profitable. These customers had used their power to negotiate low prices and to demand extensive services from Sanac. Some of the loss customers had three to four deliveries per week per delivery site.

The largest customer had a 14 percent loss on sales. De Creus communicated the information to the account manager and told him to renegotiate the terms of trade, indicating that the company's objective was to maximize net profits, not sales revenue. The account manager, considered one of the best in managing relationships with large customers, was astonished and initially did not believe the numbers. But De Creus walked him through the time equations so that the manager could learn about the high time and cost associated with multiple small deliveries to the customers' many locations. Believing the numbers, but not knowing how to solve the problem, the manager even considered quitting his job.

De Creus asked the manager to set up a meeting in which the two of them could talk with the customer about the economics of the existing delivery practices. The customer concluded that the number of deliveries per week and the number of delivery sites per delivery could be reduced without adversely affecting its operations. De Creus used the time-driven ABC model to simulate the effect of the new delivery conditions on customer profitability and learned that the new conditions would reduce the loss to 2 percent of sales. In addition, he learned that a large part of the delivered volume came from a limited number of suppliers, some of which also were experiencing a negative profitability with that customer. De Creus renegotiated prices and delivery conditions with these suppliers. At the conclusion of all these negotiations, the large customer's cost of ownership of the delivered products decreased, and it had become a profitable customer to Sanac and other suppliers. The economics of everyone's operations improved once the TDABC information was available to facilitate frank, open, and fact-based discussions among all the parties in the supply chain.

Sales representatives now understood how customer profitability information was being calculated, and how they could, in principle, use this information to create new win-win situations with the customer to increase the profitability of everyone in the supply chain. But De Creus still found it difficult to change the culture of his sales team from a volume- and revenue-driven organization toward an organization that used TDABC to continuously improve Sanac's profitability.

De Creus led with a visioning process with his management team that culminated in formulating a new profit-focused company strategy. The team then translated the strategy into a Balanced Scorecard. The TDABC customer profitability reporting system was integrated into the scorecard, which enabled De Creus to use the customer profitability information interactively during formal performance review meetings. Action plans to renegotiate terms of trade with customers and reduce cost of processes were incorporated as strategic initiatives in the Balanced Scorecard. Sanac's controllers used the TDABC model to calculate the profit effects of the strategic initiatives. In this way, the model became an important engine in Sanac's new corporate performance management system.

With customer profitability now embedded more securely in the company culture, Sanac began to use its TDABC model prospectively to calculate competitive offers for key accounts. This new process increased the time required to respond to bid requests from large customers, as well as running a risk that Sanac would lose new business to a competitor. But the disciplined process enabled Sanac to take on important new business only when the economics were favorable.

IMPACT

The new performance management process had a positive and near-term impact on profitability and on the value of the company. Sanac established an image as a well-run company with increasing profitability in a highly competitive market. Its profit turnaround, at least in part, led to Sanac's becoming an attractive acquisition candidate. In December 2005, AVEVE, the sector's market leader, acquired Sanac. During the due-diligence process by AVEVE, Sanac used its Time-Driven ABC system to show profitability by process and product group. The time equations revealed some idle capacity, facilitating the reorganization of some business processes and the preparation of the company for the planned acquisition. De Creus commented that he would never have imagined that the Time-Driven ABC project would have played such an important role in creating shareholder value.

SUMMARY

The Sanac case applies TDABC in a complex distribution company as it made a strategic transition from a sales-driven company to a profit-driven one. The Sanac project team confronted complex contingencies in its operations. The company purchased from different vendors and provided varied services to different types of customers. Sanac also operated in a seasonal business and needed to use cost rates that accurately reflected peak and slack periods in capacity utilization.

Sanac's initial attempt to capture its complex, contingent operations with a conventional ABC model failed. Abandoning conventional ABC, the company adopted the time-driven approach because TDABC could drive costs by transactions, not just products and customers. The new time equations enabled the project team to reflect complex contingencies in resource-consumption times. The case has several examples of how to translate an extensive verbal description of a process, such as would typically be provided by a frontline employee, into a time equation using Boolean logic.

Sanac's TDABC model, as at Kemps, led to management's taking quick actions to improve inefficient processes and transform unprofitable customer relationships. The near-term profit improvements led to immediate benefits, as Sanac became a highly attractive acquisition candidate to a large competitor.

NOTES

1. In the Acorn TDABC software, this time equation was written as follows: $1 + 1 + 0.17 \times$ (number of line items) $+ 2.5 \times$ (number of received pallets) $+ 1 + 10 \times$ (pallets reusable containers) $+ 3 \times$ (empty pallets)$/15 + 1 \times$ (homogeneous pallets) $+ 15 \times$ (heterogeneous pallets) $+ 1$.

2. W. Bruggeman, P. Everaert, Y. Levant, and S. Anderson, "Modeling Logistics Costs Using Time-Driven ABC: A Case in a Distribution Company," in Operations and Global Competitiveness, ed. K. Demeter, EurOMA Conference Budapest, Diamond Congress Ltd., 2005: 949–958.

## CHAPTER TEN

COMPTON FINANCIAL

Using Time-Driven ABC to Accomplish a Profit Turnaround

COMPTON FINANCIAL (disguised) is a leading financial services firm offering low-cost stock trading services, online trading, no-load mutual funds, insurance, and financial advisory services. Its 2005 annual revenues were more than $2 billion, it had $500 billion in assets, 3 million active clients, and 10,000 employees in more than 200 offices around the United States.

The company consisted of three primary segments: individual investor, institutional investor, and trust. The individual investor segment, the original focus of the company, still generated more than half the revenues. The segment had four subsegments: (1) active traders—self-service investors who traded frequently, (2) independent investors—infrequent self-service investors, (3) advice—fee-based consulting, and (4) global investors—offshore operations and foreign-language services. While Compton's origins were to serve small investors, it now had a large number of customers with assets in excess of $1 million. The advisory segment was also growing in importance, contributing a higher proportion of revenues each year.

COSTING INNOVATIONS

Compton had a long tradition as an industry leader in its cost- and profit-reporting systems. In the late 1980s, it had introduced one of the first activity-based costing systems in the brokerage industry. This mainframe-based system tracked costs along three dimensions—products, segments, and channels. The system could calculate product profitability (or loss) but could not link the product cost information to individual customers. The limitation inhibited management decisions since profitable customers could be buying unprofitable products. The company continued to market and support unprofitable products so as not to antagonize and perhaps lose good customers.

In 1996, Compton updated its ABC system to assign costs down to products, channels (including branches), and customer segments. But its segment and channel profitability calculations included only directly traceable costs. The system could not accurately assign the large and growing cost of shared services, particularly information technology (IT) and call center costs, to products, customers, and channels. Shared service costs represented 40 percent of revenue. Managers remained reluctant to take action on unprofitable products and customers when high-cost components were inaccurately allocated by the company's costing system.

The system was also expensive, time-consuming, and difficult to run. Alice Gordon, Compton's ABC project manager, recalled the system's liabilities: "The customer account profitability system took fourteen people working full time for over a month to calculate. The companywide surveys could take weeks to collect. And it was already pushing the limits of our technology to run the numbers."

Managers wanted more accuracy in product, channel, and customer profitability calculations. It wasn't enough to drive IT costs down to branches. Account and product managers wanted IT and other central costs accurately drilled down to the 3 million client accounts. Gordon reflected: "The organization was asking for some kind of a miracle . . . It wanted a system that would enable all users to analyze the profitability of their individual transactions, to perform what-if scenarios, and have all the information within hours."

THE PROFITABILITY ANALYSIS SYSTEM

The bursting of the NASDAQ and dot-com bubble in 2000 led to dramatically decreased stock trading, and Compton's revenues fell accordingly. In the spring of 2002, amid the downsizing, the company launched an ambitious initiative to respond to managers' requests for detailed and accurate information that would enhance product development, promote marketing efforts, inform pricing decisions, and facilitate the needed corporate restructuring. Compton assembled a core team that was experienced in ABC concepts and technology and that included representatives from finance, IT, and operations. The team started by defining the goals for a new Profitability Analysis System (PAS):

- Run automatically, with little manual data entry or intervention.
- Tie into actual transactions.
- Reconcile with actual financials.
- Be available for daily use by employees.
- Provide a view on capacity utilization as well as cost and profitability.
- Enable predictive analysis.

The team compared the capabilities of the proposed PAS with the existing costing system, as shown in figure 10-1.

The team issued a seventy-five-page request for proposal to eleven leading software vendors in the business intelligence domain. The project team wanted a system capable of running an enterprise-profitability model that could be quickly implemented, was easily maintained, and provided robust and accessible reporting. After evaluating five leading candidates using proof-of-concept pilots and scalability testing, the team selected the Acorn Systems solution as the platform for PAS. Acorn's solution, running on a Microsoft SQL server, demonstrated a capability of running all

FIGURE 10-1

Compton Comparison of Legacy and Profitability Analysis System (PAS)

Legacy System	PAS
• Retail-centric model developed in the early 1990s	• Integration of legacy cost systems
• Information is not available in a timely manner to users	• Information available to users within 48 hours of GL closure
• Costing changes are time consuming to enter	• Information easily accessible by everyone within Compton
• Costing based on average rates	• Framework to support "what-if" and forecasting analysis
• Has no concept of capacity	• Information automatically extracted from data warehouse (and other sources) at month-end close
• Restatements are difficult to handle	• Track resource capacity
• No "what-if" or forecasting capabilities	• Client P&L reports available via Web
• Large support staff required	• Costing based on time rather than averages
• Does not provide timely and easy access to client P&L reports as user need to write SQL to get information	• Easier to restate
	• Reduce number of resources to support profit reporting system

monthly transactions data within twenty-four hours (this time was subsequently cut in half, by optimizing the performance of Microsoft SQL).

Anticipated Challenges

Management envisioned several challenges. Compton's costing systems for the previous fifteen years had been developed completely in-house. Alice Gordon was unsure whether Compton's internal ABC team and business managers would work effectively with the outside consulting and software firm. This concern was accentuated by the objective to achieve a far more automated system, which would probably reduce the need for her group to remain at current staffing levels. The project team would also have to protect the company's highly proprietary client information. Most importantly, the amount of data to be fed into the Acorn/Microsoft application would be far greater than before. Gordon wondered whether IT resources and staff could handle on a regular basis the volume of data from 3 million active clients and 10,000 employees spread across 200 offices. She also questioned whether the business units were prepared to act on the information produced by this far more detailed reporting system.

IMPLEMENTATION

The PAS project got increased visibility when a new CEO, David Peterson, was appointed in January 2004. Peterson immediately reaffirmed Compton's historic commitment to individual investors by decreasing commission fees, focusing on customer service, and forging customer relationships, not just offering low-priced transactions.

Peterson recognized that a critical ingredient for the new strategy was more accurate and responsive cost and profitability information by product, channel, and customer segment. The existing cost and profit measurement systems did not offer an enterprisewide view of cost and profitability, a necessity if Compton were to extract hundreds of millions of dollars from its cost structure and still grow profitably. According to Ron Braxton, vice president of profitability analysis at Compton, "You can't make it in the discount brokerage industry with a lot of bureaucracy and fat." The PAS project, initially launched as the next-generation cost and profitability system, had now been elevated to greater strategic significance.

The PAS implementation team included existing company ABC personnel, Acorn consultants, and external subject matter experts on ABC implementation in financial services (figure 10-2).[1] The team wanted to

FIGURE 10-2

Compton PAS Project Organization

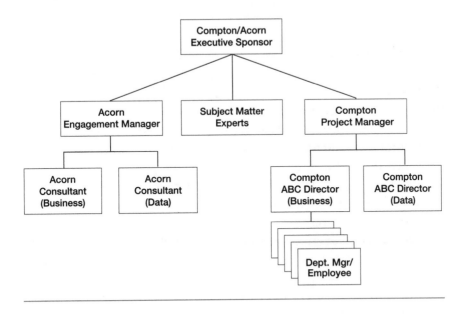

leverage existing cost assignments as much as possible to maintain a Compton look and feel for continuity. The team had worked hard over the last two decades to create understanding for cost and profitability measurement systems, and it wanted to minimize confusion and disruption to the organization. As much as possible, the external consultants worked behind the scene.

The project team emphasized three critical characteristics that had to be achieved by the new PAS: credible data, timely reporting, and clear accountability.

Credible Data

Credible data meant that customer and branch profitability had to reconcile both operationally and financially to the company's financial systems. This required the profitability calculations to be derived from actual transactions. The linkage to transactions would make it easy to generate and maintain the data and would allow easy access to both management and operating personnel. The requirement to link to actual transactions seemed obvious, but given Compton's considerable scale and scope, the task was not trivial. Monthly, the company could have tens to hundreds of millions of transactions. Users wanted access to historical information, which required maintaining twenty-four months of records and led to a model size in excess of a terabyte (a million megabytes). The system needed to scale with Compton's anticipated growth. Company management envisioned the number of accounts growing to 20 million and conducting more than a billion annual trades.

The team addressed how to streamline data collection for cost assignments. The previous ABC costing systems required extensive surveys of employees' time spent on various activities. Clearly, the time requirements for nontransactional activities, such as providing advice, or for activities for which transactional data were not available, still required employee surveys. But most activities could be associated with transactions. These would be migrated from the percentage-survey approach to time equations based on transaction characteristics. The more direct link between the resources consumed and transactional activity would enable users to understand how their organizations' transactions affected costs. Then the users could better propose actions to enhance their organizations' profitability.

The TDABC team would use the system's time equations to perform capacity analysis of the company's different processes. This visibility would enable the company to supply sufficient resources to meet peak demands during the busy trading hours of the day.

Timely Reporting

If users were to make the right decisions, they would need timely reporting. A manager needs to be aware of an unprofitable trade as it is occurring, not six weeks later. The PAS system would integrate tightly with existing operating systems. Reports would be run monthly. Drill-down capabilities would enable users to extract data to Excel spreadsheets for further analysis to pinpoint the underlying drivers of cost and profitability.

Clear Accountability

Clear accountability would ensure that all managers know how and where they were responsible.[2] If call center IT costs increase, for example, operating department managers must accept responsibility for identifying the source of the cost increase and how they can contribute to a solution. The call center will be charged for IT services through time-driven modeling of the IT processes. In this way, user departments and groups get charged for the cost of meeting their client's demands. They can then collaborate with customers to develop strategies for improvement. At Compton, client organizations determine the level of service they want to consume because they recognize that they will ultimately have to pay for it. There is an ongoing dialogue and communication about service levels and costs that gives operating departments ultimate profit responsibility. The support departments are mindful to hit their expense targets commensurate with the agreed-upon service levels.

TIME-DRIVEN MODELING OF IT SERVICES AND CALL CENTERS

The accurate costing of Compton's extensive IT resources was a central focus for the PAS project. IT resources had escalated dramatically to support online trading. End-use customers expected online access to view their account statements, execute trades, and conduct their own research. Compton now provided customers with online access to macroeconomic data and company-specific financial information, stock prices, and trading volumes. Internally, the organization consumed IT resources to run the latest software-modeling tools for corporate valuation, prepare hedging strategies, predict trends, and optimize pricing.

Compton had invested significantly in IT infrastructure to handle not only contemporary needs, but also future growth. Referred to as the *cost of readiness,* this excess capacity in the system network was maintained by Compton to handle capacity surges. But all this investment and protective capacity had led to extremely high IT expenses. Effectively managing IT to provide the same level of service at a lower cost would be an important component of Compton's profit turnaround strategy.

Pricing Daily Peak Capacity

The team used the model's time equations to predict the actual capacity utilization of IT resources and its variation on the basis of the volume and nature of transactions processed during each 24-hour period (figure 10-3). The data indicated a significant quantity of "strategic and unsold capacity," in excess of current needs. The costs of this unused capacity would not be assigned to today's products and customers. The strategic capacity represented an investment for future growth.

The system assigned only the costs of capacity actually being used to business units and their clients. Figure 10-4 provides a more detailed

FIGURE 10-3

IT Capacity Daily Utilization

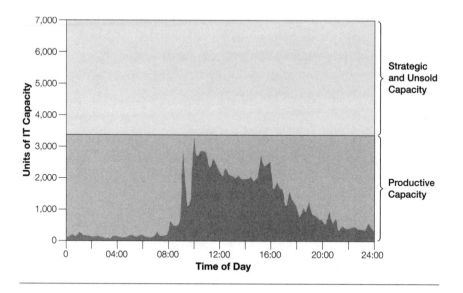

view, showing the four capacity-utilization periods during the day. The morning peak occurred as traders made their investments during the initial 60 minutes after U.S. markets opened. A secondary peak occurred during the 60 minutes at the end of the trading day, as traders closed out their daily positions. The third level of capacity utilization occurred in the remaining 4.5 hours that U.S. markets were open, between the opening and closing peaks. The lowest level of utilization occurred in the 17.5 hours when markets were not open. During this time, the computing resources handled after-hours settling of transactions, mutual-fund transactions based on closing prices, account updates, account maintenance, and other nonpriority tasks.

The PAS calculated four costing rates for the different periods of IT capacity demands (figure 10-5).[3] The cost rate for the morning opening peak period (zone 4) includes the full cost of the 200 units of capacity used only during that one-hour period, 50 percent of the 500 capacity units required to meet the demands for the opening and closing peak periods (zones 3 and 4), 1/6.5 of the 2,000 units needed during the nonpeak market trading period (zone 2), and only 1/24 of the 500 units supplied for the after-hours IT demands. In contrast, the hourly cost rate for transactions handled during the after-hours period would be only 1/24 of the 500 units of IT capacity. Thus, transactions processed in the hour after

FIGURE 10-4

Daily Demands for IT Services

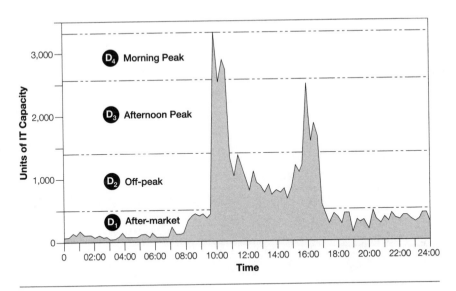

markets opened and in the hour before their closing would be charged much higher IT costs than a mutual fund transaction processed during the 17.5 hours when markets were not open.

Figure 10-6 shows how the daily IT resource cost of $436,000 ($9.6 million monthly) was assigned to the four capacity-utilization periods under this peak-pricing method. Compton could now accumulate all the IT demands by customer and assign costs to each transaction on the basis of the time of day it was processed and the quantity of IT resource time required to process the transaction. Figure 10-7 shows a sample calculation for two customers in a monthly period.

While the costs originated at the transaction level for an individual customer, they were eventually aggregated into a few customer segments (figure 10-8) since Compton did not consider it desirable to manage 3 million client accounts on a monthly basis. But the system had enough transparency for each client account representative to see the daily and monthly IT costs assigned to each of his or her clients.

Time-Driven Modeling of the Call Center

The team performed similar time-modeling for the call center (figure 10-9). Clients used the center to get quotes, execute trades, and request reports.

FIGURE 10-5

Identify Cost of Capacity Supplied Throughout the Day

Cost per hour of Zone 4: 100% of 200 units + (1/2) of 500 units +
(1/6.5) x 2,000 units + (1/24) x 500 units

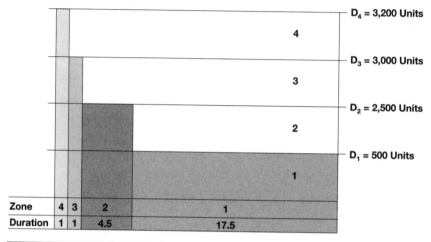

Each of these processes required various amounts of time, depending on a number of attributes of the transaction, such as whether it was a new client, the payment method, and the number of shares traded. The process time equation of the call center allowed the center's costs to be assigned on the basis of the actual time demands for its resource capacity

FIGURE 10-6

Calculated Hourly Cost of Supplying Different Levels of Capacity Throughout the Day

Total cost of capacity (monthly) = $9,600,000
Total cost of capacity (daily) = $436,364 (22 days)

Time Zone	Capacity Used	Hours	Zone Rate ($/MIPS*)	Cost per Hour of Capacity	Cost of Capacity (Daily)
1	500	17.5	5.7	$2,841	$49,716
2	2,500	4.5	17.9	44,800	201,595
3	3,000	1.0	26.3	78,890	78,890
4	3,200	1.0	33.2	106,163	106,163
					$436,364

*Millions of instructions processed.

FIGURE 10-7

Calculate IT Cost per Client

Account #	Trans- action	Time	Number of Trans- actions	MIPS per Trans- action	MIPS Used	Cost per MIPS	Total Cost
37382001	Trade	Off-peak	7	0.4	2.8	$17.90	$ 50.20
37382001	Trade	Morning Peak	14	0.4	5.6	33.20	185.80
37382001	Ask quote	Morning Peak	23	0.1	2.3	33.20	76.30
37382001	Balance transfer	Off-peak	1	0.7	0.7	17.90	12.50
37382001	**Total**						**$324.80**
37382002	Balance transfer	Off-peak	2	0.7	1.4	$17.90	$25.10
37382002	Trade	Afternoon Peak	1	0.4	0.4	26.30	10.50
37382002	**Total**						**$ 35.60**

by different clients and different types of requests and transactions. It also enabled the team to predict capacity utilization on the basis of forecasted volume and mix of customer transactions. The model had the additional advantage of transparency and auditability should any user question the cost assignments to its department or customers' accounts.

SYSTEM IMPLEMENTATION

Altogether, the project involved a team of nearly fifty full-time and part-time professionals over a twelve-month period. The team conducted comprehensive business analysis, completed a technical architecture design, and implemented a straight conversion of the existing cost and profit measurement systems. At that point, the team conducted extensive performance testing to ensure that data input, calculation, and reporting processes could be automated, that the desired cycle times could be achieved, and that the migration to a stable production environment could be completed. The team also identified sources for historical data, so that twelve months of history could be calculated and put online when the system was brought up live. Finally, the team tuned the performance of the terabyte-size database to ensure a smooth operation of the application in an ongoing production environment.

FIGURE 10-8

Aggregate Cost of Monthly IT Cost by Segment

Segment	Aggregate Cost of All Clients	Percentage of Assigned Cost
Independent foundation	$3,159,950	34.6
Independent signature	1,544,371	16.9
Advise foundation	1,102,933	12.1
Advise signature	556,004	6.1
Global	152,695	1.7
Active trader	2,629,431	28.8
Unassigned	454,616	
Total	**$9,600,000**	**100.0%**

FIGURE 10-9

Process Modeling of Call Center

Map Resources to Processes and Determine Capacity

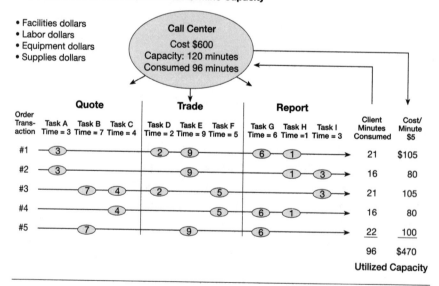

After the transition into the production environment, Compton continued to run monthly calculations until a full three years of history was in place for reporting. The team wanted to create a stable and consistent cost-modeling environment. The model would be changed, and data rerun, only when a significant reorganization of the business structure, such as reorganizations of departments, products, channels, or segments, occurred.

Once the model was up and running, the team members quantified how the new PAS model, even with its greatly increased power and flexibility, had achieved major savings in time and effort. Some statistics are the following:

- Dynamic time equations replaced time-consuming surveys.
- There was no counting or loading of driver data; all transaction data were seamlessly linked to the TDABC software solution.
- The system required 16 hours to generate comprehensive enterprisewide profit reports, versus 5 to 7 days to calculate only account-level profitability under the previous system.
- The model reduced the lead time for monthly business reports from 33 days to 3 to 5 days.

WHAT DID NOT GO SO WELL?

The PAS project successfully met all its goals but did encounter some difficulties. First, the isolation of the external consultants from the actual business users led to delays in the model preparation and validation. The expertise from the external consultants had to be filtered through project personnel. Second, the internal ABC specialists often disagreed with the recommendations of the external consultants. The Acorn time-driven methodology proved difficult to explain to the internal ABC people, who were experts in implementing conventional ABC models. In the words of one Acorn consultant, one of the most frustrating aspects of implementing the new TDABC methodology at a company with an existing conventional ABC model is, "The client doesn't know what he doesn't know." Given the fast pace of the Compton project, trying to bridge this gap in knowledge was not a priority and thus was never achieved. Third, once the system started operating successfully, the demands from internal customers for new reports overwhelmed the project team. Many business users still wanted all their old reports, calculated with the new data, while other managers requested reporting that did not yet exist. Compton had to keep several of the consultants on site after the system had been successfully installed just to assist the Compton ABC and finance team in meeting these expanded reporting requests.

PERFORMANCE AND USAGE OF THE SYSTEM

Despite the modest implementation difficulties, the vice president of technology for finance believed that PAS represented a dramatic upgrade in performance from the previous system:

The new system for profitability analysis has several key advantages over past systems. First, it is timely; the data are generated only five days after the books are closed on the prior month. Second, it is flexible, making it relatively easy to change the allocation rules to incorporate new information. It also is a pragmatic system; it uses drivers that are already collected in the data warehouse system, and if an event that drives resource consumption is not available in the system, we select another event with similar behavior. Also PAS requires fewer people to manage the system, and as a vendor-provided solution it presents an upgrade path that's more cost-effective. In general, better costing methodologies have been implemented and the data are more accurate.

This endorsement of PAS was not trivial. The system was far more comprehensive and processed orders of magnitude more data into reports encompassing the entire enterprise. The reports covered the specific transactions and profit-and-loss statements (P&Ls) of individual accounts, all products and services, and the performance of operating and support departments, including capacity utilization and benchmarking. The capabilities of PAS to collect, process, and report significantly more information yet run in much less time, and with fewer resources, were not widely expected either by the team or throughout the company. The timely reporting in PAS transformed management's use of detailed profitability data from an infrequent analytic exercise to an embedded management tool. The PAS cost and profitability information gained so much credibility that management soon linked compensation and rewards to the reported results.

Today, PAS is used on a daily basis throughout the Compton organization. The core team continues to generate management reports on costs, profits, and capacity utilization for strategic decision making and policy setting. Operating departments use it tactically for staffing decisions and process improvements. The field branches use it for customer, product, and transaction profitability analysis. A client representative in the Valley Forge, Pennsylvania, office, commented: "The new system has transformed our business . . . We can now view the actual profitability of each account. So when we are on the phone, and the customer is asking for additional services, instead of giving them away for free like we used to do, we now can push back or push them toward revenue services."

Compton used the PAS cost and capacity information as part of an overall cost leadership initiative that resulted in lowering expenses by over $400 million. By seeing where unused capacity existed throughout the enterprise, Compton managers could selectively prune excess resources without compromising customer service. Senior executive involvement in the project was key to achieving this magnitude of benefit because these leaders could act to align resource commitments to organizational goals. The client-centered organizational units used the more timely and accurate information of their accounts to increase profitability by targeting more profitable customer segments and steering clients to more profitable services and products. Compton also had the confidence, from the accurate cost information, to selectively raise prices for certain services.

Eighteen months after launching the turnaround, Compton's market capitalization had climbed by more than 50 percent (a total of more than $6 billion), an increase far greater than comparable stock market indices (see figure 10-10).

David Peterson looked back with satisfaction: "We've done an enormous amount of work in the last nine months. We took out $400 million in costs. When you take all of the things that we've done, including price and cost reductions, our return on capital is climbing, and our profit margins are at the highest level in a long time."

SUMMARY

The Compton case illustrates the enterprisewide scalability of Time-Driven ABC in the financial services industry. The Compton implementation had strong senior executive support and had to cope with enormous size: several million customer accounts, ten thousand employees, two hundred offices, and tens of millions of transactions per month.

Compton already had extensive internal experience with ABC models, but its conventional ABC system was not transactions-driven and could not assign the large and growing costs of centralized resources for IT and call centers. The conventional ABC model required extensive and annoying monthly surveys of employees' time distributions; a large corporate

FIGURE 10-10

Stock Price Impact from Compton's Successful Profit Turnaround

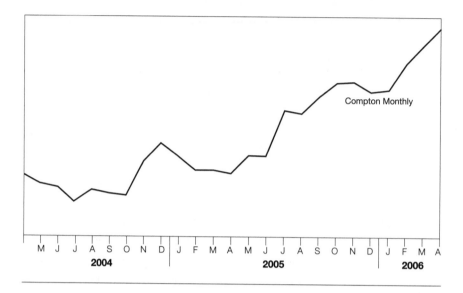

staff to collect, input, and process the data; and a 33-day cycle to produce monthly reports.

The Time-Driven ABC model overcame all these problems. Its data inputs came automatically from Compton's transactions system, producing enterprisewide monthly P&L reports within 5 days of month's end. The one-terabyte data file could be processed each month in about 16 hours. Frontline account representatives had real-time access to the profitability of their customers and their customers' transactions.

The Compton case also illustrates resource costing in the presence of highly peaked daily demands. Compton's TDABC model uses four capacity cost rates for IT and call center resources. These different rates reflect the varying demands for services during each 24-hour period. The highest peak demand occurs during the 60 minutes after the opening of U.S. markets, a secondary peak occurs in the last 60 minutes of the trading day, and the lowest level of demand occurs during the 17.5 hours when markets are not open for trading.

Compton acted immediately on the TDABC cost and profitability information and the actions, among other initiatives, contributed to a more than $400 million cost reduction without compromising customer service. Moreover, Compton empowered its customer service representatives to be more proactive in increasing the profitability of their accounts. These actions and others contributed to a 50 percent stock price increase within an 18-month period. The experience highlights the value of several elements in a well-run system:

- Strong senior executive commitment
- An experienced internal ABC project team supplemented by external solution experts in TDABC and the management of massive databases
- An organizational environment that empowers employees for action

NOTES

1. The external subject-matter experts on the PAS implementation team included Mitch Max from The Performax Group, Steve Player from the Player Group, and Sean Millane from Wright Killen.
2. S. R. Anderson and L. Maisel, "IT Value Management," Acorn Systems white paper (Houston: Acorn Systems, March 2006).
3. The Compton approach extends the peak and slack period analysis described in chapter 3 to four capacity-utilization periods.

## CHAPTER ELEVEN

ATB FINANCIAL

Guiding Profitable Growth

THE GOVERNMENT of Alberta (Canada) created ATB Financial (then called Alberta Treasury Branches) during the Great Depression to provide funding to farmers during their times of need. Fifty years later (in the 1980s), ATB began to incur losses as low oil prices and a weak agriculture sector triggered a downturn in the Albertan economy; unemployment exceeded 10 percent. Branch expansion and diversification into new services did little to eliminate the loss. ATB realized it needed to operate more like a private sector bank while still remaining under a government-owned framework. The provincial government created a board of directors, with a mandate to develop a strategy that would strengthen ATB's balance sheet, align its service levels with customer needs, invest in technology, and enhance staff training.[1]

In the late 1990s, the rise in oil and gas prices stimulated the Alberta economy, attracted new residents, and raised employment levels. These economic factors, along with the governance and management changes, restored ATB's profitability. By 2004, ATB (rebranded as ATB Financial in 2002) had strong revenue growth and had nearly doubled its asset base from 1997. But economic growth brought new competitors, and ATB management knew that downturns could occur again in the future. Executives developed a new business plan to address future opportunities and challenges (figure 11-1).

As part of the business plan, ATB expanded its product offering. The Personal Services business offered credit card products, mortgage services,

FIGURE 11-1

ATB Business Plan

- *Modernizing* our core Personal and Business Financial Services
- Diversifying our revenue and growing Investor Services Corporate Financial Services opportunities
- Building and promoting the ATB Financial brand
- Building an *outstanding team of associates*
- *Improving productivity*
- Implementing a risk-management program

Internet banking, travel protection, loans, and retirement products. The Business Services group offered investment products, tax filing services, merchant processing services, brokerage services, foreign correspondence, and debt financing. And the newly formed Investor Services group offered a portfolio of savings and investment vehicles, such as mutual funds and fixed-date deposits, registered educational savings plans, and retirement savings plans.

The increased diversification of products and services led to higher demands for corporate support. The bank gained economies of scale by shifting many transactions-processing resources (and costs) from branches to regional and centralized units that now processed transaction previously launched and completed at a local branch. ATB's existing costing system, however, could not accurately assign the significant costs of corporate and regional resources to transactions, products, and customers. Jim McKillop, chief financial officer since 2004, explained: "We had the ability to do corporate financial statements and functional analysis against budget, but we had no real capability to look at product profitability or process costs. To operate effectively, we needed an ability to drive costs against the parts of the business that drove performance."

Amolak Grewal, ATB's chief operating officer, expressed a concern that the bank's focus on revenue growth in a booming economy had blurred its focus on the bottom line: "When the top line is growing fast, it is easy to hide a ton of sins—we run the risk of overbuilding and giving away profitability." ATB needed an accurate assignment of corporate support costs to processes and products if it were to be a competitive operator.

Lenka Stuchlik, vice president of finance at ATB, believed that activity-based costing should be introduced into the corporate performance management system. The more accurate information would enable managers of the various business units to identify new profit-improvement opportunities with processes, customers, and services. McKillop, however, was initially skeptical about an ABC initiative, having experienced limited success with past ABC implementations. He wanted to be assured that the project would focus on creating value, could be delivered in a timely and efficient manner, and would provide usable, practical information. Gaining support for the ABC initiative also had to overcome the skepticism of others in ATB and compete for resources with many other existing projects, including a major overhaul of the branch operating network.

McKillop asked Stuchlik to lead a team to provide proof-of-concept before committing to a large-scale ABC implementation project. Stuchlik hired Acorn Systems and a financial services consulting firm, The Performax Group (subsequently combined into DecisionVu), to conduct a pilot study to demonstrate that ABC could be effectively implemented and would add value to ATB.

The consulting team decided to demonstrate the feasibility of ABC by building a cost model for the branch loan application process within ATB's central services group. This group had productivity metrics, such as the number of applications an agent could process per day, but was unable to assign its costs to the branches it supported. The team migrated the existing operational and productivity data into an Acorn Time-Driven ABC model. This information enabled the model to calculate and accurately assign the cost of the central services group loan application process to individual branches.

The study revealed, for example, that the cost to process loan applications depended on the quality of an application transmitted by the branch. The team learned that branches differed in their rate of held mortgages and that the cost of a "held" application (one requiring rework) was significantly higher than a "clean" application. Some of the highest-volume branches required one-third of their applications to be reworked. The project team communicated this key cost driver to the branches and suggested that branches be charged more for processing their held mortgages. Immediately, branches began to focus more carefully on the quality of the applications they sent to the central services group. Through this pilot study, the team succeeded in demonstrating the feasibility and benefits of an accurate, comprehensive cost and profitability measurement system. The pilot TDABC model's accurate and transparent calculations, based on existing productivity data, created operational buy-in for a wider implementation project.

With feasibility established, the consulting team formulated the key requirements for an enterprisewide TDABC project (figure 11-2). McKillop

FIGURE 11-2

ABC Project Requirements

- Understand costs incurred within the organization and how they support delivery of services and products
- Understand and manage drivers of costs by process across the channels of our organization
- Provide information to help manage profitability of customer relationships
- Provide cost transparency and accountability for management of profitability
- Provide accurate cost information and operational metrics to enable profitability and operational analysis under a corporatewide performance management framework

approved the project. ATB formed an ABC project team consisting of experienced personnel from finance and systems. The external consultants from the pilot study would provide assistance for large-scale model development and software implementation. McKillop also created an ABC Project Steering Committee of senior executives to guide the process through an ambitious project completion timetable of nine months.

BUILDING AN ENTERPRISE MODEL

At the time of the project, ATB had 160 branches and a total of 2 million accounts, offered 200 products, and processed 12 million transactions per month. The TDABC model would have to assign most bank costs down to the transaction level and include the interaction effects between branch, regional, and corporate units. For example, a customer may establish his or her accounts at a branch close to home, conduct transactions at other branches or ATM machines near work or during shopping trips, call a central customer-service line for questions about products and services, and use the Internet to make account balance queries, merchant payments, and funds transfers. Fortunately, ATB already had an excellent information system on customer transactions and activities. The TDABC model provided an integrated, analytic system that could scale to handle ATB's huge volumes of transactions, products, and customers.

The project team formulated a four-phase implementation approach that incorporated interim checkpoints and value generation throughout the project (figure 11-3).

Phase 1, establishing proof of the value of the model, had been accomplished by the pilot study, which assigned central loan-processing costs to branches. In Phase 2, the team focused on assigning the remain-

FIGURE 11-3

Implementation Plan

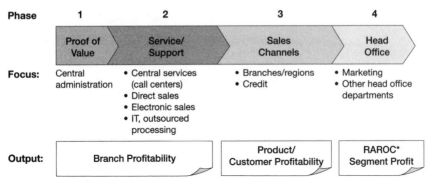

Phase	1	2	3	4
	Proof of Value	Service/ Support	Sales Channels	Head Office
Focus:	Central administration	• Central services (call centers) • Direct sales • Electronic sales • IT, outsourced processing	• Branches/regions • Credit	• Marketing • Other head office departments
Output:	Branch Profitability		Product/ Customer Profitability	RAROC* Segment Profit

*RAROC: Risk-Adjusted Return-on-Capital, a standard banking profitability metric.

ing centralized operating expenses to individual branches. By accurately assigning these costs to transactions and branches, the ABC model would provide a more accurate view of branch, product, and customer profitability. In Phase 3, the project team would drive costs down within branches to produce product and customer profitability reports, by branch and region. The team recognized that full profitability numbers would not be produced until the end of Phase 4, when all corporate overhead costs would be incorporated into the cost assignments to branches, products, and customers.

Figure 11-4 shows the overall structure of the enterprisewide ABC model. The enterprise model contained two submodels, Model 1 for corporate shared-service expenses, and Model 2 for branch-specific expenses. Model 1 assigned expenses to processing departments and then assigned each department's costs to the activities it performed. Each activity had a process and a channel designation. Therefore, similar process activities such as setup, termination, and maintenance costs could easily be grouped together and analyzed.

Some Model 1 expenses, such as those incurred to process loans, were assigned on the basis of the time they required. In this way, branch costs would reflect the quantity of loans generated by a branch and the time and cost incurred by the corporate office to process the loans. The team calculated the time required for each activity, added up the times on the basis of the quantity of activities performed by each branch, and assigned

FIGURE 11-4

ABC Model Structure

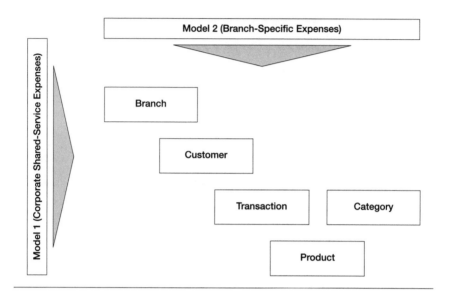

costs according to each activity's total processing time. Additional branch and product costs incorporated the costs of contracted activities triggered at the branch, such as the processing of automated bank transactions. The costs that could not be easily assigned according to time were then transferred to Model 2, where they would be assigned on the basis of other cost drivers. For example, human resource costs were assigned to branches on the basis of head count.[2]

Model 2 focused on costs incurred within the branches. In a given period, the percentage of time a department spent on an activity varied with the demand for a product or service. Requiring each department to estimate the percentage of time spent on an activity per month was "old ABC," an extremely subjective, time-consuming, and unreliable method of assigning costs. The TDABC model calculated the time required for each activity according to the number of transactions performed each period and the time required by each branch to perform the service. Since every department had a finite set of activities that it performed, the model calculated the sum of all departmental times and apportioned the total cost of the department on the basis of each activity's calculated percentage of the department's total time.[3]

The project team reached the end of Phase 4 in nine months. The TDABC system was now producing cost and profitability each month, and the team was beginning to integrate the information into ATB's management information systems and processes. The project had accomplished the following:

- *Cost analysis:* completed a set of fully loaded cost analyses across all processes, products, and channels
- *Shared services:* provided the capabilities for assigning the costs of centralized service areas, including processing, call centers, and IT, to profit centers on the basis of their specific consumption of those resources
- *Process analysis and benchmarking:* provided the ability to benchmark key activities against other units within ATB or external organizations
- *Channel analysis:* facilitated the comparison of costs and performance across alternate service and delivery channels

WHAT DID NOT GO SO WELL?

The ABC team had much to be proud of, though it still experienced a hollow feeling at the end of the project. First, organization buy-in and adoption had been much slower than expected. At the start of the project, the team members had high hopes that the study would be a transforming event for the company and their own careers. They felt that the potential profit impact from the new TDABC information was great, but the team members had to spend an inordinate amount of time educating the rest of the organization about how to capture this potential. Second, TDABC time equations were so flexible and powerful for modeling complexity that the team members continued to search for additional drivers to add to the model, rather than freeze the model at its current, quite high level of accuracy and declare success, at least for a while. Third, some key team members left. The most visible departure occurred when the primary external consultant, who had built the model, left for law school. This loss slowed momentum for the entire project.

KEY FINDINGS

Operational Improvements

ATB had previously been through many operational improvement initiatives. Despite these initiatives, the new TDABC cost and profitability information stimulated numerous cost and revenue improvement actions, which are described in the following paragraphs.

Cost Reduction Ideas in Outsourced Activities

ATB had been outsourcing many routine functions. The invoices received from vendors were accurate and auditable but did not reveal the drivers of total invoice costs. The ABC team investigated the drivers of vendor costs to learn where and how these costs could be reduced. For example, the team learned that a large component of the outsourced cost of producing monthly statements for customers was the number of print lines. Working with the customer service organization, the team modified the report to reduce the number of print lines without sacrificing content. The cost of statement production decreased immediately.

Cost Avoidance for Internal Processes

The time equations in the TDABC model revealed how call-center process times varied by type of call. For example, the team learned that calls to reset passwords were expensive and frequent. After the team developed new procedures to address the root cause for these calls, the volume and cost for this type of call soon plummeted.

Responses to Customer Requests

ATB was spending significantly more resources to handle trace requests (customers requesting an adjustment for items they didn't recognize) than it was charging customers for this service, and often more than the amount in dispute. The bank established a procedure to either increase its service fee or authorize an adjustment in lieu of handling a trace request on small items.

Revenue Enhancements

The team identified several products that had been expensive to develop and introduce but for which little revenue had been generated to date. ATB initiated a new training and awareness campaign that would educate the branches about the new products so that these offerings could be more effectively marketed to customers.

Branch Performance

The team could see, and demonstrate to others, that the considerable variability in branch cost and profitability was caused by customer demographics, product mix, cost structure, and branch efficiency. The team discovered that the number of branches achieving targeted efficiency ratios (costs divided by revenue) was insufficient. Neither branch type nor branch size appeared to correlate with efficiency. The TDABC model enabled the team to discover that differences in capacity utilization explained much of the variation in branch efficiency. The model identified where excess capacity existed by process within each branch. Management could then downsize its branch service and delivery platform to expected demands.

Product Performance

The system calculated the revenue and cost for each major product, revealing significantly more variation than had previously been measured or believed. ATB had proliferated its core deposit product into many different variations, and several variations were particularly low margin or unprofitable. After stratifying activities by cost, the team explored the most time-consuming and costly account maintenance activities for deposit products (figure 11-5).

As the team studied the highest-cost activities—taking deposits, processing withdrawals, and handling bill payments—it noted a marked difference

FIGURE 11-5

Deposit Account Maintenance Activities

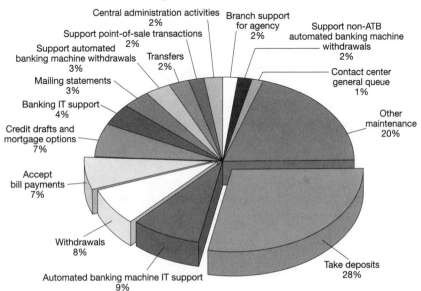

"Maintain" Activities—Selected Deposit Products

Central administration activities 2%
Branch support for agency 2%
Support non-ATB automated banking machine withdrawals 2%
Support point-of-sale transactions 2%
Support automated banking machine withdrawals 3%
Transfers 2%
Contact center general queue 1%
Mailing statements 3%
Banking IT support 4%
Other maintenance 20%
Credit drafts and mortgage options 7%
Accept bill payments 7%
Withdrawals 8%
Take deposits 28%
Automated banking machine IT support 9%

in the rate of human-handled transactions compared with electronic transactions in many branches. The team learned that the use of one human-handled transaction often led to another: customers who had already waited in line to make a bill payment were likely to make a deposit or withdrawal at the same time. Some of the most efficient branches used "greeters" to direct customers to banking machines or Internet terminals for these activities. This insight was incorporated in branch redesigns, and the "best practice" disseminated across the network.

IMPACT

On seeing the near-term impact from the actions suggested and implemented by the project team, ATB's Steering Committee formed a task force of key managers to mine the information further, develop insights and hypotheses, and begin to implement changes. The task force shared the information more broadly within ATB. Employees began to generate suggestions for profit improvements. Over two hundred suggestions were received, with nearly 20 percent of them implemented within a year. By the end of 2005, the bank identified nearly $2 million in annualized profit improvement through revenue enhancement and cost reductions, with higher amounts still being investigated for implementation.

Amolak Grewal commented on the impact:

> *The true cost of exception processing became visible. We had been tolerating these from a customer service perspective, but now we had an opportunity to look at the exceptions more completely.*
>
> *We have changed our approach from adding new capability to optimizing the capabilities that we have. That means [fewer] new products and optimizing our existing product portfolio, and simplifying our sales environment.*

Sharon Bell, vice president of marketing, concurred. Her marketing team was completing a product portfolio analysis, which was based on the new, complete product profitability information. She expected that the team would streamline the product portfolio, and implement more customized pricing, by channel. ATB's original profitability work had identified a "True Blue" category for its best customers. The new ABC information helped classify a True Blue customer more precisely, through the use of a more complete and accurate view of the cost to service each customer relationship. Bell claimed, "ABC allowed us to replace guesswork with science."

As the team moved into 2006, it was exploring options to integrate the TDABC systematic view of profitability—by product, channel, and customer—into business decisions and performance management and incentive systems. McKillop summarized the journey:

ABC is part of our evolution to build a rigorous commercial capability to drive and manage profitability, helping us make the right decisions to drive performance. We have other building blocks—capital allocation, training, governance, technical architecture, a more disciplined decision-making process, and improved incentive programs. All of these will fit together in helping to build the longer-term capability to sustain our franchise and help meet corporate goals.

SUMMARY

ATB Financial's existing cost system operated only at the branch level. Since the company had been centralizing many of its processes, the cost system could not assign the large shared-service costs in regional centers and corporate headquarters. The TDABC approach enabled these costs to be accurately and transparently assigned on the basis of the transactions initiated at more than one hundred branches.

The project team encountered considerable skepticism that it could produce a defensible cost-assignment methodology for regional and centralized resources. To gain credibility, the team conducted a pilot study of a single process, loan approval. The study revealed that having to reprocess a loan application led to much higher costs relative to processing a defect-free application. Since the branches had considerable variation in their percentage of reworked loans, the finding had high significance for branch profitability, indicating the value of performing a pilot study on a high-profile, expensive process for which considerable variation exists across the organization.

After the success of the pilot, the project team scaled up to an enterprisewide model that quickly led to $2 million in annual savings from the following improvements:

- Reduced costs of outsourced processes
- Cost reduction in shared services
- Benchmarking and the sharing of best practices across various branches' processes
- Capacity adjustments at the branch level

The project experienced some difficulty when an external consultant, who was the lead technical person on the project, unexpectedly left to return to academic study. The incident illustrates that companies should have an internal employee as the TDABC project leader, allowing for an orderly transition to an internal replacement should the project leader depart. ATB Financial, like Compton (chapter 10), reveals the high payoff of applying TDABC to retail financial services. The homogeneity of retail outlets enables a model built at one branch to scale quickly to the entire enterprise. Also, retail financial services enjoy economies of scale from centralizing IT and back-office processes. But unless companies use a TDABC model to drive these centralized costs to transactions, customer accounts, and branches, the organizations will not be able to accurately measure the profit or loss from their diverse operations, products, and customer accounts. Accurate customer-level P&Ls are critical for allowing customer account representatives to manage the introduction of new products and services to their clients.

NOTES

1. This chapter includes contributions by Mitchell Max (Partner, DecisionVu) and Sehyung Lee (Consultant, Acorn Systems).
2. Indirect support costs, such as for human resources, could have been assigned directly by the time-driven methodology. The project team decided to use more readily available cost drivers at this phase.
3. Again, as with several other case studies reported in this book, ATB used the percentage-allocation approach for assigning departmental costs to activities rather than calculating capacity cost rates for each department (as described in chapter 3) and using these rates to assign costs to the various activities performed.

## CHAPTER TWELVE

CITIGROUP TECHNOLOGY INFRASTRUCTURE DIVISION

Financial Strategies for Managing IT as a Business Within a Business

CITIGROUP, one of the largest financial services organizations in the world, offered, through four global sectors, a broad set of products and services to numerous and diverse customers. Citigroup's corporate center provided administrative support and information technology (IT) services to the global business units. Within the corporate center, Citigroup Technology Infrastructure (CTI) operated 75 to 80 percent of the company's technology infrastructure to provide reliable, secure, and cost effective services to about sixty units in the global sectors and the Corporate Center. CTI managed all the global mainframe data centers and most of the distributed computing.

In 2004, CTI embarked on a major shift in strategic focus to redirect its business model from a utility to a service model. The division summarized the change as follows:

The rationale for managing IT as a business within a business, as opposed to as an internal corporate utility, was to demonstrate how we create value to the businesses that we support. If we cannot add value to our customers, they will look elsewhere for their technology services. We introduced product managers, client relationship managers, service-level agreements, benchmarking, and service catalogs.

As part of this change, the CTI finance organization made a parallel transformation from scorekeeper and cost overseer to active business adviser for CTI's operations managers. The policy decision to transform itself necessitated an in-depth review of its existing financial practices to plan and track product costs and develop pricing for its chargeback revenue system. The review revealed that product costs were derived from numerous source documents, so product cost could be measured only as aggregated amounts derived from a series of linked spreadsheets. CTI finance could not trace sources of cost information, utilize cost-based pricing, or provide cost and price transparency to its user community. These deficiencies conflicted with CTI's strategic goal to become a trusted adviser to business unit leaders.

CTI started by acquiring new technology to replace its use of spreadsheets and to provide a foundation to deploy critical new applications. Two of the more significant applications were: (1) product profit and loss (P&Ls) and (2) a Time-Driven Activity-Based Costing system to better manage labor capacity, such as staff levels and utilization. The TDABC methodology could establish the causal linkages between the time consumed by that staff to perform assigned activities triggered by transactional drivers and the level of staff required.

CTI FINANCIAL MANAGEMENT CYCLE

Figure 12-1 illustrates the four components in the financial management cycle that are at the heart of managing technology infrastructure as a business within a business: operational productivity, product P&L statements, benchmarking, and customer recovery and chargeback.

The operational productivity component strives to lower the costs—salary, occupancy, hardware, and software—of operating the technology infrastructure. Labor capacity planning and capital planning help determine the correct size of CTI in light of current and projected productivity and the demands for its services.

Product P&Ls match the customer charges for technology products and services with the costs of producing those products and services. These costs were based on traditional departmental budgets for cost categories such as hardware, software, facilities, salaries, and planned levels of transactions. The product P&Ls are distributed to client relationship managers and product managers. Beyond their financial responsibilities, these managers ensure that products' features and functionality are best in class, and manage new-product introductions.

FIGURE 12-1

CTI Financial Management Cycle

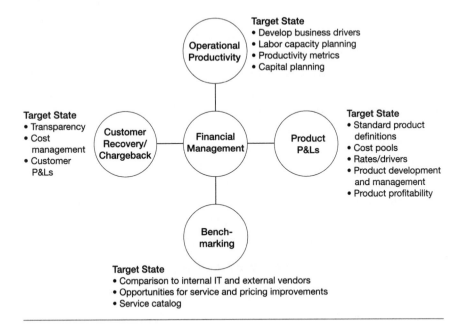

Benchmarking, the third component, compares CTI products and services and their internal pricing against other internal IT organizations and external vendors.

Customer recovery and chargeback, the fourth component, enables CTI to recover its annual operating expense. CTI's people expenses are 25 percent of total costs, much lower than the typical 50 to 55 percent experienced in other Citigroup divisions. The CTI chargeback to the global sectors and businesses generates many comments, says Jeff Nachowitz, chief financial officer of CTI: "Probably the biggest noise we get from the businesses is around cost transparency. A typical comment is 'I don't understand what you're charging me for or how to manage the cost.' It seems that whether an assigned cost is transparent depends on where you sit in the organization."

WHY BUILD A PERFORMANCE MEASUREMENT AND MANAGEMENT SYSTEM?

CTI wanted to be responsive to the concerns that its internal customers expressed about the lack of transparency in its cost-recovery charges. It also wanted to have an analytic tool to help reduce costs and improve operational productivity. CTI finance launched concurrent initiatives. One initiative addressed the management of product profitability. The second initiative, to address the needs of operational managers, would use Time-Driven ABC to produce reports on activity-cost and labor-capacity management. The TDABC model would be at the core of CTI's comprehensive business performance management system. This enterprise system became known as the Performance Measurement and Management (PMM) system and was designed in two modules:

1. *Product Profitability Management* to plan and manage product revenues and costs at required levels of detail
2. *Activity-Based Business Performance Management* to capture time-driven activity-based costs, track labor capacity and staffing data, and measure and report cost and operational productivity

Product Profitability Management

CTI's existing cost system estimated the charging rates for products and services annually. It used these rates to charge customers on the basis of their volume and mix of usage of CTI products and services. But the system did not allow users to understand how the rates were calculated, how the rates compared with actual monthly costs, or why CTI's total expenses were either over- or under-recovered in any given month. Apart from its opacity, the system was also manual and cumbersome. It calculated product and service P&Ls in Excel spreadsheets, with some twenty or thirty spreadsheets required just to do the P&Ls for one business unit. Any changes had to be entered separately on each spreadsheet.

CTI's proposed Product Profitability Management system would overcome the limitations of its spreadsheet-dependent system. Figure 12-2 illustrates how the product P&L would interface with other systems, such as the multiple general ledgers and other data feeds. Total gross expenses would be fully assigned to the product P&Ls to assure managers that all expenses were being assigned to products and customers. In that way, revenues, recoveries, and expenses matched the general ledger and under- and over-recoveries could be tracked to products and services.

Activity-Based Business Performance Management

CTI decided to include, within the Performance Measurement and Management system, a module to implement TDABC and to create an

FIGURE 12-2

Product Profitability Management

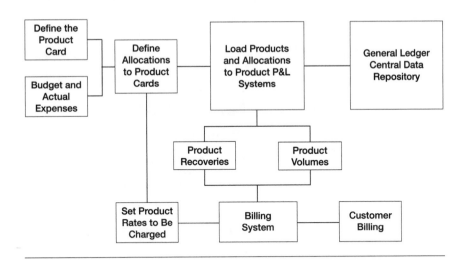

activity-based Business Performance Management (BPM) system. The enhancements would integrate strategic and operational data for better operational decision making, customer service, and financial planning and control. The division's CFO selected the Global Network and Security Operations (GNSO) section as the pilot for implementing the new approach. GNSO's management team was receptive to this approach and had an excellent track record for capturing and using data to manage the business. Figure 12-3 illustrates the multistep approach to implementing TDABC within GNSO.

In step 1, *business analysis,* the project team conducted interviews with managers and supervisors to define each department's major activities and activity groups. Additionally, the team identified transactional drivers and their source system and developed time estimates and adjustment factors for each activity. During step 2, *system integration,* the team collected and loaded expense and driver data from financial and operational source systems. As part of this step, it reviewed the data for reasonableness, did additional research on questionable data, and validated potential anomalies. In step 3, *model development,* the team modeled the operations of the selected department and defined and loaded the time equations into the system. In step 4, *business performance management reporting,* the team designed and developed a portal site and dashboard for reporting and analyzing the information and results.

FIGURE 12-3

Architecture for Time-Driven ABC Model

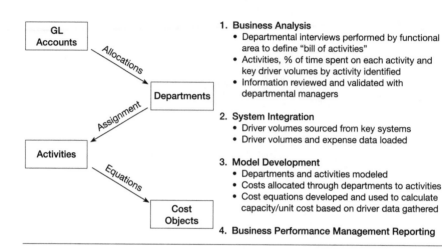

1. **Business Analysis**
   - Departmental interviews performed by functional area to define "bill of activities"
   - Activities, % of time spent on each activity and key driver volumes by activity identified
   - Information reviewed and validated with departmental managers

2. **System Integration**
   - Driver volumes sourced from key systems
   - Driver volumes and expense data loaded

3. **Model Development**
   - Departments and activities modeled
   - Costs allocated through departments to activities
   - Cost equations developed and used to calculate capacity/unit cost based on driver data gathered

4. **Business Performance Management Reporting**

RESULTS

The new Performance Measurement and Management system generated benefits to CTI by providing two key tools:

- Product P&L system
- TDABC Business Performance Management system

Product P&L System

The new product P&L system allowed CTI to capture, for each user organization, the monthly usage volumes and the quantities and prices of supplied products and services that were billable out to clients. Additionally, CTI could now capture monthly actual expenses by cost center and major expenditure category such as staffing expenses, hardware, software, and occupancy. The matching of revenues and expenses formed the basis for product P&Ls.

Monthly, the financial managers analyzed these costs for under- and over-recovery and compared them to other internal and external cost benchmarks for selected products and services. Where appropriate, the analysts adjusted recovery rates for the current year's operations. This information provided a reference for the next year's budgeted rates and expense planning.

Activity-Based Business Performance Management System

The BPM system utilizing TDABC methods was initially piloted in the GNSO operating department to complement the P&L reports. The system assigned a department's costs to activities by calculating the minutes of effort for each activity and assigning costs based on the proportion of minutes spent on the different activities performed. The system allowed CTI to understand its costs at the activity level rather than the department level. Moreover, activity-based BPM provided more transparency by tracing costs based on the specific transactions that consumed the department's capacity. For example, the system tracked trouble tickets by type of problem, level of severity, and region, enabling managers to take targeted actions to address the specific causes of the problems. In the future, CTI envisioned extending the data capture to include customer-driven events, which would give greater cost transparency to customers and empower them to improve their processes and modify their practices to reduce their billable costs from CTI.

Managers also used the new BPM system to compare the operating productivity and cost efficiencies between groups within GNSO, such as the productivity between the European and North American regions, for common processes related to the diagnosis and resolution of reported trouble tickets. Such comparisons in the past were performed on an aggregate basis by dividing a designated cost center's cost by the total volume of trouble tickets. In the new system, these data could be analyzed at a more disaggregate level of detail. This ability to peel away the layers provided managers with a better understanding of the causes of productivity differences so executives could transfer best practice between units and regions. Managers were also beginning to link the data to business planning since they now had a more analytic basis for determining the necessary level of staffing to deliver superior customer services.

The BPM system offered a comprehensive, easily navigable, and Web-accessible site to access and analyze performance management information. Configured as an executive dashboard, the system had three integrated views: departmental, activity, and labor capacity. A single source of data drove the three views, a considerable improvement over the previous system, which required three separate spreadsheets to capture the data for each monthly period.

The system also incorporated drill-down capabilities by activity group and cost driver. In addition, the system included analytical tools that could highlight trend lines and operating anomalies and analyze usage volumes and unit costs. The system also integrated with office productivity systems including e-mail, word processing, and spreadsheets.

IMPLEMENTATION CHALLENGES

The team and CTI faced several important challenges to implementation:

- The user organizations initially resisted changes to the costing methodology. CTI viewed the conversion of its IT services-costing model to the TDABC approach as a technical, not a managerial, project. The project team did not spend sufficient time explaining to the users how to leverage the accuracy and depth of information that the TDABC system could now supply. Team members wished they had spent more time up front with user organizations, explaining the overall concept and value of TDABC.
- The limited availability of machine-readable data for the TDABC model required continual manual interventions. For example, while the group knew the number of servers it had in its distributed business, it had inadequate information about which applications were installed on which servers, and for whom. Nor did it have readily accessible data on the quantity of server time associated with a given application. Detailed data on customer service levels were also unavailable online. CTI planned to automate the capture and validation of source system data so that it could eliminate data errors and minimize manual data entry.
- Business unit managers were focused on the daily demands of their operations and were not accustomed to having access to detailed data on measuring and analyzing their operating results. Planned training sessions had not been conducted to facilitate the users' ability to rapidly report and analyze operating results.

The project team also modified its approach for capturing business requirements. Initially, the team interviewed senior department managers and reviewed numerous monthly operating reports to determine business requirements and better understand reporting needs. However, this process only revealed a limited portion of the actual reporting and analysis needs of operating managers. In the future, the team would use a more interactive approach to identify the underlying role for IT to drive value at business units.

At time of writing, CTI was in the process of aligning the business resources to perform a more extensive deployment of the initial activity-based BPM system built for the GNSO group. CTI has identified the key business areas within its North American operations as the next major segment for the deployment. CTI established three expectations for the managing director of the next units to receive the BPM system. First, the director had to understand the value of the data generated by the system. Second, he or she needed a vision for how the information would be leveraged to better manage the business. Finally, the manager had to be willing to dedicate the resources required to complete the deployment.

The new approach of managing CTI as a "business within a business" is gradually gaining acceptance, as noted by Jeff Nachowitz, Chief Financial Officer of CTI: "Transparency of costs is an elusive concept and in a large, complex organization there will be 'winners and losers' creating a political element to any chargeback methodology. As such, dealing with facts and data that are reliable and recognizable is key in building integrity and trust with internal customers."

SUMMARY

CTI learned that to achieve its intended financial management transformation, the group had to embark on a long-term strategy based on a clear vision of its role and capabilities. To support its vision, CTI needed to better define its financial cost and revenue practices, effectively use benchmarking data to support its pricing decisions, and acquire technology that allowed for detailed cost and revenue data capture and that supported time-driven ABC.

CTI learned that it must involve its users in the development of its Performance Measurement and Management system. Their continued involvement and support would be critical to sustaining the benefits derived. An example was the use of CTI's labor capacity planning and management system, which was originally developed using traditional costing methods. This approach was not widely accepted by operating managers, because it used estimated time as its cost driver. The disciplined TDABC approach replaced the highly subjective time estimates, with specific time drivers and explicit time equations to calculate resource consumption. This made the labor capacity management system within the PMM more credible and relevant and therefore more valuable to operating managers.

CTI learned that to introduce change required the broad-based support of its executive leadership team and a continual open dialogue among designers, users, and financial managers.

## CHAPTER THIRTEEN

GLOBAL INSURANCE COMPANY PRIVATE CLIENT GROUP

Forecasting Key Employee Staffing Levels

IN 2002, GLOBAL INSURANCE COMPANY, one of the world's largest financial services and insurance companies, formed the Private Client Group (PCG) within its Personal Lines Division. PCG's stated business objectives were to meet the insurance needs of high-net-worth clients by providing specialized products and services:

Flexible coverage: insurance products and services flexible enough to meet the unique needs of high-net-worth clients.

Innovative insurance products: a breadth of quality products for a comprehensive approach to risk-management needs. The products included insurance for automobiles, homeowners, excess liability, kidnap and ransom, aviation, watercraft, and private collections of jewelry, art, and other fine collectibles.

Extraordinary services: distinctive risk-management services that would complement the portfolio of insurance products.

Competitive pricing: a benefit offered for all products and services, including high-deductible options that help clients control their risk-management costs.

This chapter was written by Lawrence Maisel (Partner, DecisionVu), David Michie (Consultant, Acorn Systems), and Scott Skorupsky (Consultant, Acorn Systems).

Access to a global leader: harnessing the resources, underwriting acumen, and risk-management expertise of Global Insurance Company, a world leader in insurance and financial services.

The group's offerings were well received by its targeted market, and the group experienced rapid growth from 2001 to 2005 (figure 13-1).

Responding to its explosive revenue and policy growth, PCG had to add professional staff for its major client service functions: underwriting, client care, claim processing, risk-management services, and billing and collections. The group wanted staff who would exceed the expectations of its high-net-worth clients. But PCG faced the tension between delivering premium levels of services and the business reality of delivering profitable

FIGURE 13-1

Global Insurance Private Client Group: Head Count and Revenue, 2001–2005

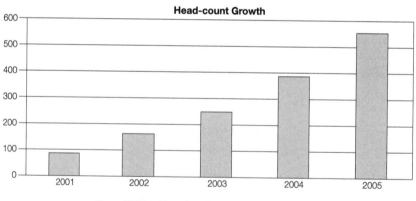

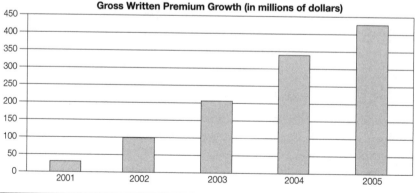

results to the shareholders of its parent, Global Insurance Company. PCG had been following industry practice by estimating staff requirements with a simple, linear, heuristic model that calculated the number of people required per thousand policies issued. This approach was inherently flawed since it did not reflect the skill mix required by its varied policies and geographic regions. Additionally, PCG built its simple staffing models on spreadsheets that were cumbersome, inefficient, and prone to error.

PCG's president and chief financial officer wanted a more analytic staffing model that would work from detailed revenue and policy forecasts to estimate the required staffing levels by skill set for each region and product line. The executives wanted adequate time to hire and train employees to handle the anticipated demand for service in future periods. Ideally, the supply of trained new employees would coincide with the increase in policies and the predictable lags associated with the incidence, filing, and processing of claims by policy type. The forecast had to be region-specific so that fully trained professional staff could be deployed as needed to the different offices throughout North America. Having too few employees available with the requisite skills would lower the quality and service level experienced by clients in a region. Conversely, having available more trained employees than were actually needed would lower the region's profits.

The group's executives also wanted the staffing model to be transparent enough that managers could measure the cost productivity of each core process and compare staff productivity with industry benchmarks. The leaders believed that such a model would highlight opportunities for process improvement.

The idea of developing a better staffing model coincided with a major initiative to enhance PCG's business planning, analysis, and reporting capabilities, including an automated revenue system and a performance management system for brokers. The chief financial officer wanted the staffing model to support critical decision making by examining what-if scenarios based on assumed changes in revenues, product mix, processing policies and procedures, and new technologies and software applications.

As an example of the challenges of developing a staffing prediction model, consider a client filing an automobile collision claim. Figure 13-2 lists the various activities performed to process a new auto collision claim. Each activity requires some quantity of time, expressed in minutes of effort. The overall prediction of claims-processing time includes two contingencies: whether the policy includes auto rental coverage and whether the incident led to a total loss of the insured vehicle.

FIGURE 13-2

Time Equation for Automobile Claim Processing

2.2 New Claim—Auto Collision
   2.2.1 Input to policy insurance system, set
       reserve, send letter (A)
   2.2.2 Notify additional parties (B)
   2.2.3 Auto rental (C)
       2.2.3.1 Reservation
       2.2.3.2 Payment
   2.2.4 Repair assignment (D)
   2.2.5 Estimate review (E)
   2.2.6 Total loss handling (F)
       2.2.6.1 Send paperwork to insured
       2.2.6.2 Receive paperwork and title
       2.2.6.3 Send payment to insured
	Time (in minutes) to process new claim for auto collision
	
	= 35 [A]
	+ 10 × no. of parties involved [B]
	+ 15 + 15 {if auto rental included} [C]
	+ 20 [D]
	+ 10 [E]
	+ 60 + 30 + 60 {if vehicle is total loss} [F]

ORGANIZING THE STAFFING AND RESOURCE MANAGEMENT SYSTEM PROJECT

Global Insurance formed a project team consisting of internal staff, outside consultants from Acorn Systems, and Larry Maisel, from DecisionVu (formerly Paramount Consulting). Maisel, who served as the project manager, had experience and expertise in financial services and was already assisting PCG in the design, development, and implementation of an enterprisewide business planning and analysis (BP&A) system. As project leader, he initiated and facilitated stakeholder meetings, managed the overall execution of project tasks, and reviewed the project results. The project team facilitated the review and validation sessions, documented process flows, defined the model's activities, and developed the model's structures and architecture.

PCG's project team performed the following five tasks in building the staffing system:

- Analyze business processes
- Define the model architecture
- Build the model
- Develop organization roles and responsibilities
- Establish governance and change management

Analyze Business Processes

The project team led a series of review and validation sessions for PCG managers and staff. Before each session, the team documented in detail the processes performed in a particular functional area, region, and line of business and then identified the required skill sets. Figure 13-3 illustrates the degree of complexity resulting from the need to integrate the four dimensions into the staffing and resource capacity model. Resource demands would be examined by region (e.g., East zone), business process or function (e.g., new business quote, bind, issue, renewals, and claims), skill set (e.g., claims adjuster), and line of business (e.g., auto).

Define the Model Architecture

Figure 13-4 summarizes the model architecture selected for the staffing system. Each functional area had its own structure so that it could define and modify its own model assumptions and perform scenario analysis of staffing needs by varying any of the key inputs to the model. Additionally, each functional area assigned a manager to operate and maintain its model structure and update activity time estimates and work standards.

The model architecture shown in figure 13-4 allowed PCG to assign a single coordinator within finance to consolidate the output from each functional area into an overall BP&A system. The system had a single data warehouse for storing business data and results. PCG assigned a single IT administrator to maintain and upgrade the software and applicable IT production environment.

FIGURE 13-3

Four Dimensions of Resources Required: Region, Process, Skill Set, and Line of Business

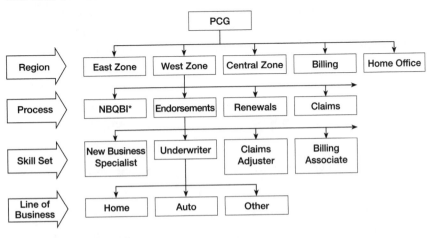

*New business quote, bind and issue

FIGURE 13-4

Model Architecture

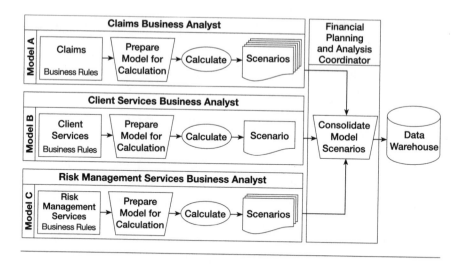

Build the Model

Figure 13-5 highlights important components of the model structure, including operating expenses, activity and tasks, and structural elements such as drivers, factors, and time estimates. The financial system supplied operating expense data. For each activity within each business process, the team developed time equations based on drivers, factors, and specific time estimates to predict the minutes of effort. These estimates enabled the PCG team to assign operating expenses to activities according to the time consumption of specific employee resources. Once the team had built the time equations for the model structure, it could then forecast staff and resource utilization on the basis of forecasted volume and mix, and productivity and business process improvements. Senior managers could then authorize the hiring and training of staff to meet the anticipated demands for quantities of staff by region, skill set, and product line.

Develop Organizational Roles and Responsibilities

The project team defined and developed organizational roles and responsibilities to operate and maintain the staffing system. The team wanted to use existing staff for these positions. It identified six key process steps and assigned each step to an owner in a functional department (figure 13-6). The team developed for each functional role a process flowchart and

FIGURE 13-5

Model Structure

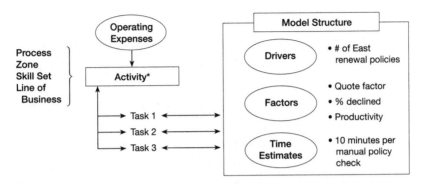

*Activities are where the model collects both time and cost.

FIGURE 13-6

Organizational Roles and Responsibilities

Role	Capture Operating Expenses	Capture Operating Statistics	Update Model	Reporting and Analysis	Model Maintenance	System Maintenance
Financial systems manager	X			X		
Operations analyst		X	X	X	X	
System administrator						X
Time frame	Monthly	Monthly	Monthly	As needed	As needed	Periodically

process narrative as a means to document and train the individuals as-signed to perform these steps.

Establish Governance and Change Management

PCG formed a stakeholder committee consisting of the chief underwriting officer, chief financial officer, chief information officer, executive vice president of risk management and claims, executive vice president of client care, and vice president of performance management. As the executive sponsor for the project, the stakeholder committee established the priorities for the project team.

IMPLEMENTATION PROCESS AND PROJECT TEAM

The initial implementation of the staffing system had two principal phases, design and development. Figure 13-7 identifies the major tasks performed within each phase. At the conclusion of the project, the project team provided a series of training sessions, one-on-one walk-throughs, hands-on usage sessions, and follow-up and on-site support.

The project leader conducted biweekly status and decision meetings with the committee. The committee reviewed and approved critical decisions such as model architecture, activity detail, and time estimates and equations. It provided continual support to the project team and to the PCG staff who would operate and maintain the system in the steady state.

PCG staff members supplemented the dedicated project team. They led one of the most critical tasks—the review analysis and walk-through

FIGURE 13-7

Project Implementation Process

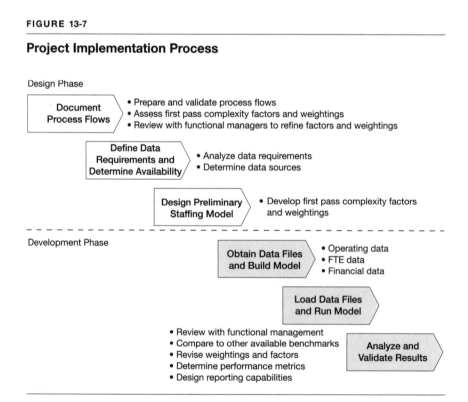

Design Phase

- Document Process Flows
  - Prepare and validate process flows
  - Assess first pass complexity factors and weightings
  - Review with functional managers to refine factors and weightings

- Define Data Requirements and Determine Availability
  - Analyze data requirements
  - Determine data sources

- Design Preliminary Staffing Model
  - Develop first pass complexity factors and weightings

Development Phase

- Obtain Data Files and Build Model
  - Operating data
  - FTE data
  - Financial data

- Load Data Files and Run Model

- Analyze and Validate Results
  - Review with functional management
  - Compare to other available benchmarks
  - Revise weightings and factors
  - Determine performance metrics
  - Design reporting capabilities

sessions. These sessions used an adaptation of the Delphi method to validate activities and tasks, identify key drivers and factors, and estimate the time required to perform each task within an activity. The interactive Delphi process contributed to the reliability and credibility of the time-driven activity-based staffing and resource capacity management system. The team developed similar time equations for claims processing in each product line. Using a forecast of claims by region, the team converted the aggregated forecasted minutes of effort into the number of full-time equivalent people (FTEs) required by region. A further extension involved identifying the skill levels required for each type of claim. Only individuals with specialized skills could properly adjust an auto collision claim or an excess liability claim. Thus, the team designed a model that could predict the requirements for personnel—numbers, skill level, and region—for a forecasted volume and mix of claims.

IMPLEMENTATION CHALLENGES

The team and PCG faced several challenges in implementing the project. Some of the more important challenges include the following:

- Maintaining a consistent vision for the staffing system
- Establishing the right balance between activity detail and an unwieldy model structure
- Integrating with other PCG initiatives, including a salary-forecasting system and several new systems for customer relationship management and BP&A
- Coordinating with various functional groups such as finance, IT, claims processing, and human resources
- Rapid changes and turnover in PCG staff members assigned to operate and maintain the system as well as executive sponsorship

This last barrier, the continual reassignment and turnover of key staff members and executives, introduced significant delays. The project team had to retrain those newly assigned to operate the system. New executives made new requests for system capabilities—requests that PCG staff found difficult to fulfill. The executives had yet to receive sufficient training in the objectives of the staffing system's design. This lack of full appreciation of the capabilities of the system was exacerbated by the ongoing demands of executive management to develop and implement other new systems (e.g., customer relationship management and the redesign of issuance systems).

With too many competing priorities present at the same time, the priority for the design and implementation of the staffing system kept being pushed down.

In the future, executive managers and staff members will resume using the staffing system to plan and forecast staffing and resource needs. The project team will establish a series of process standards to measure staff productivity and utilization against internal management targets and external industry benchmarks. Additionally, the system will allow PCG to calculate unit costs and cost productivity using monthly actual or forecasted operating expenses. These capabilities will help PCG executives better manage staff and cost as well as ensure the effective delivery of superior client services and continued profitability in an environment of rapid growth. Ultimately, these systems and the business information they contain should produce key business benefits, including increases in revenues, improved penetration of broker-agencies, more effective staffing levels and thus better expense and operating ratios, and profitability.

PCG extended the claims-processing staffing model into a comprehensive employee planning model for all its major functions, one that eventually reached more than 75 percent of its staff. The employee-planning model would encompass PCG's eight insurance products, three regional offices and home offices, and numerous functional skill sets—such as underwriting, inspection, and billings—that were involved in designing and issuing client policies and servicing brokers. The model would evaluate activities performed within each major process and function and then convert the activities into a series of subactivities expressed in levels of effort (measured in minutes), just as in the claims-processing examples in figures 13-2 and 13-5.

SUMMARY

The Private Client Group (PCG) of Global Insurance was experiencing explosive growth and wanted an analytic tool to help it plan for future resource capacity, particularly the professional staff that would be required to service the anticipated growth in policies. Hence, unlike the previous case studies, the focus was not on the profitability of existing products, services, and customers.

While limited in scope to forecasting the claims-processing staff, the PCG model at Global Insurance is among the first to deliver on the time-driven activity-based budgeting approach described in chapter 5. The case study describes the straightforward process of building an "as-is" model using a system of time equations to represent the demands for employee staff, by skill set, needed to process claims for each product line. This was not a difficult task, since insurance processes tend to be predictable and standardized. The team then fed the operating model with forecasts of product volume and mix, by region, to produce the specific professional staff capacity that must be supplied, by skill level and region, if the aggressive growth plans were to be realized. Since insurance employees serving sophisticated customers require considerable education and training, the analytic model gave executives adequate time to hire and train employees to meet the anticipated demands in future periods. Although the application was still limited in scope in 2006, the company plans to extend the approach to all PCG processes.

The case illustrates (1) how to integrate a staffing forecast system with the enterprisewide business planning, budgeting, and forecasting system; and (2) how to apply TDABC to budget and forecast resource consumption by skill set, product mix, and region to reflect planned and forecasted levels of revenue and transaction volumes and product mix by region.

## CHAPTER FOURTEEN

JACKSON STATE UNIVERSITY

Introducing Business Concepts into Education

JACKSON STATE UNIVERSITY (JSU), located in Jackson, Mississippi, the capital and largest city of the state, was founded in 1877 as a teachers college to provide a quality education for antebellum black students. The state awarded the college university status in 1977 to recognize its evolution into a research-intensive institution. During the next twenty-five years, JSU experienced steady growth in undergraduate and graduate students. In 2005, it ranked first among historically black institutions in acquiring federal research funds.[1]

Jackson State still faced serious competition for top students from the prominent, historically black colleges in the U.S. South, and from many historically white institutions, now eager to diversify their student population. State and federal funding of postsecondary education was being reduced. The university also faced its own diversity pressures when the Mississippi legislature passed a law requiring JSU to raise its nonblack enrollment to at least 10 percent, a challenging target for this historically black university.

In 2001, Ronald Mason, president of JSU, launched the Millennium Agenda, a strategic planning exercise designed to elevate the university to a new level of efficiency, accountability, and quality. Mason challenged his management team with the following questions:

- Are the *academic enterprise and academic excellence goals* of Jackson State being advanced to the point to make JSU a leading urban institution of higher learning in the [United States]?

- Are a superior set of *support services* from preadmission through and beyond graduation being delivered with effectiveness and efficiency?
- Are Jackson State *resources being managed* in the most effective and efficient manner possible?
- Are the *lives and livelihoods* of the many stakeholders in the external Jackson State community being improved?
- Is the Administration embarking on its initiative in a responsible way?[2]

JSU would have to attract significant new funding to support the hiring of world-class faculty and invest in new facilities and infrastructure. Mason also wanted a new information system to achieve his goals of superior support services, efficiency, and optimal management of resources. He believed that JSU would have to be run like a business if it were to prosper in the challenging twenty-first-century environment.

To lead his management agenda, Mason hired Troy Stovall as senior vice president of finance and operations. Stovall, an experienced consultant from McKinsey & Company with an MBA from Harvard Business School and a master's degree in computer science from Stanford University, had extensive work experience in business analytics, operational improvements, and technology management.

True to his McKinsey background, Stovall framed the challenges faced by Jackson State with a bulleted slide (figure 14-1). The objectives on the left summarized the Millennium Agenda. The key success factors on the right highlighted the need for new information, organizational buy-in, departmental commitment and discipline, and strong process management. Unfortunately, Stovall soon discovered that the university had almost no discretionary money to fund new projects. The university budget was totally consumed by departmental spending and projects. Beyond finding new resources of time and money, Stovall knew that JSU needed a much-improved information system. "We are trying to navigate, manage, and plan blind right now," he explained at a preliminary planning session.

Stovall noted the enormous inertia in state budgets for higher education. Once a given level of funding had been authorized, the recipient could expect to continue to receive it as long as the money had been spent and the recipient continued to ask for that level or more. School deans and department heads continually asked for more money to improve the educational quality and experience of the students and to support the research agenda of faculty. But each department's and school's request was submitted without regard to the competing demands from other univer-

FIGURE 14-1

The Challenges Facing Jackson State University

Objectives

- Restructure academic programs and *budgets*
- Accelerate *technology*
- *Fiscal management* and increase available resources
- Enhance *image*
- Model working/learning *environment*

Key Success Factors

- Better visibility on costs
- *Increased investment* in technology
- Greater *accountability* on resources
- *Discipline* on cost control
- *Raise $$$* to invest in high-profile opportunities/*construction*
- Flawless execution

sity units or the overall budget constraints of the university. During periods of generous funding, the process spawned new courses, new laboratories, new facilities, and new departments. The 6 percent average annual rate of growth in new departments exceeded JSU's revenue growth rate. In just the past few years, nearly thirty new departments, including Epidemiology, Entrepreneurship, and Environmental Health, had been added. Furthermore, a department could add a computer lab with the latest technology to support project work, with the cost of the lab supported by general university funds, not the department's budget.

Stovall noted an alarming trend of the decreasing number of students per department. The increase in number of departments and classes had outpaced the growth in the number of students. Similar increases had occurred in JSU's administrative and auxiliary areas.

A major driver of JSU's spending was the increased use of information technology in academic and administrative departments. Students were enrolling, learning, sharing, downloading course materials, conducting research, and even attending lectures online. JSU had responded to this increased demand by investing in expensive information technology infrastructure and support. To gain some economies of scale, JSU, like many other educational institutions, had established a centralized IT department and treated it as a separate cost center, with its own budget. The IT department's costs, however, were not assigned to user departments and schools. Naturally, with little accountability for costs, departments demanded more and more IT support and services, and IT spending continually increased. The IT department met the demands from academic and administrative departments with no signals or feedback about the value of the services it provided.

Mason's team clearly saw the need for change. Jackson State could not compete under its current financial duress. Processes had to be made more efficient, and resources had to be redeployed if funds were to become available for the Millennium Agenda and future growth. The president considered it dangerous to rely solely on federal and state funding for new initiatives. And annual tuition could not rise fast enough to make up the difference. With these limitations in mind, Mason and Stovall set a target of identifying $5 million to $10 million in real cost-savings opportunities across the university, an ambitious goal for a school with a $120 million budget.

BUILDING THE TIME-DRIVEN ABC MODEL

In his previous business life, Stovall had become familiar with Activity-Based Costing for tracing costs and analyzing opportunities for improvement in the telecommunications industry. But he wondered how the approach would be accepted at Jackson State, where academics would probably be reluctant to participate in surveys of how they spent their time and were certainly not accustomed to being held accountable for their efforts.

Stovall formed an ABC project team of internal staff—including finance, IT, and operations—and external consultants. The external consultants, from Acorn Systems, educated and guided the team about building a Time-Driven ABC model. Senior management at Jackson State provided access to key employees and data systems. Student analysts gathered the needed information. Given the tight academic schedule, most team members worked only two days per week on the project. While most did not have accounting backgrounds, the team members quickly learned the fundamentals needed to build the model.

Early Challenges

Implementing a cost model for the university posed several challenges. Academic departments enjoy significant autonomy. Having outside consultants model and monitor their cost and performance was likely to create waves. Also, few staff had private sector experience; most were unfamiliar with even the basics of a costing model. Universities use budgets to control departmental spending, but rarely attempt to link their spending to the outputs they produce. The staff was also unfamiliar with the basic data available from the school's general ledger and accounting system.

The executive team decided to go slowly, with a phased approach. In Phase 1, the project team would establish feasibility and impact, validate the effort, and set the direction. If a pilot study did not reveal significant opportunities for cost savings, the project could be terminated at that point. Phase 2 would enable the university to attack noncontroversial opportunities in administrative departments, leaving the analysis of academic departments for Phase 3. Figure 14-2 shows the nine-month project plan developed for Phase 2.

Many team members were frustrated about the delay in addressing the most likely source for large cost improvements in the academic departments. The project team had been briefed by James Johnson, economic model manager for Indiana University, who related his experiences in implementing ABC at his school, "Most of the value for ABC is with the academic departments. The problem is that these are extremely difficult to model. And you are not likely to get a lot of cooperation from professors and department staff as to where they spend their time." The JSU team believed that the time-driven approach would avoid some of these difficulties by relying less on interviews and surveys. TDABC would work from transaction data available directly from university databases.

FIGURE 14-2

Project Plan

Phase 2 Work

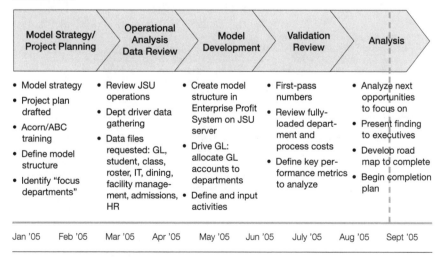

Model Strategy/ Project Planning	Operational Analysis Data Review	Model Development	Validation Review	Analysis
• Model strategy	• Review JSU operations	• Create model structure in Enterprise Profit System on JSU server	• First-pass numbers	• Analyze next opportunities to focus on
• Project plan drafted	• Dept driver data gathering	• Drive GL: allocate GL accounts to departments	• Review fully-loaded department and process costs	• Present finding to executives
• Acorn/ABC training	• Data files requested: GL, student, class, roster, IT, dining, facility management, admissions, HR	• Define and input activities	• Define key performance metrics to analyze	• Develop road map to complete
• Define model structure				• Begin completion plan
• Identify "focus departments"				

Jan '05   Feb '05   Mar '05   Apr '05   May '05   Jun '05   July '05   Aug '05   Sept '05

IMPLEMENTATION

By early 2006, JSU had just completed Phase 2 and was embarking on pilot runs for Phase 3. We will describe the project through Phase 2 and the anticipated work plan for the next phase.

The project started by assigning costs accumulated in the university's general ledger (GL in the figure) to the core academic, administrative, and auxiliary departments. Core departments were those that directly touched the ultimate cost objects, the students.

Administrative and auxiliary departments, such as legal and human resources, provided infrastructure and support for the academic units and students (figure 14-3), and the costs of these departments also needed to be driven down to academic units and their students.

As an example of an early run, figure 14-4 shows the top ten high-cost academic departments. The project team was surprised to see how tracing all of a department's support costs caused the total department cost to be much higher than its direct general-ledger assignment. For example, one department, 528, consumed large quantities of space, IT support, housekeeping, and security and safety assistance. Its total cost per student taught was nine times higher than its direct faculty costs.

Stovall examined closely the costs of the dining activity. Dining, supposedly a stand-alone business, was budgeted to operate at a small profit, which could be used to fund other parts of the university. But the Dining

FIGURE 14-3

Model-Building Process for JSU

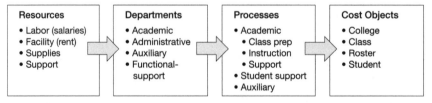

Resources	Departments	Processes	Cost Objects
• Labor (salaries) • Facility (rent) • Supplies • Support	• Academic • Administrative • Auxiliary • Functional-support	• Academic • Class prep • Instruction • Support • Student support • Auxiliary	• College • Class • Roster • Student

- *Departmentalize GL.* 8,000 accounts have been driven to 230 core and 100 support departments
- Shared expenses (e.g., rent, supplies) are departmentalized based on known data (e.g., square footage, # employees, # terminals)

- Drive fully loaded department expense to the *department* (easy because usually a department has only one process)
- Study the process and build the *time-based algorithm* (over 400 process algorithms)

- Drive fully loaded process expense to the appropriate cost objects (easy because time-driven model pulls directly from *class roster and student files* to populate its algorithms)
- More accurate because cost information is built from the bottom up

| Phase 1 | 3,000 accounts | 130+ departments | 170 processes | 0 cost objects |
| Phase 2 | 8,000 accounts | 300+ departments | 400 processes | 3 cost objects |

FIGURE 14-4

High-Cost Departments at JSU

ID	GL Amount In ($)	Support Amount In ($)	Total Amount In ($)	Outgoing Amount ($)	$/Student
528	491,610	3,827,383	4,318,993	4,318,993	414
537	1,978,277	2,087,281	4,065,559	4,065,559	390
534	427,550	3,550,368	3,977,918	3,977,918	382
399	158,695	2,995,672	3,154,367	3,154,367	302
525	835,020	2,017,200	2,852,220	2,852,220	273
531	499,837	1,952,535	2,452,373	2,452,373	235
426	585,788	1,758,207	2,343,995	2,343,995	225
543	229,089	1,813,420	2,042,510	2,042,510	196
489	446,043	1,588,514	2,034,557	2,034,557	195
420	967,914	850,096	1,818,010	1,818,010	174

Department operated within university buildings that required maintenance. The IT Department tracked food purchases and sales, and the Finance Department analyzed Dining's budgets and actual financial performance. Figure 14-5 presents a sample calculation done by the ABC project team to estimate the full cost of serving a meal. The calculation revealed that Dining operated at a considerable deficit.

The analysis clearly identified that restoring Dining to breakeven operations would generate considerable savings to the university. Stovall commented, "The losses in Dining were a big surprise to us. Knowing the truth is the first step to identifying the opportunity."

Once all the costs had been accumulated in the departments, the project team planned to drive costs to five core processes for each academic department:

- Research grant and development
- Class preparation
- Instruction
- Student support
- Academic improvement

Since the time spent by the department varied for each of these processes, this cost assignment required a TDABC approach if it were to be done correctly.

FIGURE 14-5

Opportunities for Cost Savings at Dining Hall

	Price[a]	Cost[b]	Margin	Semester Profit[c]
Industry	$5.00	$4.00	$1.00	$149,826
JSU (GL costing method)	$5.00	$13.20	($8.20)	($1,228,573)
Difference	—	($9.20)	($9.20)	($1,378,399)
JSU (TDABC method)	$5.00	$27.14	($22.14)	($3,317,148)
Difference	—	($23.14)	($23.14)	($3,466,974)

Average price per meal that universities charge students is just under $5.00. Using the general-ledger (GL) cost of the dining department and the number of meals prepared, JSU's cost per meal is $13.20. Using the fully loaded department cost (from the TDABC model) and the number of meals prepared, JSU's cost per meal is $27.14.

[a]Assuming that JSU's price per meal is close to the industry average.
[b]Assuming an industry gross margin of 20 percent.
[c]Assuming 149,826 meals prepared per semester.

Once the full expenses had been accumulated in each academic process, the team would study each departmental process to determine the activity steps, the key drivers, and the average time spent per step and driver. Figure 14-6 displays an example of a time equation for teaching an accounting course.

Getting the data for the model proved to be difficult. Jackson State had just installed a new general-ledger system, and the IT people were still getting familiar with how to access and export data elements. After waiting several months without receiving the data, the external consultants became more proactive and worked directly with IT personnel to gather the data.

PROPOSED ACTIONS

Once the initial runs of the model had been validated, the project team, working with Stovall, made several observations and identified several near-term actions for cost reduction.

1. *Improve capacity utilization across departments.* The team wanted to identify and eliminate unused capacity—in people and facilities—throughout the university. The challenge was to determine how much capacity actually existed and how it was being used, department by department. On their own initiative, departments

FIGURE 14-6

Example Time Equation at JSU

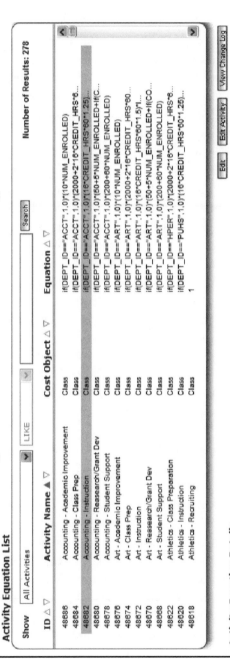

JSU Costing Model: Acorn's Time-driven Algorithms

Activity Equation List

Show [All Activities] [▶] [LIKE] [▶] [_____] [Search]   Number of Results: 278

ID △▽	Activity Name ▲▽	Cost Object △▽	Equation △▽
48686	Accounting - Academic Improvement	Class	if(DEPT_ID=="ACCT",1.0)*(10*NUM_ENROLLED)
48684	Accounting - Class Prep	Class	if(DEPT_ID=="ACCT",1.0)*(2000+2*16*CREDIT_HRS*6...
48682	Accounting - Instruction	Class	if(DEPT_ID=="ACCT",1.0)*(16*CREDIT_HRS*60*1.25)...
48680	Accounting - Reasearch/Grant Dev	Class	if(DEPT_ID=="ACCT",1.0)*(50+5*NUM_ENROLLED+if(C...
48678	Accounting - Student Support	Class	if(DEPT_ID=="ACCT",1.0)*(200+60*NUM_ENROLLED)
48676	Art - Academic Improvement	Class	if(DEPT_ID=="ART",1.0)*(10*NUM_ENROLLED)
48674	Art - Class Prep	Class	if(DEPT_ID=="ART",1.0)*(2000+2*16*CREDIT_HRS*60...
48672	Art - Instruction	Class	if(DEPT_ID=="ART",1.0)*(16*CREDIT_HRS*60*1.5)*1...
48670	Art - Reasearch/Grant Dev	Class	if(DEPT_ID=="ART",1.0)*(50+5*NUM_ENROLLED+if(CO...
48668	Art - Student Support	Class	if(DEPT_ID=="ART",1.0)*(200+60*NUM_ENROLLED)
48622	Athletics - Class Preparation	Class	if(DEPT_ID=="HPER",1.0)*(2000+2*16*CREDIT_HRS*6...
48620	Athletics - Instruction	Class	if(DEPT_ID=="PUHS",1.0)*(16*CREDIT_HRS*60*1.25)...
48618	Athletics - Recruiting	Class	1

[Edit] [Edit Activity] [View Change Log]

Activity Equation Details

This is a read-only display of the selected activity's equation and a description of the equation. To edit them, click the Edit button above.

Activity Name	Accounting - Instruction	Activity ID	48682
Cost Object	Class		

Description

Equation   if(DEPT_ID=="ACCT",1,0)*(16*CREDIT_HRS*60*1.25)*if(NUM_ENROLLED>20,1,2),1)

These algorithms estimate time spent on an activity (e.g. instruction) for a cost object (e.g. class). This enables us to drive a specific department's instruction cost to a particular class, and then on to specific students

were unlikely to volunteer when they had excess capacity. The TDABC model, which reflected time spent on core activities such as research, grant development, class preparation, and instruction, would enable the team to determine each department's under- and overcapacity resources.

2. *Not all academic departments and subjects are equally "profitable."*[3] The ABC project team assigned revenues to each department. Revenues were calculated as the tuition dollars generated by teaching students in courses within the department, plus the research and grant dollars the department produced. The team could then calculate departmental profitability by subtracting the department's direct and TDABC-assigned administrative and support costs.

   JSU would not use the information to shut down unprofitable departments. But the calculation would be shared with deans and department heads to suggest how they could reduce the need for university subsidies. For example, the team suggested that departments could reduce their losses through offering better courses and instruction that attracted more students, generating more academic majors in their unit, and finding ways to lower the per-student cost of instruction. Of course, all contemplated actions must be taken without compromising the fundamental mission of the school for high-quality education and research.

3. *Not all students are equally profitable.* Costs and profits for individual students can also vary considerably. Cost variation occurs in recruiting, tuition differences, housing choice, financial aid status, and choice of coursework. For example, out-of-state students pay higher tuition, but they are also more expensive to recruit and attract. The TDABC model incorporated time equations to capture the costs of recruiting and admitting students, including travel to attract students from out of state.

4. *Not all professors or classes cost the same.* The team observed that while the overall academic processes performed by professors were homogenous across departments, the time professors actually took to perform these tasks varied greatly. New classes required more class preparation than existing courses. Large classes took more faculty time—for counseling and grading—than small classes. Some classes required expensive IT support or laboratory space, while others could be taught in standard, large lecture halls. All the factors that caused variation in faculty time or facility space

would be incorporated into the ABC model's time equations. The estimates would be validated by comparing predicted capacity utilization to available capacity. The team envisioned using the TDABC model to evaluate how grant dollars, space assignment, and support services could be adjusted to support the needs of both faculty and students and to ensure profitability of the programs.

Implementation Barriers

The largest challenge for the TDABC team was data integration. Universities tend to have lower-quality data than their private-sector counterparts. Departmental data on square feet occupied, number of full-time-equivalent faculty and staff, and the quantity and cost of assets, such as laboratory equipment and computer terminals, can be missing, fragmented, or in multiple formats. JSU also lacked information on work orders performed by support departments, such as facilities management. Most of the information existed somewhere in the university, but it was usually incomplete and in varying formats. The overworked IT department could spend weeks or months to acquire the requested data and to get work orders into a compatible format.

The attention of senior leadership also varied during the course of the project. Crises often erupted that demanded all the time of President Mason and his team until they were resolved. These distractions slowed down the project since implementing the TDABC approach requires senior-level support to build accurate models and gain access to relevant data. The project team eventually shifted its focus away from the IT department, where senior managers lacked interest and commitment, and the dining hall operation, where comprehensive data were lacking. The team concentrated on the Facilities Management Department, where managers had more interest and time to support the effort.

Finally, building an enterprisewide model for the entire university can be extremely challenging when not all parts are built in unison. Because of the phased approach, certain parts of the model would be ready quickly. Yet, the time-driven model is hungry for all the data from the start (e.g., entire general ledgers, class roster file, student file, and work order files). The team faced two choices: build the entire model, but only turn on certain parts, or build a number of separate minimodels and integrate the results later. The team decided to do the first because there is still value in having a view into the impact on certain departments (e.g., IT) before an enterprise model had been fully completed.

EARLY VALUE CAPTURE

After completing Phase 2, the project team selected three departments within the university's shared-services group for immediate attention. For each of the three departments, the TDABC model identified services or activities whose costs were much higher than expected. The team traced the cause of the higher costs to the academic or administrative departments that were making unusually high demands for the department's services. Stovall began a process to set specific service levels for each of the three support departments and manage the service expectations for consuming departments. This initial value-capture exercise became one of the project's first wins. Both service providers and receivers now had a clear view of the cost to supply a given service and could internalize this cost in their decisions for the quantity and quality of service demanded.

Stovall emphasized from the beginning of the TDABC project that "understanding true cost analytics and resource allocation optimization at Jackson State needs to be a journey, not a destination." Much like its peer universities, JSU will always face the daunting challenge of managing a complex organization with increasing operating costs and shrinking public funds to supplement its budget. TDABC analytics will become embedded in the school's management approach.

SUMMARY

The Jackson State University case features the application of TDABC in a nonprofit setting. While nonprofits may not seem to need a system to measure and manage customer profitability, in fact many nonprofits, including JSU, are extremely complex enterprises. A research university has multiple product lines (e.g., arts, humanities, engineering, sciences, and business), multiple services (research, teaching, administrative support), and multiple client types (e.g., a physics major requires very different resources from an early-child-education major). Like many of the featured private-sector case studies, JSU had been experiencing significant growth, but its growth rate of costs exceeded that for revenues (from tuition, state support, and federal research grants). The JSU president was willing to make tough decisions, but he recognized the need to understand the institution's true cost drivers before attempting the challenge of redirecting an institution as resistant to change as a university.

JSU, like Compton Financial and ATB Financial, focused initially on its IT costs since the existing cost system gave operating and support departments no visibility or accountability for the cost of IT resources they were demanding and using. The system initially drove costs to support units, deferring the more controversial full assignment of costs to academic units to a subsequent phase. The project delivered an early win when it learned that Dining, previously thought to be operating at a small profit, was actually losing substantial amounts of money. The administration could act quickly to eliminate the losses in this noncore department and at least restore it to breakeven so that it would not drain resources that could be better spent in academic departments.

The JSU implementation, while still in progress in 2006, teaches us that operations in educational institutions, indeed in many large, complex nonprofits, are not significantly different from those in the private sector. Large nonprofits need to understand the drivers that create demands for their expensive indirect and support resources. These institutions have similar opportunities for assigning accountability for resource spending, cost savings, and setting client service levels. Understanding the true cost-to-serve by university departments greatly improves visibility into opportunities for process reengineering, resource reallocation, and capacity planning based on actual and affordable needs. As CEOs of universities and other nonprofits become more publicly accountable for their costs and performance, having a Time-Driven ABC model of their resource demands provides them with a powerful tool for guiding expansion plans, determining service levels, and managing budgets.

NOTES

1. Troy Stovall (Senior Vice President, Jackson State University) and Snehal Talati (ABC Engagement Manager, Acorn Systems) contributed to this chapter.
2. Ronald Mason, memo to Millennium Agenda Committee, Jackson State University, October 2003.
3. Economic profit is defined as inflow (tuition fees plus grants) minus outflow (department direct costs plus department's portion of shared services).

TRANSFORMING UNPROFITABLE CUSTOMERS

Acting on the profitability information from a Time-Driven ABC model is the same as from a conventional ABC model. Both models give managers a better picture about process costs and the cost and profitability of individual products and customers. As we argue in this book, however, the TDABC approach generates more accurate data at lower cost. In this appendix, we review the types of actions managers take on the basis of the output from their ABC models. Specifically, we focus on how to improve customer profitability, a common application for TDABC.

We find that the single best picture from an ABC model is the "whale curve" of cumulative customer (or product) profitability (figure A-1). The whale curve ranks products and customers from the most profitable on the left side of the horizontal x-axis, to the least profitable, or largest loss, on the right side. The vertical axis, or y-axis, displays the cumulative profitability of the products or customers.

Most empirical phenomena, including sales, follow the famous Pareto 20-80 rule: 20 percent of the products or customers provide 80 percent of the sales. But the whale curve for cumulative profitability violates Pareto's rule. Typically, the most profitable 20 percent of customers generate between 150 and 300 percent of total profits. The middle 70 percent break even, and the least profitable 10 percent of customers can lose 50 to 200 percent of total profits, leaving the company with its 100 percent of total profits.

Often, some of the largest customers turn out to be the most unprofitable, since a company cannot lose large amounts of money with small

FIGURE A-1

Cumulative Customer Profitability (Whale Curve)

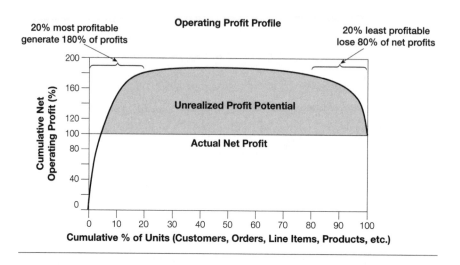

customers. A company doesn't do enough business with a small customer to incur large (absolute) losses. Only a large customer, working in a particularly perverse way, can incur large losses. Large customers tend to be either the most profitable or the least profitable in the entire customer base. It's unusual for a large customer to be in the middle of the total profitability rankings.

For service companies, customer profitability is far more important than product profitability because the costs of providing a service product are usually determined by customer behavior. Take the example of a standard product like a checking account. One customer may make very few deposits, withdrawals, balance inquiries, and service requests and may use only electronic channels—ATMs and the Internet. Such a customer imposes low demands on the bank's resources. A second customer, however, may manage a checking account balance very closely, keeping only the minimum amount on hand and making many in-person branch withdrawals and deposits. This customer's checking account may be highly unprofitable under current pricing arrangements. Service companies need to identify the differential profitability of individual customers, even those using standard products. In a bank, unlike the situation in a manufacturing company, the customer almost completely determines the quantity of demands for the organization's operating activities. For this reason, the variation in demand for a bank's organizational resources is much more customer-driven than product-driven. Customer balances or sales volume are poor proxies for profitability. Small-balance customers can be quite profitable, and large-balance customers can be highly unprofitable. To complete the picture, financial service companies need to integrate information about the transfer price of funds and the cost of risk (e.g., loan loss provisions and reserves, and risk-adjusted cost of equity) when calculating individual customer profitability.

Many service companies, such as financial institutions and telecommunication companies, offer a full line of products or services to customers. Often an entry product, such as a checking account or a commercial loan, operates at breakeven or loss levels. The product and its pricing are justified as a strategic product, since the product enables the institution to leverage the customer relationship by selling financial products and services that are more profitable. (When companies call a product strategic, it is a sure sign that the product is unprofitable.) But many companies lack the ability to track all the services used by individual customers. To manage the complete customer relationship, the company must know the profitability of each product or service used by an individual customer, and the total profitability of the relationship, which is the sum of the profits or losses on each product used by the customer.

TRANSFORMING CUSTOMER RELATIONSHIPS

Companies have three primary levers for transforming breakeven and loss customer relationships into profitable ones: improve processes, modify customer relationships, and reprice services.[1]

Process Improvement

Suppliers first look internally to see where they can improve their own processes to lower the costs to serve. If most customers are migrating to smaller order sizes, companies should strive to reduce batch-related costs, such as setup and order handling, so that customer preferences can be accommodated at lower cost, without a rise in overall prices. Electronic systems greatly lower the cost of processing large quantities of small orders. If customers like variety, manufacturing companies can introduce modular designs and use IT to enhance the linkages from design to manufacturing so that greater variety and customization can be offered without cost penalties.

Customer Relationship Management

Before taking any action with unprofitable customers, companies should expand the customer profitability measurement to encompass all the relationships that each customer has with the company. In a bank, for example, a customer may have, in addition to a standard checking account, a savings account, a credit card, a mortgage, and a personal loan. Bank managers need to understand the profitability of the total relationship between the bank and its customer and act on the total relationship profitability, not just the profitability with a single product. While such total profitability calculations were difficult and expensive with legacy computer systems, modern systems of enterprise resource planning and customer relationship management can identify and link all customer relationships. For a commercial bank, a standard corporate loan may break even or lose money (after an appropriate risk-adjusted cost of capital is applied). The loan, however, is the entry-level product that establishes a relationship between the bank and its customer. The bank may make enough profit on other banking relationships, such as trust services, corporate money management, and investment and merchant banking services, to produce a highly profitable total relationship. But a marginal borrower who uses no other commercial or merchant banking services is a prime candidate for repricing, aggressive marketing activities, or deletion (if all other attempts to generate a profitable relationship fail).

At one commercial bank, the loan officer tried to "fire" an unprofitable customer, who had only a single banking relationship and did not use its banking facility intensively. The officer shared the economics of the unprofitable relationship with the customer and suggested that it seek other financial institutions for its borrowing needs. The customer, however, wanted to retain its relationship with the bank and offered to find ways to increase the bank's profitability on this account. The CFO of the customer company offered to travel to New York for periodic meetings, rather than have the loan officer visit its Midwestern headquarters. He also offered to do more business with the bank so that the relationship could be transformed into a profitable one for the bank.

Menu-Based Pricing

The real opportunity for mediating conflicts between suppliers and customers, and for transforming unprofitable to profitable relationships, arises from pricing individual orders and transactions. Customized pricing policies should be at the heart of any strategy to manage customer profitability. When companies know the actual cost of providing their services, they can establish prices that motivate more efficient behavior of both suppliers and customers, mediate the demand for services between suppliers and customers, and transform unprofitable relationships into profitable ones. Valid cost and pricing information motivates customers to shift their ordering, shipping, and distribution patterns in ways that lower total value-chain costs, to the benefit of both suppliers and customers.

Prices of special services can be set simply to recover the cost-to-serve, allowing the customer to choose the menu of services it wishes and allowing the supplier to recover the cost of serving. Alternatively, the supplier may choose to earn a margin on special services—an inherent feature of becoming a differentiated supplier. The supplier would then price its specialized services above the costs of providing the service. For example, the supplier could price the service up to the point of the costs saved or costs avoided by the customer from the special service. Suppliers could even try to estimate the value created (revenue enhancements) from the special service and price up to that created value. Some companies estimate a second TDABC model—of their customers' internal costs and profits—to be explicit about how far above this floor the price can be and still provide a net benefit to the customer. In the consumer packaged goods industry, collaboration on cost-to-serve pricing has been used by leading companies such as Procter & Gamble. In addition to covering their internal costs with a margin, the companies share cost savings with their customers.

Suppliers that are first to exploit the opportunities for activity-based pricing gain clear short-term advantages, as indicated by the above examples. They recover costs that their competitors are absorbing, and change customers' behavior to lower the cost of serving them. Moreover, they can gain additional market share by offering lower prices to customers who wish just the basic level of services, and shed customers that are not willing to change their behavior to allow a minimum level of supplier profitability.

NOTE

1. For additional discussion of the actions to transform unprofitable customer relationships into profitable ones, see R. S. Kaplan and R. Cooper, *Cost & Effect: Using Integrated Cost Systems to Drive Profitability and Performance* (Boston: Harvard Business School Press, 1998), 183–201, and R. S. Kaplan and V. G. Narayanan, "Measuring and Managing Customer Profitability," *Journal of Cost Management* (September–October 2001): 5–15.

FREQUENTLY ASKED QUESTIONS

1. Is implementing Time-Driven Activity-Based Costing (TDABC) worthwhile, even for a small company, with few departments and transactions?
In our experience, all organizations benefit from the discipline of building a TDABC model. But some companies benefit more than others. What governs the fit has less to do with company size than with other factors, such as these:

- *Standardization of processes:* The more repeatable the process, the easier it is to model with a time equation.
- *Diversity of products and customers:* If you have only a few products or customers, and they are relatively similar to each other, then the accuracy of a standard cost system or conventional ABC may be sufficient. If, however, you have high- and low-volume products, standard and custom products, and both simple-to-serve customers and complex ones, then the benefits of a more accurate costing model more than justify its cost.
- *Large and growing overhead costs:* You can get a clear sign of when even a small enterprise could benefit from a TDABC model by examining the magnitude and trend of your company's overhead costs. Without an accurate costing model, even small companies tend to add too many variations to their product and service offerings and accommodate too many special customer requests, all of which lead to escalating support resources. The Sanac case study in the book is a good example of how a small, seemingly simple

business introduced far too much complexity into its operations prior to the adoption of a TDABC model.

- *Data availability:* A TDABC model requires transactional data. If such data are not readily available or easily retrievable, then building a time-driven model could be expensive.

2. With the incorporation of more process characteristics and drivers into the model, it seems as if TDABC is even more complicated than the conventional approach. How can a TDABC model be simpler than conventional ABC?

Time equations should be understandable and grounded in actual operations. We do not recommend building time equations with drivers that are not already easily available. Nor do we recommend building equations for processes that operational personnel cannot describe in simple terms. Also, not all process equations require the same rigor to build. Low-cost or low-variability processes are addressed with single time estimates, not a complex equation. The TDABC modeler expands a time equation as needed and will do so only when the additional drivers are readily available. As discussed in chapter 4, most models are fed by standard files from a company's enterprise resource planning (ERP) or equivalent system. Adding drivers to an equation can leverage the same data file. Thus, the TDABC achieves its simplicity by building time equations based on observable processes, using existing databases and systems, and avoiding the costly step, required by conventional ABC, of interviewing and surveying employees about their time distributions.

Some complexity from a TDABC model comes from interpreting and acting on the output. Coca-Cola Belgium now measures profitability for all its 425,000 deliveries. The Comcast Philadelphia Metro Region has customer profitability data for all its 6 million customers. Managers must be prepared to act on these more granular data if the benefits from a TDABC model are to be captured.

3. How can we leverage our existing ABC system?

Many companies' existing ABC models already define core processes and activity structures. The companies have learned how to drive general ledger expenses to departments and processes. The previous ABC implementations also gave good insight about the identity and data source of key activity drivers, information that became the inputs to the time equations. This experience facilitated a more rapid rollout to an enterprisewide TDABC model.

4. Do existing ERP systems have the capability to perform TDABC?

Most leading ERP systems offer modules or functionality to perform conventional ABC. By 2006, we had not yet seen any ERP system that could handle a fully functional TDABC model. An ERP-based TDABC system would need to incorporate process modeling and time equations of the type described in chapter 2 and in the Kemps and Sanac case studies in chapters 8 and 9. Such a system would also need the ability to accept transactional data feeds. Currently, companies prefer to have dedicated TDABC software sit on top of (i.e., be fed by) their ERP systems. This provides a simpler and more robust application.

5. What if my company does not have an ERP system?

We use the term *ERP* to refer to any computer-based management information system that tracks transaction information. Transaction information is often available even in homegrown legacy systems and off-the-shelf accounting packages like Peachtree or Quickbooks. Data can also come from spreadsheet packages like Microsoft Excel and Lotus 1-2-3. The basic requirement for a TDABC model is a system that tracks transaction data that can be exported into a time equation.

If a company does not have a convenient source for transaction data, building a time-driven model may be difficult. Simplified TDABC models can be constructed for one-time analytical purposes, but rolling such models out on a wider scale may prove cumbersome if a company does not have some form of ERP system to capture and export transaction data.

6. What if our company is about to implement a new ERP system? Should we wait until the new system is up and running before we install a TDABC model?

The implementation teams for both projects should communicate with each other. TDABC models require specific types of data, so its implementation team needs to communicate these requirements to the ERP implementation team as early as possible. It is much easier to supply the capability for specialized data fields and capture before an ERP is installed than afterward. If the ERP is to be completed in the distant future, the TDABC team can conduct a quick pilot to identify high-cost and inefficient processes and to get a quick win by delivering near-term results. Tree of Life, a large food distributor, worked with IBM Global Services to build an "as-is" TDABC model that reflected the company's current processes. This model was then fed actual transaction data to verify that the "as-is" model reconciled operationally and financially. The team identified several areas in which large improvement opportunities existed, and it developed a framework for a proposed "to-be" TDABC model. The proposed model had new requirements not originally considered in the choice of ERP modules.

7. What advice do you have on the selection of the pilot location?

If your company has many locations, we recommend selecting a facility whose general manager is enthusiastic about the potential benefits from a TDABC model. The recommended pilot facility should also have many processes that are common to other facilities. TW Metals opted to conduct a pilot in five facilities in the Ohio region. The regional manager was highly respected and understood the need for the TDABC project, and the region's facilities encompassed all the major processes performed at the forty other locations. Both conditions led to a successful pilot, which subsequently facilitated a rapid, strongly endorsed rollout to the entire company.

If your company does not require a rollout strategy, choose a pilot location that has the most visible opportunity for demonstrating impact and success. At Compton Financial (disguised), management perceived that the IT Department would benefit greatly from an analysis of capacity utilization (chapter 10), and the initial project was done there.

8. Who in the organization needs to understand how to build a time equation?

The TDABC team leader has to be able to build a time equation. The individual or individuals responsible for maintaining the model as it goes forward also should have this capability. Typically, these individuals reside in the finance organization. We also recommend that managers of core departments and processes where time equation accuracy is particularly important understand time equation construction.

9. How are support departments' processes handled?

The accounts receivable example in chapter 3 illustrates how time equations can be constructed for support departments. As another example, consider the time spent by an HR department processing paperwork for new employees. Once the average time per new employee has been estimated, the HR resource costs associated with this process can be driven to departments according to the number of new hires in each department. Similar time equations can be estimated for all HR processes. Thus, the total cost of this department can be assigned based on actual work performed for the company's various operating units. This will provide a more accurate and transparent assignment of HR costs than simply allocating HR costs according to the head count in each operating department.

10. Should a TDABC model reflect the variation in practical capacity (number of minutes per period) and time performance among individual employees?

Variation can exist among employees performing the same process. We don't want such variation to influence product and customer costs. We recommend using department or process averages when measuring practical capacity and the parameters in time equations. Identifying variation due to employees who are less well trained or less skilled is important for operational improvements, but should not influence the costs used to manage products and customers. An added benefit of our recommendation is obviating the need to track individual employee availability and performance for strategic costing purposes.

11. How is waste quantified in TDABC?

The TDABC model systematically tracks and quantifies the amount of capacity supplied but not used for processing transactions, making and delivering products, and serving customers. The TDABC practitioner can also often identify waste by benchmarking (chapter 7) and examining the time equations for obvious inefficiencies in processes. As the project team conducts interviews to estimate the parameters for a time equation, as described in chapter 4, it can categorize process steps as value-added or non-value-added. The time and hence cost associated with non-value-added process steps then become targets for lean management and process improvement methodologies.

12. How does TDABC enhance process improvements beyond those identified by lean management?

Both TDABC and lean management identify process inefficiencies and waste (see chapter 7). The TDABC model extends lean management by calculating total process costs, which helps set priorities for process improvement efforts. Knowing the existing cost of inefficiencies also justifies any front-end investments that may be required to reduce or eliminate non-value-added work. Without the guidance from an accurate cost model, lean-management work groups might focus on processes whose improvement will not contribute much to total cost reduction.

By incorporating actual transaction data, TDABC calculates the capacity utilization for all processes and departments, thereby revealing an additional source of waste: the consistent supply of resources in excess of actual needs. The capacity utilization data also enable process cost benchmarks to be calculated according to actual capacity utilized, practical capacity, and theoretical capacity.

13. How is the TDABC model for supply-chain analysis different from conventional ABC?

A conventional ABC model can provide only process cost-rate data, such as cost per shipment or cost per receipt. TDABC also provides these aggregate cost rates, but additionally gives the detail behind the drivers of these costs so that a supply-chain partner can work to lower process time and cost. For example, a components supplier learned that its customers were spending extra inspection time (and cost) when they received the supplier's products because of chronic quality problems. The company realized that it could help its customers by improving its own quality assurance processes before shipping the product.

Another company, Daily Provisions, a grocery distributor, identified high costs in its delivery process to customers. A principal driver was its current internal redistribution process, which moved products from a central warehouse to eleven local distribution centers prior to shipping to customers. Most competitors were servicing the region from one warehouse, not eleven. The TDABC team realized that it would be suicidal to ask customers to change their delivery schedules to compensate for Daily Provisions' internal delivery inefficiencies. Daily Provisions set up a task force to streamline its internal product movement to reduce the time and cost of getting product to customers in this region.

14. How do we know which supply-chain partners to collaborate with?

Supply-chain collaboration using TDABC can be rewarding, but also time-consuming. It requires both the supplier and its customer to become knowledgeable about the methodology and to be willing to invest in their own process modeling. Such collaboration is easiest with supply-chain partners that already have experience with ABC. Typically, these are larger companies and those with which you currently have or hope to develop a long-term strategic relationship. Pioneer Controls (disguised), an industrial controls distributor, chose to partner with Momentum Products, Inc. (disguised), an $8 billion company with significant ABC experience. Furthermore, Momentum Products, Inc. was launching an ABC initiative with its suppliers to uncover process improvement opportunities. While Momentum Products was not necessarily familiar with TDABC, the company understood the value of sharing accurate cost information with its customers.

15. Can time-driven benchmarking be performed without constructing a companywide TDABC model?

Yes, a company can evaluate and understand the process steps and the time component for each step without preparing a comprehensive enterprise model. Time equations can be prepared for selected processes that are common for several facilities. This exercise will highlight best and worst practices for those processes and facilities and will promote the transfer of best practices. An enterprisewide TDABC model, driven by transaction data, provides benefits beyond process improvement opportunities. Such a model calculates capacity utilization and complete product and customer profitability. This additional information facilitates decisions that generate significantly more opportunities for profitability improvements.

INDEX

Jones, Daniel, 147

Kaplan, R. S., 20, 21, 40, 105, 163, 249
Kemps LLC, 36, 69, 159
  complications of ABC analysis at,
    159–160
  customer relationships at, 161–162
  evolution of, 152
  history of, 151
  milk cooler line loading time equation,
    157–158
  order and pick time equation, 155–157
  process improvements at, 160
  product mix at, 160–161
  standard cost analysis of, 152–154
  TDABC analysis of, 154–159
  warehouse time equation, 158–159
Kerr, Greg, 161
Kunkel, Paul, xiv, 155, 159

lean management
  brainstorming stage in, 126
  data collection and process analysis in,
    124, 129
  implementation stage in, 126–127
  philosophy of, 123–124
  principles of, 124–129
  stages of, 124
  and TDABC, 128–129, 130, 132–133,
    255–256
Lean Six Sigma, 80, 124
  integrated with TDABC, 130, 132
  sample process map for, 131
Lee, Sehyung, 208
letters of intent, 108, 121
Levant, Y., 178
Lewis-Goetz, 13, 85–86

Maisel, Lawrence, xiii, 21, 195, 219, 222
Mason, Ronald, 231, 232, 234, 241, 243
Max, Mitchell, xiii, 132, 148, 195, 208
McKillop, Jim, xiv, 198, 199, 200, 207
McPherson, J., 148
menu-based pricing, 248–249
mergers and acquisitions
  fast-track profit modeling for, 107–120
  results of, 120
  strategy implementation for, 119–120

Michie, David, 219
Millane, Sean, 195
Miscelli, Aldo, 79
Modigliani, F., 65
Moreels, Kris, xiii, 165

Nachowitz, Jeff, 33, 217
Narayanan, V. G., 249
Nationwide Metals case study, 142–145
  TDABC implementation in, 142, 144
Norton, David, x

Oak Forest Ventures, 109–110, 112,
  116–118
occupancy costs, 42, 44
Ohno, Taiichi, 123, 147
operational productivity, 210
order processing, time equation for, 28–29
overhead, 4, 5

Pareto 20–80 rule, 245
peak-load capacity, 55–57
Performance Measurement and
    Management (PMM) system (at
    CTI), 212–216
  benefits of, 214–215
Phoenix Capital (disguised), 115–118
pilot model
  action plans based on, 77–78
  components of, 74–75
  validation of, 75–77, 83
Pioneer Controls (disguised), 256
  case study, 109
  TDABC modeling at, 110–112
planned maintenance, costs of, 63
Player, Steve, 195
practical capacity
  arbitrary vs. analytical approaches to,
    52–53
  distinguished from theoretical
    capacity, 53
  lumpiness of, 54–55
Private Client Group (PCG) of Global
    Insurance Company
  auto claim processing time equation
    of, 222
  business objectives of, 219–220
  business planning and analysis system

ABOUT THE AUTHORS

ROBERT S. KAPLAN is Baker Foundation Professor at Harvard Business School, where he has taught since 1983. Formerly he was on the faculty of the business school at Carnegie-Mellon University, serving as Dean from 1977 to 1983. He has authored or coauthored thirteen books, sixteen *Harvard Business Review* articles, and more than 110 other papers. His research, teaching, consulting, and speaking focus on linking new performance and cost management systems, especially the Balanced Scorecard and Activity-Based Costing, to strategy. He has received numerous honors, including election in 2006 to the Accounting Hall of Fame, the Outstanding Educator Award from the American Accounting Association, Lifetime Contributions to Management Accounting from the AAA, and the Chartered Institute of Management Accountants (UK) Award for "Outstanding Contributions to the Accountancy Profession." Dr. Kaplan serves on the board of Acorn Systems and Evergreen Energy. He can be reached at rkaplan@hbs.edu.

STEVEN R. ANDERSON is Chairman and Founder of Acorn Systems, a consulting and software company with offices in Houston, Austin, and Philadelphia. The firm specializes in profit management and other decision automation software tools that help boost the operating profits of their clients. In 1996, Mr. Anderson founded Acorn and pioneered the new Time-Driven approach to Activity-Based Costing. He used the principles highlighted in this book to more than double the net operating profit of a large percentage of Acorn's clients. He has written over thirty white papers and articles on this and related subjects. Mr. Anderson is an alumnus of Harvard Business School (Baker Scholar) and McKinsey & Company. He received a dual degree with honors in Engineering Management Systems and Chemical Engineering from Princeton University. In addition, he has a Post Baccalaureate in Accounting from the University of Houston. He can be reached at sanderson@acornsys.com.